"*The Other Side of Reality* is essential truth disguised as entertainment!"
~ *David Russell, M.A, Moja Missions/Young Life, Tanzania, Africa*

"*The Other Side of Reality* is like entering a school of philosophy and theology through the door of the imagination. Ingenious. This multi-dimensional journey into the depths of God is for … the seeker of treasures. … For years Gary Durham was my pastor. I sat spellbound as he established case after case for authenticity of the Word and the power of covenant fellowship with God. I would say he is a theological attorney who knows the Word at a level most of us would tremble to approach."
~ *Pat McNab, Ph.D., Eagle's Glen Foundation, Divide, Colorado*

"I have worked and taught with Dr. Gary Durham in many different venues over the years. He is a creative thinker and a natural teacher. …This wonderful story … is a fresh example of his ability to share important principles through creating an entertaining and engaging story that will draw you into the characters and, before you know it, into new discoveries on your own journey."
~ *Alan Scott, Senior Pastor, Trinity Church, Colorado Springs, Colorado*

"A riveting adventure story that bathes your mind and imagination in God's point of view. The high drama of this book took me captive much like The Lord of the Rings. I can't wait to read books two and three and see this Trilogy become a movie."
~ *Larry Ryan, Kingsway Foundation, Yukon, Oklahoma*

"An absolutely fascinating exploration of the deceptivity of the enemy of our souls … and our ultimate victory over him in Christ! Knowing Dr. Durham as I do, I am not at all surprised at the depth, the coloring, the brilliance of his amazing insight into the reality of what we face in our spiritual journey. I highly recommend this read to anyone who seeks a broader understanding of *The Other Side of Reality.*"
~ *Dr. Steven Fletcher, District Superintendent Emeritus*
*(and grateful friend), Church of the Nazarene*

"Gary Durham has written a sensational thriller that will keep readers on the edge of their seats. I can't wait till the next book in this series releases."
~ *Dr. Stan Toler, Bestselling Author & Speaker, Oklahoma City, OK*

# Map of Severed Lands

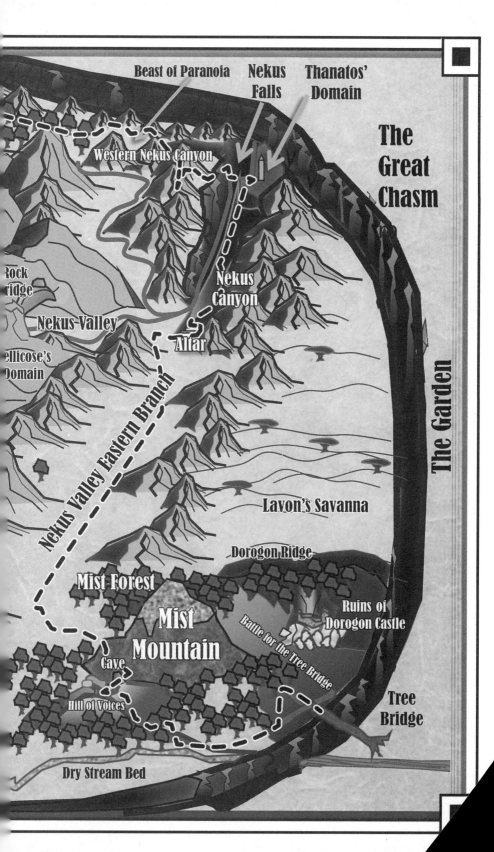

# THE OTHER SIDE OF REALITY: A TRILOGY

BOOK ONE:

# THE CURSE OF THE IMMORTAL FRUIT

*(THE QUEST BEGINS)*

# GARY L. DURHAM

**Veritas Resurgence** Media and Publishing

Copyright ©2014
*THE OTHER SIDE OF REALITY: A Trilogy*
*Book One: THE CURSE OF THE IMMORTAL FRUIT (THE QUEST BEGINS)/ Gary L. Durham*

ISBN: 978-0-9906776-3-5

**Veritas Resurgence**
Media and Publishing
3900 SW Citrus Blvd.
Palm City, Florida 34990

**www.osortrilogy.com**

Cover and Interior Design: Dust Jacket Press Creative Art Department

Printed in United States of America

# DEDICATION

To my two grandsons, Gavin and Ethan Russell
and my brand new granddaughter, Kaia Grace Durham;
and to all the grandchildren everywhere, young and old,
whom the Living One so deeply loves.

———————⬥———————

*Gary L. Durham*

*II Cor. 4:18*

# TABLE of CONTENTS

# PREFACE
## About This Book

This Trilogy is what C. S Lewis would have called "a supposal." It is a story that uses *likening*—comparing different aspects of reality to what it is *not* in order to reveal more of what it is—to pull the reader into an other-worldly adventure from which he or she may look back on this world with an enhanced objectivity and clarity.

The haunting awareness—clear to some and vague to others—that this world is pointing beyond itself, that it is even sometimes a poor mirror that gives us fleeting, tantalizing glimpses of another world, or an echo that dies away before the beauty of some majestic melody can be fully heard, often awakens us to deliciously painful longings. *The Other Side of Reality* seeks to bring the objects of these longings into sharper focus for the reader, and perhaps, for some, to awaken the experience of such longings for the first time.

These longings point to more than desire. They leave an imprint on the soul like an ocean wave leaves on a beach. The imprint testifies to the reality of the wave. When we properly contemplate the imprints left on our souls by the invisible waves that often wash over us uninvited, we are startled by an involuntary spring of hope rising within us. It is a hope that cries for life to have a meaning and purpose that comes from beyond this world and will outlive this world.

In this sense, this Trilogy is an attempt to give perspective: a perspective much needed in a culture where reductionism has shriveled the organ of meaning—our imaginations—by dehydrating the significance of life and everything it contains. If, *"this is only that"* *is* the ultimate pathway to reality, then the only possible conclusion is unrelenting despair.

But that despair, itself, raises the question: Why do we despair? Why do we hope for more? If there isn't any more, why do we long for it? Why do we pine? If we are mere accidents between two cosmic voids, why do the desires for meaning and purpose, identity and security tug so relentlessly at our souls? Are there truths beyond our senses to which this hunger and thirst point?

*The Other Side of Reality,* by means of a fascinating story, seeks to raise and focus these questions in the form of a *supposal. Suppose* someone were taken to the other side of reality and could see not only the material world but the world that lies beyond and behind it. *Suppose* they were also taken out of their time and dropped into the flow of our world's first history. *Suppose* there was a critical reason for them to be there and the meaning and purpose of all future life would hang on their willingly engaging a dangerous quest, and so forth. By means of such a story, it is my belief that this kind of *likening* can silhouette the answers—the *objects* for which we hunger and thirst—and resurrect the true passion of living.

I make no apologies for believing there is another side to reality and that it can be known because *Someone* is seeking to reveal it. What is more, I believe that the other side of reality has a very definite character and nature; that it is filled both with risk, danger and possible tragedy as well as adventure, love and possible triumph; and that you will determine which it will be for you by how you engage these unseen truths.

Welcome to the *Other Side of Reality!*

*- Gary*

# Editor's
# PREFACE

Dr. Gary L. Durham is a fascinating man—scholar, science buff, theologian, counselor, teacher, musician, even a bit of a daredevil. He's one of those guys who keeps surprising you with new facets of his personality that you didn't know were there. He's the only man I know who writes patents for fun on his "day off" and thinks zip-lining less than 100 feet off the ground is boring. Among his many other talents, I've recently discovered that Gary is an incredibly creative storyteller. I'm honored to call him my friend.

*The Other Side of Reality* is an imaginative adventure born in Gary's heart many years ago and is finally making its way to the printed and digital page. It's the tale of a young woman who is pulled into a daring quest in which the future of humanity is at stake. The quest takes place on The Other Side of Reality, the realm in which both material and spiritual realities are seen and interacted with in ways that reveal the Creator's grand Story more clearly than most of us have ever imagined. She fights intense battles, confronts many faces of evil, learns to love and trust, and is forever changed by her encounters with *the real world* like you've never seen it. The story entertains, inspires and teaches, all with one stroke. Editing this work has been a labor of love.

Congratulations on discovering *The Other Side of Reality*. This tale will enrich your life!

*- Don White, Editor*

# ACKNOWLEDGEMENTS

This book would have never become a reality without the generous, skillful and persistent help of numerous people. I wanted to write pages and pages and pages of thanks (in fact, I did!), but both my editor and publisher balked, and I am reluctantly acquiescing to their plea for brevity. Please know that my gratitude to these individuals could fill its own book.

That being said, I must express my heartfelt, though abbreviated, appreciation to the following colleagues, friends and family members:

To Joshua "Gavin" Russell, my grandson, whose brilliant, creative and imaginary mind has added untold value to the adventure. Gavin, this story is as much yours as mine, and it is a much better tale than it would ever have been without your insightful input. Papa will always be more grateful than you could possibly know! (Most of the "pages" of thanks were about you!) I will always treasure our times of reading and discussing the books on our *Man Trips.*

To my accountability reading circle: Gary & Irene Merritt and Diane Rudd, who held me to the task and provided much-appreciated feedback week after week.

To my dear friend and ministry partner, Gary Merritt, whose loyal and effective ministry as Executive Pastor has enabled me to give myself to the teaching and writing I am called to do.

To my editor, Don White, whose skillful and creative massaging and rephrasing of my original manuscript has made this work much more readable and attainable to a broader audience than my own academic and sometimes-verbose writing style could have accomplished.

To my friend, Darren Currin, who took several vacation days from his ministry at Life Church in Oklahoma City, to go through the books with me as a content editor and is now in the process of producing small group discussion materials to accompany the Trilogy.

To my C. S. Lewis reading group at New Hope Fellowship, which took several weeks off from our normal diet to read through some of the early material for this Trilogy. Thanks for being willing to descend from the joyous, intoxicating heights of *Jack* to the lowlands of Gary.

To several precious friends who have been willing to read the manuscripts and give sage feedback. Among them are Rev. Larry Ryan, Dr. Steven Fletcher, Rev. Allan Scott, Dr. Stan Toler, Dr. Pat and Mark McNab, and Lois Frazier. Lois not only read the final version, but also some of the first chapters nearly 20 years ago. Thanks to all of you for letting me impose *my* dream on *you*.

To my wonderful New Hope family who are a constant encouragement to me and my ministry. No pastor could have a more positive atmosphere of love and support in which to serve.

To Tony and Judy DeSantis, Gary and Jan Motley, and Larry and Gayla Ryan for making unsolicited financial investments in seeing this dream become a reality. Your generosity has been a blessed confirmation for me to finish strong.

To my precious, loving and supportive family. David, Janet, Gavin and Ethan, your example of sacrificial ministry and commitment to excellence as missionaries in Tanzania, Africa, continually inspires me. Ryan and Colleen, your friendship and support are a deep source of joy to me, and you now have given me the most beautiful granddaughter the world has ever seen, Kaia Grace! Ryan, your creative gift of music and composition inspires me every week and creates a Spirit-anointed atmosphere in which I can teach.

To my dearest friend and loving wife, Sheryl, without whose prayers and support I could never have prevailed. Over two years ago, the Living One used Sheryl to confirm that I was indeed to finish this project. Sheryl, you are God's gift of so much beauty and grace to me. I am indeed blessed to journey this life with you!

Above all others, my thanks goes to the Living One, Himself, King Jesus, who kept stimulating and sanctifying my imagination to His purposes through the long and sometimes-tedious hours of writing, rewriting, editing and revising. All the while, His Presence never left my side, giving me not only the imagination, but the self-control I needed to keep this hyperactive Type-A personality focused on such a long task. Repeatedly, I have looked back on something I wrote and recognized that He was saying more through me than I realized. Hidden lessons in the imagery came to light only after they had been written. I am deeply thankful for His kind and generous attention. I have grown as I have struggled to find new ways of communicating the old, unchangeable, ever-new realities of His beauty and glory. And in those months of emersion, I really did have the privilege of being sometimes on *The Other Side Of Reality!*

# BOOK ONE:

# The Curse of the Immortal Fruit (The Quest Begins)

Some important character names and
their pronunciations and meanings.

- **DIAKRINA** *(Die-a-KREE-na)*. From Diakrino. Dia means between; Krino means to judge or discern. It has both a negative and positive use. Negatively, it means to doubt (unable to discern between). Positively, it means to discern (to judge between).
- **STRATEIA** *(Stra-TEE-ah)*. Means warfare, to make war; thus, warrior.
- **ANOMOS PONEROS** *(AH-no-mos Po-NAY-ros)*. Means lawless diseased one. Anomos means lawless one, rebellious, defiant, very evil, wicked; Poneros means diseased, degeneracy, calamity, vicious, derelict.
- **HEYLEL** *(Hay-LEL)*. Morning Star; one who shines brightly.
- **SCEPTER OF KABOD** *(Kah-BAHD)*. Kabod means glory, weight, splendor, honor, greatness.
- **KINGDOM OF PARAD** *(Paw-RAHD)*. The realm of Anomos Poneros. Parad means severed self, separated self; to divide, to put out of joint, to scatter.
- **TUPHOO** *(Too-FAH-oh)*. The next to last "o" is the Greek o, the last "o" is the Greek ω. From tuphos (too-fahs) which means to wrap in smoke; by implication, to blind. Tuphoo means high-minded and puffed up with pride.
- **THANATOS** *(THAN-ah-tos)*. Fallen angel of death, lord (god) over the realms of the dead.

## CHAPTER ONE

# The OPEN DOOR

Diakrina woke with a start, aware of an unexpected cool breeze stroking her hair. Surely she had shut the window only moments ago as she climbed into bed. Determined to solve the mystery, she reached toward the window in the darkness. Suddenly her hand froze. "What's this?" she whispered, as her mind raced frantically, trying to recall her surroundings. "Where am I? Did I put flowers or something on the nightstand?"

Determined to banish this momentary, sleep-induced insanity, she reached quickly for the reading light on the headboard of her bed. Her hand found nothing but the kiss of that warm, yet somehow cool, breeze that had wakened her.

But Diakrina never noticed. For as she reached up for the lamp, she also looked up, and what met her focusing eyes dispelled any thought of the reading lamp. Even *thought* itself seemed stunned into silence, as the scene above her suddenly arrested all of her senses, brushing aside all other possible thoughts.

There, above her, sparkled thousands of stars, like dancing diamonds taking their final bow on some heavenly stage, with the curtains being slowly lowered in shafts of pale gold light. A brilliant sunrise was escorting each one into the emerging blue of a celestial ocean, as if a rising tide were steadily hiding the jeweled bottom of a vast, yet intimate pool. Half in uninhibited delight, and half in a mixture of wonder and terror, a shrill yelp pierced the air from Diakrina's lips as she fell limp to the soft green turf beneath her.

How long she lay there with dilated eyes and heaving breast, she could never remember afterwards. Whether the sun had just risen high enough over the distant mountains to throw a shaft of warm light on her hand, or whether she had simply burst from her trance into conscious awareness—like a diver breaking the surface to be greeted by the sounds above the hydrosphere—she was suddenly aware that in her left hand she still clenched whatever it was she had encountered while reaching for the window.

Lifting her hand into the warm light, Diakrina stared, fascinated, at a beautiful, yet strange sight. Tiny liquid rainbows shimmered on the soft petals of a perfect rose nestled in her palm, with the stem—still attached to a glorious rose bush—gripped gently between her third and fourth fingers. She watched obediently as one of the little rainbows, changing its colors in the morning light like a twinkling Christmas tree, slid quietly down the face of a curled petal. It paused but a moment at the edge, as if gathering itself, and then dove softly into the green carpet.

Diakrina moved her forefinger almost imperceptibly along the backside of a soft, smooth petal while she stared as wide-eyed at the harmless beauty as she would a threatening cobra. Suddenly, conscious thought came crashing in on her like a returning tidal wave. "No! No! I must wake up. This is not real!" Then leaping from her screaming thoughts came a nervous determined whisper, "IT CAN'T BE!"

As if trying to annihilate the vision of the rose by those very thoughts, she slammed it into her face with both hands, crushing it into her forehead. Two opposite sensations greeted her: the sharp sting of the thorny stem as she scraped it taut across her forearm, and the delicious, unmistakable fragrance of a crushed rose.

As she silently considered the crumpled petals in her left hand and nursed her forearm with her right, a gentle rebuke whispered in the air, "It is all real enough. Not only can it be wounded, it can wound."

Like a corrected schoolgirl caught with the evidence of mischief in her hand, she unclasped the remains of the rose, which sprang back among its unruffled sisters.

"I see you are awake."

Diakrina turned to her right and jumped to her feet to face the voice. With the rose bush and the rising sun to her back, she peered into the illuminated glory all around her.

"Don't be frightened, Diakrina. There is nothing here to fear." The voice seemed to be very near; in fact, right in front of her. But no matter how hard she looked she could see nothing that should have speech or personality.

"Where are you?" She had no sooner heard her own voice than a disquieting feeling came over her that she might not want to know *where*. After all, she did not yet know *who*.

As if having heard her thoughts, the voice replied, "I told you there is nothing here to fear. That includes what you can see and what you cannot see. And as to where I am, I am afraid there is no answer to that question which you can understand until we do something about where *you* are."

"But I don't know where I am!"

"Of course you don't. And that is why we must do something about it."

"I'm not sure I want anything done about it!" said Diakrina. "I'm not sure this is even real."

"Have you already forgotten the rose?"

This mention of the rose seemed strange to Diakrina. It was spoken as though it bore importance—an importance even a lover of roses would not normally give it. Plus, it was disconcerting to think that *her* experience with the rose, *her* thoughts and hers *alone*, were obviously known to this . . . this *voice*.

"The rose was your first lesson, your first challenge to the reality of all you see. Doesn't its wound and yours speak louder than your doubts?"

Diakrina rubbed her arm thoughtfully but said nothing.

"I must warn you that you will not be able to stay here long if you keep doubting. We have very little time before the door must be shut, and we can do nothing else until we do something about where you are."

"Well, then, for Heaven's sake, where am I?"

"Why, you are in the door, of course. And I should say that it is not for Heaven's sake, but for your own sake that you are here."

Diakrina was more confused than ever. All around her was nothing but a glorious landscape, drenched in a soft golden light. Certainly, nothing that looked remotely like a door was anywhere to be seen.

"If you will trust me, I will get you through the door."

"Trust you?" said Diakrina softly. "I'm not even sure you are real or, if you are real, whether you are someone I *should* trust."

"It is all—myself included—much more real than you can now imagine. As to whether you should trust me, I can only remind you that there is nothing here to fear."

"But how do I know you are telling me the truth?"

"Because there is nothing but truth here, except for *one*. And I am not that one."

"And how do I know you are not that *one*?" Diakrina had no idea who that *one* was, but it seemed like a possible objection. "I can't see you, and I can't see this door you speak of. If I am being asked to trust you, why can't I see you and the door first?"

"Seeing would add nothing to your present ability to believe, Diakrina. You see the garden around you, you feel the warmth of the sun and you have exchanged life with the rose. Do you believe all this to be real because you see it? No. And if you do not come to believe what you now 'see,' you will soon see it no longer. The door will close on you, maybe forever. Things do not have to be seen to be real."

"I'm so confused," sighed Diakrina in half surrender.

"Diakrina, do you believe that the room and the bed you lay down to sleep in tonight are real . . ." Diakrina started as if remembering something almost forgotten. ". . . that they really exist? I know you do. But can you see them now? No. And yet you believe they are real. Can you not understand that 'seeing' is not the measure of reality? Many things are real which are, for the moment, beyond your limited perception. In fact, almost everything that is real is presently beyond *your* perception."

The matter-of-fact tone of this last statement bothered Diakrina a little. But she had argued such a point before and, being one always determined to win any disputes, she immediately countered: "But I believe in my room and the bed because I have past experience with them. I have none with you and this place."

"That is not quite true. Have you forgotten the rose? I must ask you to remember the experience of a wound given and a wound received. But we cannot speak more of this now, for time is short. Will you meet me at the edge of the lake?"

Until now, Diakrina had only been aware of the lake as part of the whole setting, the whole "garden" as it had been called. Turning a little to her right, so that the sun was now warming the right side of her face, she observed a beautiful, still lake. Distant mountains reflected toward her from the far banks, giving way to blue sky and golden sunshine gleaming from the near shore.

"To your right, by the rose bush, is a path. I cannot lead you for you are not yet through the door. But if you follow the path, I will meet you at the lake's edge."

Turning to her right to face the rose bush, Diakrina spotted a footpath, not well defined, but visible, beginning where the imprint of her body still lingered in the soft turf.

"I am going to the lake now. You have only a few moments to follow the path and make it through the door. Please hurry!"

With that, it was suddenly obvious to Diakrina that she stood alone. An abrupt sense of loss, of loneliness, closed in on her. At first it seemed strange and then, all too quickly, it was familiar. She felt as though this *one* who had spoken with her had radiated a brilliant light that drove back some invisible gloom—a gloom that now seemed to permeate her memories of what she had always felt life to be. But it had not seemed like gloom before. Now, here, in the sudden absence of the *one* who had spoken, an unbearable darkness rolled over Diakrina like a black night. Almost before she knew what she was doing, she turned, stepped past the rose bush and ran down the path toward the lake. She was not prepared for what happened next!

CHAPTER TWO

# The CLOSING DOOR

Have you ever awakened suddenly from a sound sleep, and for a moment you can't remember where you are or where you have been or how it is that you came to be asleep in this place? Your thoughts are searching for something familiar to take hold of—racing around trying to pick up the trail of conscious memory. If you have, then you may be able to understand a little of how Diakrina felt as she took her third step past the rose bush.

It was as if she passed through something, though even to this day she cannot tell you what. On one hand, the change was sudden—as definite as entering another room. Yet on the other, the point of change was imperceptible—one did not feel the change happen, but suddenly just *knew* it had.

A powerful sense of time-defying *otherness* suddenly troubled Diakrina. She couldn't be certain if this change had happened ten seconds ago, ten minutes ago, or ten years ago. In trying to explain it to me years later, she said: "It was like I had awakened in a land where time, as we understand it, had no meaning. And yet, somehow, sequence and order had greater meaning. I knew in one sense that I had just arrived, and yet, could never be quite sure."

As she described it later, her uncertainty seemed rooted in a sense that every attempt she made to mentally organize a timeline of her arrival was mildly but overwhelmingly rebuked as, *"Unimportant."* Rebuked from where? Well, to hear her tell it, from *everywhere*. She was in a *place* where such thoughts must step aside, because there were truly important matters in the air. It was as though a King had arrived and, of course, the card game is instantly laid aside—forgotten; or the School Master had walked in unexpectedly and the former mischief scampers for the corner. However you wish to say it, it was clear that everything within Diakrina had snapped to attention.

But, don't misunderstand. It was not in the military sense of *snapping to attention*, but in the overwhelmed sense. She was instantly engulfed in a higher law of existence, a more royal atmosphere. Her whole person responded as if it suddenly remembered and rejoiced in this living, *speaking* atmosphere—a memory, the details of which it did not bother to share with her astonished mind. It was as if her heart, long crippled and sick, had leaped to its feet vibrant with life and ran dancing ahead of her pulling her in its wake.

This inner resurrection was so overpowering that an avalanche of sensations, most of which were formerly unknown to her, tumbled joyously into her and out of her at the same moment. She was so entranced, that she had run at least twenty steps beyond the rose bush before she became aware that she was in a large cave or tunnel, which turned gently to the left toward what she remembered to be the direction of the lake. From around the corner ahead of her came a liquid, golden light that washed the steel gray of the walls in a quivering warmth.

This almost tangible light flooding the cavern had a strange effect on Diakrina. While inside her this inner resurrection continued unrelentingly (until Diakrina felt as if she would burst), a sudden feeling of, well—I guess the best expression is—*homesickness* came rushing at her from the source of this light. She expected her inner jubilation to be drowned under this powerful, engulfing wave. Yet, it was not so. It seemed only to surround the celebration like a weeping and relieved father—weeping joyously and wiping dancing tears from his face as his once lost, but now found children squealed with delight at his feet.

All this was too much for Diakrina. She stopped in the path, fell to the still green turf (though I cannot explain how this turf remained green inside this cave or tunnel—unless of course it had something to do with the golden light) and began sobbing uncontrollably. She was suddenly a prodigal in the midst of a homecoming celebration in her honor. She had not known she was in anyway *lost*. Yet, at that moment, all her former life now seemed to her as if she had never been anything but always away from *home*.

"Hurry, Diakrina! HURRY!" It was *his* voice from somewhere around the turn. "The door is closing!" She looked up to see the golden light lessening. She leaped to her feet, suddenly seized with an awful dread that she would never make it *home* to this place of delicious golden light.

There was no question now of whether she wanted to go on, but only a dreadful fear that she might not make it. Though she never actually looked behind her, she knew that as the golden light faded, a hungry, evil darkness was chasing after her, determined to reclaim her.

She ran wildly toward the light, as determined to possess it as the charging darkness was to possess her. The light lessened with every moment, even though she was running toward it with a desperate abandon she had never felt before. She heard someone crying, "NO! NO! Please, NO!"

Without warning, there it was. A huge door, like one might expect to see in a castle, loomed ahead of her. It looked to be made of very dense wood, hand carved with strange and wonderful etchings of creatures Diakrina had never seen before. They were carved like a sunburst from the center of the door. Yet the effect on the eye was that it was bursting from the outside of the door to the center—like a backwards explosion.

All the carved creatures were beautiful beyond description. The ones at the outside of the door were very distinct and clear, while the ones in the center were almost totally transparent. "No, not almost transparent, they *are* transparent!" The golden light shot out like laser beams from this center.

This door was not open like doors open in our world. It was somehow open while remaining in place. It was quickly clear to Diakrina that this transparent center was the portal through which she must pass. She must leap headlong into the golden light.

She had been about 50 yards from the door when she came around the turn. With everything in her, with speed she did not know she possessed, she strained ahead to cover the distance between her and the door. As she did so, she noticed the door seemed to be materializing from the outside toward its center and that the opening (if you could call it an opening) was getting rapidly smaller every moment.

Again, she heard the same voice as before, crying, "NO! NO! PLEASE, NO!" This time she knew it was her own voice.

When she had first seen the door, the opening of golden light was about the size of a regular door in our world. By the time she was within 10 yards, it was no bigger than a small window. Already the carved figures in the center, where the golden light still poured through, were becoming more distinct. Diakrina knew she was running faster than she had ever run in her life, yet, compared to the speed at which the opening was closing, she felt she was hardly moving.

She was almost there. The opening was now only the size of a large rabbit hole. "Please, Oh God, please let me make it!" she heard herself praying.

"Jump, Diakrina, Jump!" came a commanding shout that poured through the remaining opening with the light. Without slowing her stride she planted her last step about three yards from the door and, with all the strength left in her, threw herself into the golden light.

As she did, two things happened simultaneously. She felt a terrible coldness snapping at her feet; "a cold gloom," as she later called it. At the same moment, a bronze hand shot out of the light through the door, grabbing hold of her outstretched hands. Instantly, her speed accelerated by a powerful pull, her hands and head plunged into the opening in the door. Hitting the opening, which was quickly materializing, was like hitting something slightly thicker than water. For a tenth of a second, she seemed encased. She lost all sense of motion. Then like a ball shot from a cannon she burst into blue sky, golden light, the powerful and unmistakable fragrance of roses and the strong arms of a beautiful giant.

She felt both of her foot-warming socks, which she had worn to bed, come off and the next moment she and the beautiful giant were tumbling together, end over end, in delicious green grass.

## CHAPTER THREE

# The OTHER SIDE of the DOOR

Diakrina had never heard such laughter—noble, yet unpretentious and unrestrained. The beautiful giant, who looked like the most handsome and perfect young man you could ever imagine on earth—his features finely balanced, but with a *chiseled* freedom—lay beside Diakrina in the ankle deep turf, in a fit of focused delight.

The majesty of this splendid creature fascinated Diakrina. Had she been an ancient Greek pagan, she would have surely mistaken him for a god. She lay there in the grass beside him watching his eyes flash with a golden light that radiated from his bronze face.

He was about eight feet tall, powerfully and perfectly proportioned, and dressed in a dazzling white ankle-length tunic, which looked more like it was made of light than any other substance. Around his waist he wore a three-inch wide golden belt, on which hung a sword in its sheath. The sword handle was larger than any she had ever seen or imagined and looked as if it were carved from a single ruby, though she could not imagine a precious stone so large. It was blood red, yet transparent, and flashed brilliantly in the golden sunlight.

"Now that is what I call timing," chuckled the noble giant. He was pointing in the direction of the door. It was an effort to take her eyes off this dazzling being long enough to look toward the door, yet her natural curiosity and his commanding manner would have it no other way.

Sitting up, she looked at where the still laughing giant was pointing. There in the door, hanging from the toes, were her foot-warmers. The empty socks were embedded in the now solid center of the door. Diakrina, who had always been rather self-conscious, flushed a little. Yet, somehow, she could not make it matter like she normally would. Instead, she found herself also giggling quietly at the strange sight—the homey socks did look silly embedded in such a massive and impressive work of art.

And it *was* an impressive work of art! With her attention now drawn to the door, Diakrina noticed the exquisite carving on this side of the great door and the unusual color of the door itself. It was a deep crimson red. The impressive relievo style carving, which covered the whole of its massive surface, was of a single rose, so perfect in shape and so life-like in appearance that it seemed alive.

The door was set into a small hillside, blanketed on every square inch with heavily laden rose bushes. Diakrina had never seen—or even imagined—roses of such vibrant beauty. It was otherworldly. The rose bushes extended out from either side of the great door and formed a large garden, surrounding the spot where Diakrina and the giant sat, and ended at a path that ran parallel with the shores of a lake which lay just behind them.

Diakrina's eyes were drawn back to the great door, as though following a path back to its source. The etched rose of the door, Diakrina realized, seemed not only alive and real, but even *more so* than the "real" roses all around it! You could almost imagine the door itself was the original from which every living and perfectly beautiful rose was a reflection.

As if he knew her thoughts, the bronze giant was quiet for a few moments to allow her to gaze deeply into the door from where she sat in the grass. The door's *surface*—if you could call it that—was not merely on its surface. It seemed to extend like a crimson, crystal-clear ocean away from Diakrina—"a bottomless, horizontal ocean," as she would later recall it. Yet, somehow, this bottomless depth of crystal crimson *was* on its surface and only its surface. Extra spatial dimensions seemed somehow involved in its structure—dimensions that transcended the three Diakrina had always known.

"You almost didn't make it," said the giant youth, suddenly looking wonderfully sober.

Diakrina's attention was snapped back from the crimson ocean to the immediate moment. "I know," she said as she tried to recall the former panic she had felt as the cold, dark gloom grabbed at her ankles. Yet, no matter how hard she tried, she could feel nothing but secure wonder, inside and out.

"My name is Strateia," said the bronze giant, as he rose nimbly to his feet. In the golden sunlight, Strateia's golden hair looked ablaze. He looked like a human oak tree to Diakrina as he towered over her. Somehow, though she did not know how, she knew that his name, Strateia, meant, "Warrior."

Bending over and reaching out his arms, Strateia lifted Diakrina to her feet as gently as a father lifting a small child. Then stepping back and gazing thoughtfully down on her, he announced, "I'm glad you made it."

Suddenly a powerful shaft of light fell from the sky and struck Strateia. Diakrina fell back startled, right into the very spot from which the giant had just lifted her. Strateia seemed almost to disappear for a moment as his whole being became one with the brilliant light. Diakrina could distinguish him from it just enough to see that he had gracefully fallen to one knee and raised a flaming sword in what seemed both a salute and an act of devotion, which she could only describe with the word, "Worship."

Diakrina had never seen anything so beautiful. The ruby handle of the sword appeared to generate life into the fire-red blade that Strateia held before his up-turned face.

He seemed to be in another place, isolated from Diakrina. She could look in on what was happening but could not hear a single sound coming from within the shaft of light, even though it was obvious Strateia was speaking to *Someone*. From the thoughtful responses of understanding on his face, Diakrina surmised that he must be receiving instructions of some kind.

Diakrina suddenly gasped. A beautiful, crystal-clear, diamond looking hand reached down from above Strateia and rested on the top of his up-turned head. It was surely a moment of blessing, like the reassuring affirmation of a loving father, yet also like a king commissioning a noble knight. Strateia's face glowed with radiant admiration and love.

Then, as suddenly as it had come, the light was gone. Strateia seemed to blaze more glorious than before.

Rising to his full height with his face still to the sky, he slowly dropped his sword point to the ground. Where the blazing blade touched the soil, the turf trembled as if pulsing life had entered it. At the sword's tip, a small tuft of grass slowly parted as a brilliant red bud opened gracefully and raised its head majestically about 10 inches above the ground. In what seemed only about five seconds (though Diakrina could never be sure about such considerations, for this place confounded her sense of time—it could just as easily have been five hours or days) there stood a perfect rose of unearthly radiance.

Diakrina was never sure if Strateia had even noticed the rose. He looked down at his sword thoughtfully for a moment and then replaced it in its sheath.

"It is important that we begin immediately," said Strateia's silver voice. "There is much you must learn before you undertake your quest."

Diakrina wanted to ask him about the shaft of light and all she had seen, but the very atmosphere seemed to recommend that she listen, not speak. And this . . . did he say, "*quest*"? What could he mean?

"The Living One says we have little time to prepare you for the journey. There are lies to be exposed and truths that must take their place. Only then can your quest be undertaken. But first," Strateia smiled patiently, "we must get better acquainted."

Before Diakrina could ask about the lies, the truths and the quest, Strateia once again reached down and lifted her to her feet. This time Diakrina noticed that he handled her with great care, as if she were in danger of breaking—like a fragile vase.

"As I said before, my name is Strateia. I am a servant of the Living One."

And surprising herself, Diakrina heard herself say, "Then in my language, your name is *Warrior*."

"This is correct," admitted the towering giant. "Thus I have been named."

"Who is the *Living One*?" asked Diakrina. As she spoke the Name, *Living One*, the inner resurrection she had previously experienced while in the tunnel approaching the door, with the same avalanche of unknown, glorious sensations, began anew. This time she had what she could only describe as, "a painful joy, a stab of intense longing which made me want to cry and laugh at the same time."

"How your eyes twinkle, little one," said Strateia, obviously aware of what she was experiencing. "Though you cannot yet translate it, I believe you have your answer. I can add nothing but understanding to what you now know. But that will take time."

"I must go to Him, I must be with Him," sobbed Diakrina. "I cannot bear to live unless I can."

"You have spoken more truth than your understanding can yet embrace," said Strateia, kneeling in the grass in front of her and tenderly wiping her tears with his thumbs as he took her face in his large bronze hands. "But first, your eyes must be opened so you can believe, and then know, that He is real."

"But I do believe He is real!"

"No, little one, you mistake what you feel for belief. What you feel happens to be true this time, but it has no roots in you yet. The feeling will not be constant, and neither will your belief under difficult circumstances. And the quest will be very difficult."

This all puzzled, even hurt Diakrina very much. She was sure Strateia did not understand how she felt. For the first time since she had arrived she felt misunderstood; a little like a stranger.

For a moment she thought she saw something like pity in Strateia's eyes. However, it passed too quickly for her to be certain. Anyway, she was not in the mood to be pitied, but understood.

"Come, little one." Strateia rose suddenly and began walking toward the lake and then, when he reached the path, turned right in the direction of the golden sunshine. Diakrina was so startled that she simply turned and fell in behind him.

It was soon apparent that she would have to nearly run to keep pace with the easy stride of this huge, bronze warrior. He was brilliant in the dancing sunlight. She had never seen anyone, or anything, which looked so noble and yet..."What is it that lies just below that surface?" she wondered to herself.

Suddenly, she knew! He looked *formidable*, even *fierce*. He did not look fierce in the scary sense, but in the comforting sense. In looking at him you felt as if an army of mythical dragons made real and terrible, would only fall swiftly before his blazing sword. His every movement was precision made both beautiful and terrifying by its utter naturalness and ease.

A sense of security came over Diakrina, though she could see no need for it. She could not know at that moment that in the not-too-distant future she would face days when she would cling to this sense of security emanating from Strateia's presence.

They walked along a path not more than 20 feet from the shore of the sparkling lake. The lake—mysteriously—appeared to be in constant motion, as though water were boiling out of the ground from some great depth and filling the lake. As they walked along the shore, Diakrina noted delightful fragrances she could not identify. Each one told its own story— as if begging someone to stop and listen.

Flowers were everywhere, sporting colors that were not only more intense than any she had ever seen, but sometimes unidentifiable. The mountains on the far side of the lake looked very distant, yet they were clearer to the eyes than anything that far off should be. Diakrina was not sure if it was something special about the atmosphere or if her eyes were stronger here in this wonderful place.

Their path made a slight turn away from the lake and started up a subtle incline. It led them into a grove of trees covered with red, purple and ivory colored flowers. The trees waved as the stirring breeze carried the most delicious fragrances toward them. As the travelers pressed in among the trees, the branches reached close enough to the path for Diakrina to reach out and touch the flowers. As she did, she was startled to feel each one move in her hand—as though happily responding to her touch, much like a small affectionate pet.

"They recognize a long absent master," said Strateia without slowing or turning.

"Master?" thought Diakrina, "Absent?" Before she could form her questions they came out of the trees into a clearing, which continued to rise slowly toward the sky.

Strateia stopped and turned part way around to receive the still approaching Diakrina. Placing his left hand on her shoulder and lifting his right hand toward the horizon, he pointed into the morning sun. "Look, little one. There ahead is the place of your first tutorial."

Diakrina lifted her eyes into the sunlight to the horizon where Strateia was pointing. At the top of the rise, blazing brighter than the golden sunshine, rose huge gates mounted in an ivy-covered wall that reached 300 feet into the air. As her eyes adjusted, she realized it was not the gates themselves that were ablaze, but something or someone standing higher than the gates and wall.

This someone or something could be seen towering above the other side of the gates. Whatever, or whoever it was, was ablaze like a furnace all over. The flames reached high into the air above the source. Yet, there was no smoke. There was only a golden heat that seemed to distort the light all around the dancing blaze.

"You must stay here for a moment and not come closer," said Strateia. "I will walk ahead of you a little. Do not come until I motion for you."

With that, Strateia left her at the edge of the trees and walked a few steps into the clearing. Then with a voice like a silver trumpet he called out, "Guardian of the Tree, Strateia, servant of the Living One, greets you!"

Diakrina gasped as the flaming source stirred and turned. What she had been looking at was the backside of what she later described as "a 450 foot tall man who burned like a white-hot furnace." He was both beautiful and terrible beyond description.

Unlike Strateia, he had wings of great length, much like some pictures she had seen of angels. He was dressed only in a robe of flames and held a fearsome sword in his right hand.

What she heard next sounded like melodious thunder. She had never heard words carried by such a medium. "HIS NAME IS GLORIOUS IN MERCY AND IN BATTLE! YOU ARE WELCOME MY BROTHER, STRATEIA, SERVANT OF OUR MASTER." The ground beneath Diakrina's feet trembled with each melodic syllable.

"I have with me one for whom purification and preparation for a great quest have been decreed. She is to serve on behalf of the Living One soon. His purpose I cannot share as yet. It is my sacred trust."

"YOU MAY KEEP YOUR TRUST AS I KEEP MY OWN. BUT I MUST KNOW HOW SHE WAS BROUGHT HERE, FOR SHE IS ALREADY STANDING IN THE DOMAIN OF *MY* TRUST."

"She was brought here through the Door of The Rose."

"WELL ENOUGH! ONLY HIS MERCY AND FOREKNOWLEDGE COULD OPEN SUCH A DOOR. BUT I MUST CHARGE YOU WITH MY PLEDGE CONCERNING THE TREE."

"She will be always with me during her days in the Garden. I vow that she shall not go beyond the Forbidden Barrier."

"IT IS ENOUGH! HE HAS HEARD YOU AND ME! SHE MAY DWELL HERE WITHOUT FEAR."

With that, Strateia turned to Diakrina and motioned for her to come join him. She gladly ran to his side and pulled close to him.

"Do not fear, little one. You are secured into my trust."

The flaming angel turned back around toward the sun and resumed his station.

"We will now approach the gates so the first truth about the dilemma of your kind may be known."

"But I am afraid," whispered Diakrina.

"Then the teaching has begun already. We must not tarry." Strateia reached down and lifted her into his arms as if she were a child, not a young lady, and carried her up the hill toward the gates. Diakrina noticed that with each step the heat became greater. Soon it seemed more than she could bear.

CHAPTER FOUR

# The GREAT DANCE

"I can't breathe," thought Diakrina.

Again as if reading her thoughts, Strateia spoke: "Be calm, little one, the flames will not hurt you. It will pass soon."

A sound like a roaring furnace grew louder and louder as they approached the top of the hill. Diakrina peeked out of the folds of Strateia's tunic of light, in which she had buried her face, and saw the towering gates not far ahead. Though heat rose from the surface of the doors, they were clearly not as hot as the flaming Guardian who stood just beyond them. They were not gold or shiny, as she had thought them to be when she had mistaken the fire of the Guardian as coming from the gates. They were rather very black, and each looked to be made of a solid stone that appeared to be like some kind of marble, yet, denser.

There were carvings of a man on the right door of the gates and of a woman on the left. Both seemed to be in great despair and anguish, as a huge serpent held them in its coils, pulling them where they did not wish to go.

As Diakrina looked at the carved scene of terror and sorrow, she felt as though she were remembering the terrible moment herself—as if she too were caught in the coils of the great serpent. She could feel its twisting, scaled body, heaving heavily, tightening its grip. She tried to scream but nothing came from her open mouth. She could not breathe; the coils were getting tighter. She struggled to free herself, but her wriggling only gave the coils room to grip her body more closely.

Suddenly, Strateia's bronze hand covered her face. All went dark, the carved black gates disappeared and she took a deep breath of the hot air. The serpent had disappeared and she was once again in the arms of her protector.

"You are not yet wise enough nor free enough to engage the Gates of Deprivation without fear."

Having said this, Strateia, instead of approaching the gates, turned to the left and walked alongside the ivy-covered wall for about 20 yards. There he stopped, took his hand from Diakrina's face and set her to the ground with her back to the gates.

"Do not look back, little one."

Then he took the blade of his sword and with it touched a stone in the wall. In obedience to the touch, an opening about 10 feet high materialized in the wall.

Suddenly, sounds of melodic music flooded through the opening to meet them. Beautiful, yet serious tones—which made one think both of a solemn procession and an elegant waltz—stabbed Diakrina again with an intense longing—a longing that was like pain, yet more desirable than any pleasure she had ever known.

"You may enter, little one."

Strateia stepped back so she could enter ahead of him.

"Will you be coming with me?" Diakrina looked anxiously into his clear eyes.

"If you please. But you must go through first."

Immediately on stepping into the opening, Diakrina discovered steps of deep-cut stone descending in front of her and to the left, then arching slowly to the right as they descended. The air was cool and refreshing to her skin as she took two steps down the stairs. Then, after turning to make sure Strateia was following her, she continued downward toward the sound of the wonderful *Speaking Music*.

Diakrina always used this expression, *Speaking Music*, whenever she referred to the music she heard there. When I asked her why, a faraway, otherworldly expression would come into her clear eyes as they rimmed with quiet tears of memory. (Inexplicably, Diakrina's eyes, which had been deep blue all her life, were ever after her journey almost liquid clear, with only the slightest hint of a beautiful sky blue left in them.)

Once she tried to explain why she called it *Speaking Music:* "It is music beyond our earthly understanding of music. It speaks to something deep in our nature, which the greatest music of our world only occasionally touches, ever so slightly. But this *Speaking Music* spoke to—I must say, awakened—inner domains of my soul that I had never before imagined existed. It brought to life a part of me that had always before been asleep.

"I can only say that when earthly music had deeply and greatly stirred me before, so that I felt really alive and overwhelmed, it was but a vague, passing dream. It left me slumbering still as compared to this awakening.

"This music called to me. It summoned me to a great adventure: to an ever-unfolding drama of life and beauty. And somehow I knew it was for this I was made. It gave me identity and security, significance and worth that I can only dream of here.

"We go through our lives really never knowing who we are or what we were created to become—or even that we are to *become*! We try to know our self by our self. Here we are blind and can only grope at our own face with clumsy mental hands.

"Yet, in this Music, *He*—Someone both profound and intimate—tells you who you are and what He has created you for. When He does, you not only begin to understand your true self, you begin to value Him and all the others He has placed in your life.

"Suddenly, you are but one thing known among many, and, I might add, no longer the most important thing even in your own estimation. You come to see that to know your *self*, you have to know Him and others. All selves become equally valuable and honored. You begin to see who and what they are as somehow part of who and what you are."

Always, in the end, she would grope for words and fall silent. Then she would simply shrug her shoulders helplessly and say, "I'm sorry. Words really are quite useless. You would have to hear it for yourself. And one day, you will!"

As I was saying, the steps turned slowly to the right in a gentle winding fashion. The further Diakrina descended, the louder the music became. Abruptly the stairs made a sharp right turn and emptied through another opening onto a large balcony. As Diakrina stepped through the opening, the music swelled to a sweet crescendo.

Below the balcony, some 30 feet, was a sky-blue surface, slightly transparent, on which danced thousands of beautiful creatures. I say creatures, because they were not human, yet they certainly were not less than human.

Diakrina stood transfixed, unable to take in all she was seeing. The dance was not like any she had ever seen. Diakrina had taken ballet classes as a little girl, and she loved the elegant forms of graceful dancing. "Dancing which spoke," she called it. She had often sneaked into the local ballet school to watch the professional dancers at their daily practices. It always delighted and mesmerized her.

But here, below her on the endless blue, was a dance that was more than art. It was a language of life in full three-dimensional expression. It turned the Speaking Music into a visual display of meaningful beauty. It told a story—no, thousands of stories—yet they were all synchronized and taken into a Great Story in which every individual and collective story found its true meaning and fulfillment.

Each pair of dancers was performing a dance very different from that of any of the others. Yet, like constantly changing shapes, concaving and convexing, the movements of one pair fit perfectly into the movements of a second and a third, and the three together into a larger pattern of other groups, which formed exquisite and intricate patterns, which did the same with other patterns on an ever larger scale.

No matter how you looked at it, you always saw smaller patterns making up larger ones and they, together with others, even larger ones, ad infinitum. As far as the eye could see, the dance spread in all directions away from the balcony.

Diakrina noticed that the Music seemed to find almost perfect expression in the changing patterns on the transparent blue. It was as if someone first played an idea, and then it appeared before your eyes in a kaleidoscope of changing color and form. How long she watched the Great Dance she did not know—she felt she could stand there forever and never ask for anything more than to watch in wonder the scene below her.

Then she felt the touch of Strateia on her right shoulder. "Look down, little one."

Diakrina looked almost straight down, nearly under the balcony, where Strateia pointed. There, as if just entering the Dance, was a human Couple. Such a couple she had never seen. They were not clothed in any kind of garment, yet you could not say they were naked. Both seemed to move in a garment of pure light, which had no form but their form.

The music seemed to be announcing the Couple's arrival as if they were newborn royalty. The whole Dance, each member themselves all kings and queens in their own bestowed right, burst into glorious patterns of celebration and welcome. Diakrina could not help but feel that, somehow, this regal company had just embraced her, too. Tears of joy ran down her face as she watched the noble Couple glide onto the floor and join the exquisite patterns.

It was then she noticed other creatures, which looked familiar, following the Couple onto the blue sea; moving, as it seemed, at the Couple's silent command. Patterns began to appear from these new dancers led by the Couple's graceful movements—patterns that spoke to her. It was a language she somehow knew. Unlike the other patterns, this one she understood completely.

Instantly, she was taken up into a moving story of joy and wonder. All was drenched with purpose and destiny. She watched glorious history materialize and vanish in swirling wave after wave. Diakrina was beside herself with delight. She felt as if the Great Dance had taken her in; she moved in perfect synchronization with the Couple, the creatures that were with them, and they all, along with the whole endless company, in sync with the Speaking Music.

Abruptly, someone who clearly did not belong—someone whose presence and movements mocked and defied the Dance—came weaving through the moving patterns in the Couple's direction. As he drew near, Diakrina heard a discordant sound, a countering melody of mystery and intrigue. The other creatures with the Couple did not seem to hear the contrary melody. Strangely, they did not seem capable.

The Couple, however, instantly noticed the discordant music. At first they kept in step with the Speaking Music, willfully ignoring this Intruder and his music.

Just then, the Intruder burst into a blaze of brilliant colors and began dancing a most complicated and startling pattern. Diakrina was mesmerized by his artistry. It was indeed beautiful, unusual—unique. However, she recognized at the same moment that it was unique to a fault—it did not blend with the pattern of the rest of the Great Dance.

If you looked only at this Intruder and his patterns, there was indeed a mysterious beauty about it all. Yet, when you focused outward, taking in the rest, his dance was hideously contorted—twisted and grotesque in relation to the rest. At no point did it add to the beauty of the Great Dance. Rather his dance defied it, smashing into its beauty all around, arrogantly demanding that the Great Dance give way. In this larger perspective, the Intruder's dance looked, if not silly and foolish, small.

The mysterious melody grew more intense and forceful. It sounded to Diakrina to take on some of the same melodic structures of the Speaking Music, but only in the form of a distorted echo. It did not so much mimic as mock the glorious strains that had first been played by the Speaking Music.

Then somehow Diakrina was no longer on the balcony (or so it seemed); she was included—dancing beside the Couple. How she knew what to do she could not tell. Yet, like all the others, she moved faultlessly to the Speaking Music. The Music danced through her, gently yet authoritatively guiding her every step as she delightfully willed to embrace it.

Yet as the music of the Intruder gained intensity, so now did his dance. He weaved intricate and swirling patterns around and around the Couple,

Diakrina and the creatures who followed, trying to draw them into his defiantly beautiful patterns.

He would interlace his dance a few steps with theirs, and for a moment he seemed to move in harmony with them and all the others. But then he would break step again. As he did, the Couple and Diakrina struggled to keep from following him.

Again and again, he repeated this strategy, each time staying a little longer in sync with them and the Great Dance. Each time he broke step they found it harder to stay in step with the Speaking Music.

In those moments when he stayed in step with the Speaking Music, he mimicked it like an echo that was a few milliseconds behind, and they found it easy to focus on his echo instead of the original. But when he broke step, his dance suddenly changed to glaring defiance, and they nearly stumbled as his music tugged at their limbs, demanding them to follow it instead of the Speaking Music.

At first, it was all quite unbearable—defiantly troubling and out of place. But the longer he danced in and then out of step with them, the more confused they became, until it felt almost "right" to *not* break step with *him*!

They knew that the law of the Great Dance must not be broken. Yet the Intruder's dance had become so much like the Great Dance—and yet totally unlike it in any way that mattered—it seemed that to follow him would not *really* break the law of the Great Dance at all.

"Did he not always come back in step just a few steps later?" they found themselves asking.

In fact, by the time Diakrina had reached this point in her thoughts, the Intruder did not deviate from the Speaking Music but a few steps at a time. Surely his few "liberties" were only innocent, and even desirable, embellishments. This new individualism he commended to them could fit harmlessly into the greater whole. The longer she gazed at him, the more desirable seemed his proposition.

The Intruder's music, now sweet and mysterious with red passion, began to replace the Speaking Music in Diakrina's mind. It tried to dance through her. Rather than being gentle, however, it was passionately demanding.

Before she knew it, she and the Couple had broken step with the Speaking Music, though only for a few steps. Almost immediately, they again re-joined the Great Dance. It seemed nothing of consequence had happened.

It happened again; this time for a few steps longer. A rush of what felt like personal accomplishment surged through them—they had added their "own" embellishment to the Great Dance. (Though actually it was not theirs, but the Intruder's.)

Had they been able to see what Strateia observed from the balcony, they would have realized that the grotesque features of the Intruder's dance were spreading through them in an arrogant challenge to the Great Dance, like a cancer growing in an otherwise healthy body.

The creatures that followed the Couple fell into confusion. They could not understand these new steps—steps that clashed with the Speaking Music. The creatures attempted to follow the Couple's lead, only to stumble and collide with each other.

Meanwhile, the Couple and Diakrina lost themselves in the Intruder's trance. As he danced increasingly out of step with the Great Dance, so did they.

Diakrina felt a new sense of destiny, a new thrill of adventure. The new music filled her with passion, red and sweet. She gave way to it. It danced through her the intricate steps of the Intruder. Forgotten was the Great Dance. Now she would dance HER DANCE!

In the intoxication of her newfound self-expression, she missed noticing that it was not really "HER DANCE" at all. It was always the Intruder's dance. She danced nothing truly original, only and always the mocking counterfeits of the Intruder. Real originality had been left behind in the Great Dance. What she danced now was neither original nor harmonious. It was intricately ugly.

The poor creatures were by this time in total disarray. The Couple and Diakrina did not notice that the Great Dance was moving away from them, leaving a growing distance between itself and their confusion. Soon no one danced in front of the balcony but the four who danced in a mad frenzy. The creatures who had followed the Couple had all stumbled and lay on the transparent blue in complete bewilderment. The music of the Intruder roared its mocking phrases while the Speaking Music faded with the Great Dance into the infinite horizon.

"ENOUGH!" trumpeted the silver voice of Strateia.

Deadly silence instantly filled the air. Diakrina opened her eyes as the music of the Intruder was leaving her limbs. She stumbled clumsily on the blue surface and fell.

Diakrina now lay alone on the transparent blue sea. The Great Dance was gone; its haunting music silent. The Couple, along with the dancing creatures, had vanished.

The stabbing silence closed in on Diakrina with a crash.

Suddenly she wailed as if her heart would break. "The Speaking Music, the Great Dance, it is gone and I am forever outside!"

She collapsed.

"Not forever, little one," the melodic voice of Strateia announce as he reached down and gathered her sobbing form in his bronze arms. He had leaped, unseen by Diakrina, as softly as a cat from the great balcony.

Then almost under his breath, he said, "Thanks to the Living One, not forever."

## CHAPTER FIVE

# The AWAKENING

Diakrina could never remember leaving the great transparent blue. She did recall semi-consciously feeling again the great heat of the Guardian and Gates. When she finally came to herself, she lay in cool green grass near a giggling brook with the sun, now high in the sky, peeking through the treetops above.

She lay there for several moments drinking in the beauty and peace. Colorful birds, which stirred everywhere, sang almost intelligent melodies of symphonic splendor. One could almost imagine that the breeze and the trees were somehow in agreement to interpret the birds' songs with their movements. It reminded Diakrina of the . . .

"THE GREAT DANCE! WHERE IS THE GREAT DANCE?" her mind shouted.

Diakrina sat straight up and jumped to her feet. It was then she realized she was naked. She stood there stunned, her mind racing.

"Here, little one," interrupted the now familiar voice of Strateia, "Put this on." Strateia walked toward her from the edge of a clearing.

"Where is my nightgown?" said Diakrina as Strateia handed her a green tunic. When it touched her hands, she knew it was made of skillfully woven grasses.

"You might say you danced yourself out of it," said Strateia, without the slightest sense of humor in his tone. "This will do for now."

Diakrina pulled the soft green tunic over her head. As it fell down over her body, reaching to just above her knees, the smell of fragrant flowers surrounded her. It seemed to bathe her body in gentle strength and beauty.

Strateia held out to her a simple scarlet cord with a gold carved rose bud on each end, attached to the cord by lovely silver settings. "Tie this around your waist," instructed Strateia.

Diakrina took the cord and examined the two roses. They were cut of something that looked like a diamond, somewhat transparent, yet with a deep yellow-gold color tinting the whole stone. "These are beautiful, Strateia! What are they?"

"They are chrusolithos, which means, *gold stone*. In your language you would call it chrysolite. It is the seventh of The City's twelve foundations."

Diakrina pulled the scarlet cord around her waist and tied it so the two golden roses hung together just to the right of her center. "What city, and where is it?" she inquired.

"I refer to The City, the dwelling place of the Living One."

Holding the almost living roses in her hand, Diakrina felt sweet tears rim over in her eyes, though she was not quite sure why. She watched as a single teardrop fell from her cheek onto one of the roses and then slide gently onto the other. The roses seemed to sparkle golden light in return. A deep longing, mixed with the most piercing sense of loss she had ever known, boiled up inside of her. "Please, oh, please, can we go to Him . . . to The City?"

"Indeed we will, little one," responded Strateia. "But much shall come first. You need preparation and instruction for a quest you must embrace and complete: a quest that will be woven in and among grave and destiny-altering events."

Strateia's eyes filled with a faraway look. For the first time, Diakrina thought perhaps she perceived a hint of concern in his eyes. But if so, it was so mastered by resolve that she could not be sure of it. For suddenly Strateia's whole countenance flushed back to the present moment.

"For now you must eat, and then we shall talk about the Great Dance." With that, he motioned for her to follow him.

They walked toward the little brook and, upon reaching it, Strateia waded into the sparkling water. Diakrina followed. She longed to question him about this *quest* he kept referring to, but the moment did not seem right.

All her life, Diakrina had been haunted by a sense of impending adventure that might burst upon her at any moment. As a child she had often talked of it and longed to be suddenly pulled into a grand story where she was caught in the flow of serious events in which something important was at stake.

But as Diakrina had moved into her teenage years she had begun to shrug off these deep, inner longings and relegate them to childish fantasies. She had actually become embarrassed to speak of them for fear of being thought less than grown up.

Even as she denied these longings, slandering them to herself as "childish," they still stirred inside her. In unguarded moments she found herself inexplicably and powerfully pulled back into the old longings. In those moments, she could almost admit to herself that adventure was indeed calling to her from over an unseen horizon.

Surely she had now crossed some such horizon, and she felt the old longings revive without any need to hide them. They were like a tingling message whispering of an adventure crouching just out of sight: an adventure about to spring on her at any moment.

Could it be, she mused, that these longings would prove to be important indicators after all? Had they been projected into her young heart like dancing shadows by some purposely-directed light? Were they meant to prepare her for this moment? And if shadows, what realities had cast those shadows? Who or what had directed the light which had cast these longings over her?

In coming through the Door of the Rose she had clearly crossed a horizon of some kind. It was a horizon between dimensions of perception or . . . *something*. Would she now meet face-to-face with the sources of these shadows—these longings? And was this *quest* somehow related to these longings?

It seemed—now that she no longer needed to hide these longings—that they were not childish at all. They were valid; they were *real*. They had always been valid, and she had no reason to be ashamed of them.

"Yet," she said to herself in a moment of sudden insight, "they were not valid in and of themselves. They were valid because they pointed to something real beyond themselves."

The *normal* world she had always known was constantly trying to invalidate and defame the reality to which these secret longings pointed. And if her world denigrated and disparaged what was indeed real . . . then might these secret longings point to what was actually most genuine? Could they have been her best clue all along, her most accurate perception of the true nature and meaning of life? If so, then they were more real than the world that mocked and denied them!

These longings, certainly, would need to be educated beyond the childish forms they had taken. Yet the longings themselves had a real and important task to complete, and that task could only be accomplished if the longings were obeyed as they pointed beyond themselves to their source. The purpose of the longings was to cry out, *"Not here! There!"*

Diakrina's inner conversation paused a moment, and then, in a flash of insight, she said to herself, "If these longings are recognized, not as the thing desired, but as the sensation of missing the thing truly desired, then they are indeed useful. The longings," she continued, "are like thirst calling for water."

Because this *thirst* was her only clue to the *water* she desired and needed, she had often tried to capture and recapture this sensation of *thirst*. It was her only contact with that *something* to which her thirst witnessed. She now realized she had often mistaken the thirst for the true object of the thirst. Yet, her thirst had always proven false in that regard, for it was not the *thirst* she desired, it was the incredible *living water* to which her thirst pointed. And it was to this *water* the depths of her heart now responded with excited passion.

"Why this excited passion?" she asked herself, and instantly she knew the answer. The very atmosphere of this place confirmed that such water *did* actually exist and could be obtained! Here her life-long thirst could find its source and be filled!

She longed to ask Strateia about all this. But for now she was following the handsome giant to find something to eat. Questions would have to wait.

The water was cool and sweet as it gently swirled around their feet. It was so clear it appeared to the eye like liquid flowing crystal.

When the water was about to her knees—yet hardly halfway up Strateia's shin—Strateia turned to the left and started wading up stream. The current was not strong. Diakrina did not find it strenuous to wade against.

They had not gone far when Diakrina noticed an enormous tree on the bank ahead of them to the right. A large rock sloped down into the water at a very steep angle, and the tree sat on the bank above the rock, spreading its branches out to the sky.

Branches reached across the stream, all the way to the left bank. Some of them were quite low where they crossed the stream, and Diakrina could see they were heavy with fruit the shape of a very large peach. The skin was either bright yellow streaked with bright red, or bright red streaked with bright yellow—Diakrina could never decide which.

Strateia reached up and pulled one of the heavily laden branches low, just in reach for Diakrina. "Pick one, little one. You will find it most satisfying."

Diakrina reached out and placed her hand on one of the many available. The moment her hand touched it, the fruit released its hold on the branch and dropped into her hand. "They pick so easily," said Diakrina. "How do they stay on the tree?"

"They only turn loose when chosen. You might say they respond *excitedly* to their created purpose."

Diakrina reached out and took hold of another but it did not fall as the other into her hand. She pulled harder, then as hard as she was able, but the fruit did not come loose from the tree. "This one does not seem as *excited* as the other," announced Diakrina.

Strateia's eyes danced with mirth at her. "They do not cast their pearls before swine," he chuckled.

"And what do you mean by that?" snapped Diakrina playfully.

"That when you have one in your hand, there is no need for a second. Where there is no need, there is no proper power to truly appreciate. They were not created for waste, so they resist it."

Strateia turned the limb free and it returned to its place against the blue sky.

"Are you going to eat?" asked Diakrina, looking somewhat puzzled.

"I have already done so. But this food is not for me."

"Are you not allowed to eat it?"

Strateia smiled, looking down on Diakrina with serious amusement. "My Master keeps nothing good from me. It is not a matter of being *allowed* to eat it. There is no reason to eat it when my Master has given me food which I like better."

"Would I like your food better than this?" asked Diakrina, holding up the colorful fruit.

"I'm sure you would if you were wise enough to partake of it."

"Wise enough?" Diakrina looked even more puzzled. "How is wisdom needed to eat something?"

Diakrina followed as Strateia turned and began walking back down stream. "If the food itself is truth, then wisdom is needed to partake of it."

"You eat *truth?*" Diakrina looked more mystified than ever. "How can someone eat . . . reality?"

This last statement seemed to amuse Strateia as if she had made some kind of pun. But, evidently realizing she was incapable of understanding his amusement, he only smiled a flashing grin and shook his head at her in delight.

"If you will change your expression from, 'to eat reality' to, 'to take in reality,' maybe the concept will be easier for you to imagine. To eat or to take in is basically the same idea."

Diakrina paused in midstream to consider Strateia's statement. Then, coming to herself again, she waded ashore and sat down cross-legged on the velvet green in front of the now reclining Strateia.

"How does wisdom make it possible to take in this truth-food, and the lack of it make it impossible?" she asked.

"Well," said Strateia, rising up on one elbow and turning from his back to his side toward Diakrina, "truth is taken in by perspective. Wisdom is the vantage point from which truth may be properly seen and therefore *understood*—taken in."

He paused for a moment and then continued. "It's much like climbing a mountain and looking over a landscape. Before you climb the mountain you may be confused about the layout and design of the valley, not able to understand how *this* relates to *that*. Yet once on the mountain peak, you *can take it all in* at once. You might say that as a child developing teeth gives him a new ability to take in solid food, so acquired wisdom gives one a new ability to perceive—take in—more dense and intricate reality."

As Strateia said, "intricate," he used a gesture that flavored it with the meaning of *beautiful,* or by way of comparison, *delicious.*

"Delicious reality . . ." said Diakrina, thinking out loud.

"I think you have your own piece of delicious reality to *take in*," said Strateia, motioning toward the fruit in her hand.

Diakrina lifted the fruit to her lips and the word "delicious" suddenly became experience. The fragrance of the fruit was enough to make her forget everything else around her.

She bit into its firm but cooperative skin, and sensations she had never before known in relation to tasting food burst into her body. She had not noticed being particularly hungry beforehand. Now, as the first bite of the fruit entered her mouth, it was as if hunger was aroused from a deep sleep into bright-eyed wakefulness and came stampeding to greet this wonderful source of satisfaction.

Diakrina later tried to describe to me how two sensations—quite opposite in this world—conjoined in that realm as she bit into the fruit. "In this world," she explained, "when you eat, your hunger is tamed and satisfaction gradually displaces the hunger. Here, you never experience raging hunger and full-grown satisfaction at the same moment.

"It was different there. Eating, instead of taming hunger, inflamed it. Yet, at the same moment the most complete and extraordinary sense of total satisfaction drenched your whole insides."

Then she quickly added, "But the craving was not a complaining desire. It was a passionate eagerness, delighting in satisfaction with ever-increasing strength. Each satisfying moment strengthened the vitality of the hunger. It was not," she hurriedly clarified, "a coarse, demanding hunger, like a rude child cramming food into her mouth. It was more like unrestrained, noble delight. Craving had no fear of not being satisfied or of being denied the object of its passion: no possessiveness, no hoarding greed. For the satisfaction was both constant and abundant."

After the first bite, Diakrina squealed with wide-eyed delight and lost herself in the remainder of the fruit. When she had finished it, she lay back on the green turf in sweet exhaustion. You might think she would have wanted more, but strangely (at least from our perspective) the thought never crossed her mind. It was as if the passionate hunger had reached a perfect climax. She said it was like a diver who has leaped from a 50-foot waterfall; the intensity of the experience accelerates with the increasing speed of his fall and the crescendo of the cascading water. Then, suddenly, he pierces the surface of the placid warm pool and plunges instantly into quiet and relaxed comfort.

Diakrina floated in wide-awake contentment on the green grass for several minutes.

CHAPTER SIX

# The MEANING of the GREAT DANCE

"We must speak of the Great Dance now," said Strateia interrupting Diakrina's contented leisure.

Diakrina sat up slowly and looked deep into Strateia's clear eyes.

"It troubles me much, Strateia. Please, explain to me the things I experienced."

Positioning himself on a nearby bolder—a perfect seat for an eight-foot warrior—Strateia began.

"The Great Dance, which you beheld, fills the whole of the Master's creation. Its patterns of beauty and love are ever changing, yet always harmonious. The balcony from which you observed the Great Dance was a position of wisdom granted to you."

"Like the mountain peak?" interrupted Diakrina.

"Yes, much like the mountain peak. From it you were able to take in a panoramic view of the Great Dance. You could see the distinctive uniqueness of the various dancers and how vital it is for all of them to express their individuality in obedience to the Law of the Great Dance. The harmony, order and beauty of the Dance depends on this obedience.

"Most importantly, you could see how the *Speaking Music*, as your mind called it, provides the theme out of which emerge the unity and beauty of the Great Dance. The Music communicates and directs the dancers, as its melodic and harmonious strains form the Law of the Great Dance; the dancers, in turn, translate the Music into a visual display of glory—of *Life* as the Master intended."

"The majestic human Couple with the animal-like creatures with them, who were they?" inquired Diakrina.

"They are your Great Parents. They were beguiled by the evil one: the one you recognized as the Intruder. He is known by many names, as evil has many faces. We call him Anomos Poneros. *Anomos* means lawless one, and *Poneros* means diseased or harmful one—one who is degenerate, calamitous, vicious, derelict, wicked. In a word, *evil*. He is the lawless one because he is the diseased one, contaminated by a self-inflicted malady."

The reminder of the Intruder proved both painful and intriguing for Diakrina, and one question pushed immediately to the front of her mind.

"Strateia, why did the dance of this intruder, Anomos, seem so beautiful in its own way when I looked only at him, but so ugly and out of place when seen in relation to the Great Dance?"

"Because," said Strateia, "he will not obey the Law—the Purpose—of the Great Dance. He defies the Speaking Music by mocking it with his own impoverished imitations. He cannot create true Music himself, but he insists on trying. I think he actually believes at times that he has succeeded, because his antics appear so different from what the Speaking Music is creating at that moment. But it is always, and only, a corruption of something the Speaking Music has already composed."

"Why can he not create his own Speaking Music?" asked Diakrina.

"The Speaking Music is infinite; limitless. All music—even the very fact that music exists—flows from the Speaking Music. There is no other music. As we allow it, it plays and sings through us."

Diakrina suddenly recalled the intense joy of those moments when the Music had done exactly that.

"The Speaking Music," continued Strateia, "is composed out of nothing but the will and purpose of the One who calls all things into existence. We creatures, on the other hand, can only fashion music out of what He has already created. The music we 'make' is derived from His Music, for creating something out of nothing is beyond our reach.

"Anomos is a created, thus limited, being. He, like all creatures, depends on the Speaking Music for the very idea of music. By defying the Speaking Music and trying to create his own, he only manages to patch together echoes of strains already expressed by the Speaking Music. The result is an impoverished, scrambled and cheapened distortion of the original.

"Did you not notice, Diakrina, that the Speaking Music never repeated itself?"

Diakrina's eyes widened with remembrance.

"Of course," she exclaimed. "That is why it created such anticipation in me. While everything inside me was captivated by the melody of the moment, that same melody was predicting—almost prophesying—the next emerging theme. It filled me with both utter satisfaction and a thrill of expectation at the same moment.

"In fact," and here she paused, searching for words, "it was . . . as if . . . each theme was declaring, *'I am not the whole. I have been preceded and I will be followed. Only along with what precedes and follows can you truly know me. Remember! . . . Experience! . . . Anticipate!'*"

Strateia smiled his approval.

Diakrina's eyebrows rose, and suddenly leaning forward with inquisitive expectancy she asked, "Can the Speaking Music ever repeat a theme?"

"Why would it want to?" returned Strateia.

"Well," continued Diakrina, "when I hear a beautiful song, I want to hear it again. Is it never like that with the Speaking Music?"

"The Speaking Music creates beauty endlessly," explained Strateia. "Each melody is as beautiful as the last. There is never a need to repeat a theme or 'song' as you call it, because the Music never dies. It does not go, like your songs, into the past. Instead, each theme has a point of origin and then, immortality. Each melody is eternal because it flows from the Eternal One. It is His word to us. It begins as He creates it in relationship with His creatures, as a point of communication you call time. Yet it has no end because it comes from His unfading Life."

"But why, then," interjected Diakrina, "does the melody *seem* to end and be replaced by another?"

The look on Strateia's face told Diakrina that her question could not be answered in a way she could understand completely, but he continued.

"The melody *seems* to end or fade away to *you* because of your own finite and time-bound perception. You perceive the Speaking Music in your *Now*, for that is the only place time touches eternity for you. For *you* the melody goes into the past—the previous *Nows* in which you heard it. But the melody itself has not ceased, only your access to it in time. Each melody, in fact, continues eternally, adding to the ever-increasing glory of the Speaking Music. Each melody has its eternal place and fits perfectly with all that has gone before and all that will come after, and no two melodies are exactly alike. Each is fresh and new, and adds to the perfect and beautiful crescendo of eternity."

"Wow!" is all that escaped Diakrina's lips.

"Diakrina," continued Strateia, "let me give you a simple word picture. Imagine an organist playing and sustaining a single note on his organ. Then while holding that note, he adds a second, perfectly harmonious, note. Then while holding these two, he adds a third and the beauty is increased; then a fourth, then a fifth, and so on. The chord keeps building and increasing.

"Now imagine this being done with intricate, moving melodies as you heard from the Speaking Music. Each theme is created and sustained and then a second is added and sustained, and then a third. This goes on unendingly as theme gives counterpoint to theme. The expressions of glory and joy increase forever.

"The same is true of the Great Dance. Since it reflects the Speaking Music that is ever new, the Dance is ever new, as well. The Creator sings and His creatures dance in joyful response to His song. Both the Music and the Dance are eternally fresh and new.

"In this way, His creation reflects something of His own mysterious nature, which is both singular and plural—both unique and united. He is One through a transcendent unity of His Persons. It seems, as an expression of His own nature, he wants His creatures to be unique—no two exactly alike—and yet to find their meaning in relation to all the others; each is a story within a greater story."

Again, "Wow!" was all that Diakrina could say as she shifted onto her knees and then sat back on her bare feet with her hands in her lap. After a moment of wide-eyed thought she added, "But it does seem amazing that nothing is ever repeated."

"Yes, little one, it is part of the Great Mystery of the Living One, Whom none can totally comprehend. All time and eternity are too cramped for Him to fully express Himself even once. There is no need for an encore!"

"This too, is like the Great Dance, then," said Diakrina, jumping to her feet and self-forgetfully swirling in graceful circles she had learned as a child in ballet school. "Each dancer danced uniquely and differently from all the others," she added. "Yet all obeyed the Law of the Great Dance and moved together creating a collective visual of the Speaking Music that none of them could create alone."

"Yes," interjected Strateia, "each dancer finds his or her greatest purpose, meaning and joy in their unique reflection of the Music, in perfect harmony with the whole. This is the Law of the Dance. Without it, the Dance would collapse into chaos."

With uninhibited delight, Diakrina continued to swirl back and forth in the grass. "Is *my* dance unique, Strateia?" she asked, almost playfully, forgetting for the moment to act all grown up.

"Indeed it is, little one," Strateia chuckled. "And a lovely one, at that. By finding your place in His story and choosing to move in step with His Music, your life—your dance—becomes a beautiful—and yes, unique— reflection of His beauty.

"Every creature brings a unique expression to the Dance and reflects the Master's Music in ways no other creature can. The Music itself is ever perfect and complete, and cannot be enhanced or diminished in any way, for it flows from the heart of the Living One who is eternally self-sufficient. The Dance, however, gains exquisite beauty and depth from the involvement of each dancer, and suffers when any dancer falls out of step. The Creator has instilled immense worth and value in the reflective potential of each creature."

Diakrina stopped in mid swirl. "Reflective potential?" she mused aloud, and then continued thoughtfully, "Yes, I see. Each dancer adds profoundly to the beauty of the dance as they reflect, through their movements, the themes of the Speaking Music. They find and fulfill their greatest potential— and discover their greatest joy—by reflecting His Music through their uniqueness, in mutual interdependence with all the other dancers."

"Well said, Diakrina," Strateia beamed. "You have summed up the Law of the Great Dance."

Diakrina sat down in the grass, cupped her right elbow in her left hand and rubbed her chin thoughtfully. "This has profound implications for human notions of self-identity. Help me understand this better, Strateia."

"Yes, indeed it does, Diakrina, for all creatures, not just humans. The Law of the Dance enables us to know ourselves.

"At the most basic level, the *fact* of the Speaking Music assures us that we truly exist. We hear the Music and know it comes from beyond our self. It exists separate from us—it transcends us—and yet it fills us. We know that It is not us and we are not It. To put it plainly, *Since It exists, then so must I, because I hear It."*

Diakrina, who had always taken *existing* for granted, wrinkled her nose and started to make a retort about pinheaded philosophers, but caught herself. Strateia merely raised an eyebrow and smiled briefly at her unspoken interruption, then continued.

"We've already spoken a great deal about uniqueness, but it bears to be repeated here. In the Dance, we each discover our self-identity through our individuality. No two creatures hear, reflect or translate the Speaking Music in exactly the same way. As we learn to love the authority of the Music and find our place in the Great Dance, we gain knowledge of our self. Each creature's dance, in harmony with the whole, reveals that creature's unique nature. In short, *How I dance reveals who I am.*

"Furthermore," Strateia paused a moment to let Diakrina's thoughts catch up, "self-identity develops in the exchange—the give and take—

of the collective Dance. We discover and learn to appreciate one another by observing each other's steps and moving in harmony with one another. It is in this relationship with other creatures that we grow to understand and rightfully value each other and, consequently, self. Therefore, *I discover myself in my appreciation of others.*

"Are you still with me, Diakrina?"

"Yes, I believe so," she replied, and then eagerly added, "I am fascinated! Please go on."

Strateia, shifting his enormous frame slightly on the giant bolder, continued, "Self-identity is also a matter of context. Existence loses all meaning apart from a sense of what came before and what will follow after. Each dancer dances in his or her *Now*, for, as I mentioned earlier, *Now* offers the only point at which time touches eternity. Learning to dance— to live—in the *Eternal Now* is vital, though it is perhaps a discussion for another time.

"The Speaking Music gives context and, thus, meaning to each moment—each *Now*. Each dancer's song is a line in an eternal symphony; a chapter in an eternal story. As you so aptly stated earlier, Diakrina, the Music swells and fills each *experience* with a continual summons to *remember* and *anticipate*. Each creature's *Now* is part of something infinitely greater. We discover our identity not only in relation to one another, but also in relation to the Eternal Story that forever unfolds in the Music of the Living One. One could say, *My place in His Story gives my life meaning.*

"Before we move on from this matter of self-identity, Diakrina, I must mention one more implication—an extremely important one. As we learn to love the Speaking Music and reflect it back to Him and to others through our dance, we grow in our understanding of the Master, Himself, for the Music reveals Him to us."

Diakrina, hoping she wasn't being rude, interrupted, "Is the Living One and the Music the same, Strateia? Mentions of either of them inspire the same feelings and longings inside me. Is He the Music?"

"A good question, indeed," replied Strateia cheerfully, letting her know that her interruption was welcomed. "The Music is an expression of the

Living One. Without Him, the Music would not exist. Without the Music, however, He would *certainly* exist. It is dependent on Him, but He is not dependent on It."

"So, you mean He transcends the Music," said Diakrina, still wrinkling her forehead in thought.

"Excellent word, little one! Yes, He infinitely transcends the Music just as He infinitely transcends all He creates."

Strateia watched her countenance clear, and then he continued. "The more we know and love the Speaking Music, the better we know and love Him, for it is through the Music that He reveals Himself to us. And in knowing Him we know ourselves more fully. He is the Standard by which all things are measured, the perfect Light by which all things are illuminated, the absolute Truth by which all would-be truths are appraised. Our self-identity can be nothing other than distorted apart from an accurate knowledge of our Creator. All this is to say, *I know myself only in knowing Him.*

Strateia let several moments pass before he added, "I have said much for you to take in, Diakrina. Would you like to reiterate?"

"Let's see," Diakrina began slowly. "Regarding the Great Dance and our sense of self-identity . . . Since the Music exists, then so must I, because I hear It." She paused and looked at Strateia, who nodded his approval.

She continued, "How I dance reveals who I am, for it expresses my uniqueness." At this point, Diakrina resisted a sudden urge to jump up and demonstrate. Instead, her eyes trailed off to the horizon while she tried to remember the next thing Strateia had said.

"Oh yes," she nearly blurted after several seconds. "As I learn to value others, I discover myself."

The next two points came quickly. "My place in His Story—context, you called it—gives my life meaning. And I know myself only in knowing the Living Once through the Speaking Music."

"You are a delightful pupil, Diakrina!" Strateia gleamed at her. "Well done, indeed."

This encouragement inspired Diakrina to know more. "Strateia, you started to say something about learning to live in the *Eternal Now*. Please, explain that for me."

"Imagine, Diakrina, eternity as a vast and infinite ocean, without boundaries or beaches. Imagine also a single wave moving across that ocean. That wave is time, and the point at which the wave intersects the ocean is *Now*. It is vital that you learn to live in that wave: in the *Eternal Now*, for it is where life happens for those of us who are creatures of time.

"The wave of the *Eternal Now* sets the timing and rhythm of the Speaking Music. Anomos' music drags its followers into regret over the past or fear of the future, always out of step with the Speaking Music. His goal is to spin illusions of your past and future that warp your perspective on the *Now*. These illusions disorient and distract from the Speaking Music.

"Your race has fallen for these illusions and is captive to regret and fear, constantly stumbling in the *Eternal Now*."

Fixing his gaze steadily into Diakrina's eyes, Strateia said with grave intensity, "*Being in step with eternity is the key to living successfully in time. And the only way to do that is to hear and follow the Speaking Music in the Eternal Now. That is where, and only where, all true possibilities exist*."

Diakrina felt the solemnity of these words, though she didn't quite understand them. She determined to seek the help of the Living One to grow in her understanding and learn to live in the Eternal Now.

Both Diakrina and the giant warrior sat in contemplative silence for three or four minutes before Diakrina sighed with longing, "Oh, I love the Speaking Music and the Great Dance, Strateia."

Then her countenance clouded. "When I was dancing with the Couple and the creatures that followed them, why did the Great Dance leave us?"

"It did not leave you, Diakrina. You left it when you joined the discordant dance of Anomos," reminded Strateia.

"But it *seemed* so right at the moment," Diakrina retorted with a hint of defensiveness in her voice. "His dance was so much like the Great Dance that it seemed harmless."

"Breaking step with the Speaking Music is never harmless," replied Strateia sternly. "It always leads to death, because no life can exist severed from the Source of Life."

Softening his voice, he added, "Evil often *feels* harmless because it echoes the Speaking Music. Every step of Anomos' dance mimics some step in the Speaking Music, for Evil does not create, it merely distorts. Much that is evil is not inherently *wrong*, but is *out of place*."

"Out of place?" Diakrina leaned toward Strateia, eager to hear more.

"Imagine a grand story, Diakrina, composed of millions of words. Each word has a noble place in the story. Each word is good, beautiful, purposeful—reflecting the intentions of the author and bringing joy to all who read it.

"If you were to become enamored with a particular word and insisted on interjecting it throughout the story wherever you fancied, without regard to the author's purposes, the story would suffer and the word, though beautiful in itself, would become an obscene distraction. You may be so enthralled with the word that you sincerely believe it adds richness to the story—you may even beam with pride at your 'creative contribution' —but to any discerning reader your rogue use of language amounts to vile vandalism. The value of each word flows from its placement within the sentence, within a paragraph, within a chapter, within the story. That which enhances beauty, joy and purpose *in its place*, destroys and defames when *out of place*.

"Anomos' dance *felt* harmless because each step, in itself, is borrowed from the Great Dance. Convinced of his own power to create, he vandalizes the Great Dance by rearranging the order and cadence of the moves. Like a toddler scribbling with crayons on the nursery wall, he thinks he is creating something meaningful. After all, letters and words and stories are made up of circles and curves and lines and dashes. The crayoned scrawls are merely bits and pieces of a story all out of place."

"I know I have done much scribbling of my own," Diakrina reminisced soberly. "You said this always leads to death, Strateia. That troubles me."

"And so it should, little one. The prospect of being severed from the Great Dance is profoundly troubling."

"What do you mean by *severed*?" she asked.

"Think of it like this. Words that are written into the Great Story that defy or distort the purposes of the Author must be edited out. Or, in the language of the Great Dance, discordant music cannot be allowed to pervert the beauty and meaning of the Speaking Music. The Living One's Story *shall* be told, His Music *shall* be heard. All that defames or interferes will be removed—severed—from the Source."

"Severed from the Source of Life," Diakrina said softly. A wave of sadness swept over her as she thought of many friends and family members who seemed to be plodding along mindlessly to the defiant themes of Anomos, completely unaware that they are severed, dancing the dance of death. She longed to see them again and warn them.

"Strateia," she asked quietly, "Is it true that scribbles and misplaced words can occupy the whole of one's life, leaving them with nothing when the edits are made? Can an entire life be edited out?"

"Sadly, yes, Diakrina. Some are so defiant and proud—so full of self-deluded independence—that they refuse to learn the language of reality. They dismiss the Living One's every attempt to teach them, and insist on blurting out their own version of reality. They gyrate to the displaced and dissident music of Anomos and demand that their childish antics be applauded. Objective judgment will see it for the waste that it is, and the Living One will have no recourse but to edit them from His Story: the *only* Story that is or can ever be."

These words hung solemnly in the air for nearly a minute before Diakrina broke the silence with a question that had been gnawing its way into her consciousness. "Strateia, if my Great Parents were severed from the Dance and my entire race with them, *is there any hope for us?*"

"Ah, little one, you see the great dilemma. The answer, I am very pleased to say, is yes, there is hope. The reason for that hope is a story too wonderful for you to grasp today. In time, you will see and rejoice. For now, I will only say that it involves the grand miracle that has already happened in your time, by which the Living One Himself—the Source of the Music—has descended into the Dance and has become, Himself, a Dancer."

Something in Diakrina's heart leaped with intense excitement and longing. She sat up suddenly straight and clapped her hands together. "Oh, please tell me!"

"In time, my eager pupil. In time," was all that Strateia would say.

"For now, you would do well to rest and enjoy this remarkably lovely day. We will speak more later this afternoon. In the meantime, I have some things to do. While I am gone, embrace the beauty around you."

With that, he stood and was gone.

Diakrina was so full of thoughts of the Great Dance and all its meaning, she simply lay back on the soft green grass and watched as a few small, white clouds floated by in the blue sky. Images, jumbled together with thoughts, mingled and danced in her head.

After about half an hour, she roused herself from her trance, got up and walked back to the stream. Finding a waterhole deep enough for swimming, she dove in. The water was so crystal clear and the temperature so perfectly refreshing that she felt wonderfully renewed.

Soon, schools of colorful fish had gathered at the edge of the waterhole, looking in her direction as though awaiting her invitation to approach. Diakrina took a deep breath and dove under the water. She swam over to the fish and beckoned with her hands. Within seconds they surrounded her, swimming and jumping as if playtime had been announced. When she surfaced, the water around her boiled like a delightful cauldron of playful fish.

She dove back into the water and, together with her school of colorful friends, swam around exploring the bottom of the stream. For over an hour they splashed and played and swam in lively formations. Diakrina felt like a princess mermaid, accompanied by a hundred dancing children.

After a delightfully refreshing romp, Diakrina got out onto the bank of the stream and stretched out on the soft grass in the warm sunlight. She must have dozed off for about an hour, for she and her grass tunic were mostly dry when she awoke.

"I see you had a relaxing time," said Strateia from somewhere behind her.

Diakrina got up and stretched slightly. She felt amazing.

"Are you ready to continue our discussion of the Great Dance?" asked Strateia.

"Yes, Strateia. I feel quite refreshed and eager to continue."

Strateia took his place on the large rock again, and Diakrina sat down on the grass in front of him.

All the things Strateia had been teaching her had fermented into a question that was bothering Diakrina. Before really meaning to do so, she blurted out what was on her mind.

"How did Anomos come to be? If the Living One is the Source of all that is, why would He create one to mock and corrupt the Great Dance of Life?"

"That is a rather long story, Diakrina. Much of it will be the subject of another day. Be assured, however, that the Living One did not create Anomos evil. All that the Master creates is good, and Anomos originally danced in perfect step with the Speaking Music as one of the greatest of dancers.

"But he turned his attention inward, away from the Maker. Like Narcissus, he fell in love with his own reflection. Instead of reflecting the perfection of the Living One, he chose to reflect himself. He reasoned, absurdly, that by reflecting himself and deceiving others into reflecting him, he could become like the Living One. Unsatisfied with being a reflection, he foolishly longed to become an autonomous source, a creator in his own right.

"In his self-obsessed blindness, he failed to see the obvious: that no creature possesses the capacity for self-existence and essential creative power. These are virtues of the Creator alone.

"The creature is necessarily dependent on the Creator. All but the Creator is contingent; unnecessary. We *are—we exist*—because we have been created out of love, to be loved and to learn love, but our value is found only in our reflection of our Creator.

"Anomos' independence is an illusion. He cannot even distort anything without being, first, a thief. And his illusion is a contagious form of insanity. A whole realm of creation suffers his infection, and many are deluded into following him into the madness of this parasitic existence."

Strateia paused to allow these thoughts to sink in and then added, "Do you remember how he made you feel that you were creating independently, dancing your own dance?"

Diakrina nodded.

"It was an illusion, a lie. You were dancing his dance, the dance of corruption. And only the corruption is original with him; none of its content is.

"True creativity is only possible to us within the Law of the Great Dance. Outside of it, we can only distort and destroy. To reflect Him, who is infinitely creative, is our only access into the realms of creativity. His endless creativity is a constant act of love and joy, and He invites us to participate.

"Diakrina, we are made so that we—in step with His Speaking Music— can create out of what He has already created. And in doing so, we reflect Him. And in delighted, loving, humility He weaves our reflections back into the reality of all He is causing. And wonder of wonders, He calls us co-owners and co-authors. Such is His loving humility."

Then Strateia paused and fixed his eyes on Diakrina so as to hold her gaze. He clearly wanted her complete attention.

"Diakrina, true creativity and the joy of discovery are only found in connectedness with the Speaking Music. One of the great tragedies of being severed from directly hearing the Speaking Music and dancing in the Great Dance is the loss of wonder. Wonder probes and investigates and seeks explanations, enchanted with the ever-unfolding mystery of life.

"In the Great Dance wonder never ends, for it leads to knowledge that is both a satisfying answer and a new enticing question, which in turn points to a greater unfolding of beauty. Each arrival *is* an arrival. But each arrival is not an end. Rather it is the first step to more wonder, to a new beginning.

"Being severed from the Great Dance has limited your race to a kind of *wonder* that is killed by knowledge. Explanations become a terminus to mystery; analysis becomes the death knell of curiosity. The *this is only that* explanation becomes a reductionistic solvent that reduces all of life to a featureless plain. Arrivals become dead ends. Like a magician's trick that enchants the audience before its secret is revealed, but loses its wonder and appears simplistically commonplace once the technique is unveiled, knowledge of any one particular thing appears trivial and mundane when severed from its context in the Great Story.

"Some among your race have become lost in the minutia of this reductionism. They survey the perfect perpendicular of the letter *L*, discuss in great lengths where the circuit of the *O* begins and ends, argue the ideal angle of a *V* and expend vast quantities of resources determining the precise thickness and length of the three-pronged *E*. They stake their positions and form committees, organizations, sects, religions and nations to defend and even make war over their findings, all the while never realizing that the objects of their scrutiny are letters of a language greater than the sum of its parts. Instead of reading *L-O-V-E*, they see only marks on a page and obsess over each curve and crease. They refuse to believe in a language beyond their own, but instead reduce every jot and dash to its rudimentary elements.

"Far too sophisticated for crayons and scribbles, they cover their walls with intricate and exquisite prints of *X*s, *Z*s and *Q*s, unaware that vestiges of a wondrous alphabet hang displayed before them. This they call knowledge and revel in its calculations and formulas, plunging ever deeper into the abyss of disconnected trivia.

"Some, bent less toward knowledge than toward pleasure, fashion the jots and dashes into an endless parade of new toys. Cut off from the Source of Life, these toys generate a momentary thrill and then succumb to the entropic inevitabilities of a severed existence.

"Of course, the young, dream-filled soul will simply drop the now disenchanting toy and reach for another. But the result is the same. No thing, no person ever leads beyond itself because in the realms of death the proper interconnectedness is lost—severed. Each thing or person or experience is pursued for what it can never be: an end in itself. These unfulfilled expectations spiral downward as each new thing promises what it cannot deliver, until a heart-devouring spirit of discontentment consumes the soul.

"The Living One is the eternal connection between all things as Creator, and He has created all things to find their complete meaning in relation to all other things in Him. In Anomos' severed kingdom each thing or experience is stolen from the Great Dance, torn from its proper context within the overarching mystery and joy of creation. Everything is *out of place.*

"You were never intended to know dead, disconnected knowledge. In the Great Dance, knowledge of one thing leads to knowledge of another . . . always pointing to a beauty beyond itself. Each jot is part of a letter, a word, a sentence, a paragraph, a story, and everything finds its significance by its place in the Great Story.

"Dead, severed knowledge creates cynics and skeptics. To them, wonder always leads to a dead end; to sterile knowledge, like a fruitless branch. Mystery and enchantment give way to bitterness and disillusionment as the human soul loses its far horizon. Without this far horizon calling it to adventure, the soul is dead even while it exists.

"Do you understand, Diakrina?"

"All too well, Strateia. I have felt the disappointment so many times. After the presents are unwrapped at Christmas and everything that seemed to whisper wonder into my heart is being packed up; when the vacation is over and all the anticipated adventures are now past experience; when the great moment of achievement for which I had worked so hard came, and the thrill of the accomplishment fizzled like a dying firework; no matter how great the momentary delight, it did not last.

"Yes, Strateia, the elusive grasping at sand, which leaves one so exhausted, I know this. It makes real contentment a promise always receding just out of sight.

"I have seen it in the faces of the pleasure wearied who have pursued each sensual passion down countless dead end alleys. Their eyes betray their gnawing disappointment as yet another promise fails to deliver. Yet, like thirst-dazed men chasing a mirage into the desert, they stagger on, following the ever-allusive promise of fulfillment.

"Anomos has killed the wonder. He has filled my race with dead knowledge and has trapped us in an endless cycle of empty pursuits," Diakrina sighed sadly.

Strateia placed his hand on Diakrina's shoulder reassuringly. "Soon," he said, "the Living One will seal up Anomos so he cannot feed on the Great Dance any longer. Then he will no longer be able to sever and twist truth. He will have his wish: he will be 'independent'—alone with his corrupt 'creation'—and it will forever twist, distort and consume him. Until then, he is already defeated and serves unwittingly the Master's purpose.

"How does he serve the Master's purpose?" asked Diakrina.

"That is another and higher point of wisdom which must come, for you, later. For today, you must remember that you are a daughter of the Couple—touched by Anomos' corruption and excluded from the Great Dance by your own actions. Your Great Parents' failure has become yours. You only hear the Speaking Music second-hand and distorted by Anomos."

"You said there is hope. Will we ever get back into the Great Dance and hear the Speaking Music directly again?"

"This is the great quest of our Master: to break down and destroy every claim by which Anomos isolates your kind from direct involvement in the Great Dance. Some who trusted and were willing have found it again. And some who will trust and are willing will find it."

"Willing to do what?" asked Diakrina.

"You must be willing to break step with this Intruder."

"And how do I do that?" cried Diakrina, who was now on her feet and looking up into Strateia's clear eyes like a begging child.

"Little one, you must be cured of your deep, inborn suspicion of the Living One so you can deeply love the Speaking Music."

"But I do love the Speaking Music," cried Diakrina with the tone of one who had just been falsely accused. "I do love it!"

Strateia smiled warmly. "Yes, Diakrina, you love its beauty. But you do not yet love its authority. But we will speak of this later."

With that said, Strateia rose, indicating that the time of explanation was over. He walked away into the forest leaving Diakrina with her thoughts.

(See, *Appendix to Chapter Six*, for more of Strateia and Diakrina's discussion about identity.)

CHAPTER SEVEN

# The SEVERED LANDS

Diakrina spent that afternoon playing happily along the banks of the little brook. The fish and birds had not the slightest knowledge of fear. More than this, they seemed to possess some wonderful ability to know when she wanted them to come to her, as though they could hear her thoughts.

She would see a beautiful rainbow colored fish in the brook and think to herself, "Oh, how beautiful. I wish I could touch it." Instantly, as if her wish were its known delight, it would swim up to Diakrina's feet dangling in the water and rub against her ankles in an excited manner. When she would reach down to touch it, it would nestle up under her hand and respond to her touch like a purring kitten.

Diakrina had loved to feed the fish on her grandfather's farm, but she had never known fish to respond like this, even the ones she had made the best pets. A clear stream, full of fish, ran across the long driveway that led to her grandfather's farmhouse. A short wade upstream from the driveway swirled a beautiful swimming hole framed by rock cliffs on one side, and on the other a pleasant stone covered bank gave way to grass only a few feet from the water. Diakrina, toting a small sack of cornbread, would go down to the swimming hole on summer days and feed the small perch.

By the end of each summer, she had several of them trained to come and feed from her hand, and she always enjoyed giving them names that matched their manners. She christened them names like *Tim* for the timid one that was overly cautious, and *Toro* for the larger, bright colored perch that always pushed in to steal the cornbread from the others.

But never had she seen fish behave like *this*. Diakrina lost herself in the wonder of these tame and even affectionate creatures of the crystal waters. She wanted to touch every fish she saw, and soon was sitting in the sparkling stream up to her waist and squealing with delight as hundreds of them, of every description and color, caused the water to boil with excitement.

"Strateia, they like me," she giggled.

"They have been separated from their master so long. Of course they are excited to see you."

Diakrina was too caught up in her frolic with the fish to give Strateia's comment proper thought. Just then she noticed that several birds had landed on the bank near her. One bright yellow parrot with a silver beak and silver tipped wings caught her eye. "Oh, come," Diakrina thought aloud. Without hesitation the glorious cat-size bird spread his silver wings in the golden light and landed softly on Diakrina's outstretched hand.

Diakrina stroked his yellow head and kissed his silver beak as the fish played tag at her feet. "I wonder if you can be taught to speak?" said Diakrina.

A mimicking voice repeated, "I wonder if you can be taught to speak?"

"Why you are absolutely amazing!" cried Diakrina.

"Why you are absolutely amazing," squawked the parrot.

Diakrina giggled with delight. So did the parrot, which only made Diakrina giggle more, and so the parrot more. Soon both were in a fit of laughter as if they were being tickled beyond forbearance.

Strateia, who had been watching the scene, was soon roaring with noble laughter along with them. The fish, too, seemed to jump with delight.

"You cause the Garden to dance, little one," chuckled Strateia as they were both regaining their composure.

The golden sun was soon setting in the multi-colored sky. Diakrina mused, as she watched it descend below the low mountains in the distant valley, that every possible shade of blue was painted somewhere in the sky overhead—deep blue straight above her gave way to ever softer blues as she looked toward the setting sun.

Dancing on the different shades of blue gleamed the most brilliant golden yellow sunlight Diakrina had ever seen. No tints of red touched this sunset. For the first time, Diakrina realized how angry the red of most sunsets looked. This sunset laughed with golden laughter as it rollicked against the changing blue. Diakrina could not help thinking of the Great Dance.

Soon there was only a soft golden glow behind the mountains and the sky began to twinkle with hundreds of glorious stars. Something in the air made them seem closer and bigger than Diakrina had ever thought stars could be. A soft darkness rested gently over the Garden and a slight cool breeze mixed wonderfully with the warm night air.

Diakrina stood to better take in the last faint flush of light on the distant horizon. Then strangely, her shadow, definite and elongated, fell on the lush turf in front of her. Soft gold light seemed to wash itself over the whole glorious landscape of the gently sloping valley below, expelling some of the shadows and making others in between look darker and deeper.

Diakrina turned quickly around. There, as yellow and golden as the sun which had just disappeared, putting a faint halo on the leisurely rising slopes which stretched to the high, distant mountains of the east, rose the moon. So large and full was it that Diakrina stood in stunned silence. It was like watching a royal procession make its entrance onto the Garden stage.

A dreamy peace settled over the whole of the Garden. Birds grew quiet, and the sounds of the whispering brook and the soft rustle of the gentle breeze emerged with crisp clarity. The talented song of a faraway nightingale accented the demulcent silence—a silence itself a soothing lullaby.

"You must rest now," whispered Strateia as his bronze hand gently touched her shoulder. "Your first day is at a close and your strength is spent. There is a mat of soft green heather under the large tree there."

He led Diakrina a few steps to a little depression in the turf under a large spreading tree. Diakrina found the heather soft and comfortable—more so than any she had ever touched. "Will you sleep, too?" asked Diakrina.

"There is no need of it."

"But what will you do?"

"More than you know, little one," smiled Strateia. "Yet, I have some instructions for you before you sleep. Listen carefully. When you awake in the morning things will already be in transition and your purpose for being here—and the fruit of your exclusion from the Great Dance—will begin to unfold."

"Will I at least be able to see the Great Dance again tomorrow?"

"Reality seldom comes as we imagine. Now sleep, little one." And with that Strateia placed his hand on Diakrina's head and said, "The blessings of His light fill your dreams with joy."

Diakrina nestled into the comfortable heather and watched as Strateia walked a few paces and seated himself once more on the rock. His garment of light shimmered a soft white in the dark; his golden belt and sheath reflected the rich moonlight as the ruby-red sword handle glowed with steady warmth and cast a red halo on the ground around him.

Diakrina soon drifted off into sleep. She could never be sure if it actually happened or if it was only a dream, but she thought she saw two others like Strateia suddenly appear in front of him. They must have conversed long into the night, speaking to one another in a language ancient and beautiful, for every time Diakrina could remember stirring slightly it seemed that the music of their voices played on in quiet tones. But she could never wake herself fully enough to be sure. Besides, she was dreaming of the Great Dance and did not wish to wake.

The eastern sky still glowed pale with golden light when she did awake, lying on her side facing the rising sun. The birds had begun their morning conversations and she heard the fish splashing above the brook's surface. Bluish-gray squirrels scampered here and there playing tag among themselves. Every so often they would stop and chatter excitedly as if making up new rules to the game. Then the chase would be on again. From tree trunk to tree trunk; up one side and down the other; round and round a trunk they would chase one another.

At first, Diakrina didn't move, but lay there drinking in the glory of it all. Then she noticed that several of the squirrels had stopped their game and were lined up like little soldiers side by side, sitting on their back legs about twenty yards away, looking at her with bright brown eyes. Diakrina sat up and motioned for them to come. Obediently, they dropped to all fours and started toward her. But they never made it.

Without warning, the whole Garden began to shake. The ground trembled up and down and back and forth from east to west. The squirrels scattered toward the rising sun. Diakrina jumped to her feet, the first rays of golden light reflecting from her wide eyes. An unbearable *r i p p i n g* roar began somewhere off in the distance to Diakrina's left. She turned to see billowing clouds of earth and trees rising into the air as a terrible ear-splitting rumble raced in her direction.

Suddenly the earth where the squirrels had congregated split from left to right. A chasm yawned open, widening and deepening as the earth-shattering roar raced past Diakrina and out of sight, throwing trees and earth before it. Had Diakrina not been sheltered by the large tree she had slept under, she might have been buried by descending debris.

Just as she began to hope the violence may have spared her, a massive tree, some 500 feet away but over 600 feet tall, came crashing down in her direction, determined to pummel her under its spreading limbs. At the last moment, the falling, crushing timber caught in the gnarled forks of the great tree that sheltered her, sending a shower of broken branches down on her but diverting the enormous trunk off to her right in the direction of the still-rending earth.

"Strateia! Strateia!" she screamed.

Just then a cloud of dark earth descended down on her and all went black. Diakrina fell face first into the heather of her bed and buried her face in the mat to keep from choking on the thickening atmosphere, all the while screaming into the mat the name of her guardian.

An old, unconquered fear of darkness rose up inside her. She had always had an intense need to be in control. To her, feeling secure meant being in charge.

She desperately wanted to see, to assess her surroundings and regain control. Yet she had no say in what was happening. Somewhere in the sheer panic she gave up all pretense of being in charge and admitted deep inside that her need for control was only fear in disguise. Screaming uncontrollably into the heather of her bed, she tossed all disguise aside and gave full vent to her fear. The darkness—deep, rolling and thick—enveloped her in a prison of total and disorienting helplessness.

The earth continued to shake violently, ripping and rending around her on all sides. Diakrina covered her ears to try to stop the deafening roar. It was no use. The low groans and roars of the splitting, quaking earth turned her whole body into a vibrating eardrum. She felt as if her skin would not be able to contain her insides much longer. She wanted to go on screaming, but it now took all her concentration and strength just to find a breath.

Then suddenly, it was over. Overwhelming silence rushed in to fill the void left by the almost-liquid avalanche of noise. Diakrina waited motionless for several moments before she dared to stir. When finally she raised her head, the air was still thick with dust, and she was covered with branches and leaves.

Slowly she worked her way free of the pile and crawled out into sprinkles of golden sunlight streaking through floating gray earth. The air was clearing quite rapidly as a breeze blew gently through the chaotic tangle of branches strewn all around her. Huge limbs, which she took to be the top of the giant fallen tree, enclosed her. Enough sunlight bled through the limbs that she could see the main trunk of the great tree to her right as she faced the sun.

The old panic to get out of the darkness and back into the sunshine rose up in her, demanding with frantic urgency that she find a way up and free of the debris. She quickly formed a strategy to work her way through the large branches toward the trunk, climb the branches until she could get on top of the trunk, and then walk east on the top of the trunk to where the branches would stop. As the fallen tree was the kind that only has branches at the very top, and from there down the trunk is long, straight, and thick, she determined the lower end of the trunk would make a good perch from which to get her bearings and take inventory of the landscape around her.

The top branches of the tree, which had reached some 60 feet out from the tree in all directions when it stood, were, on the underneath side, broken, but still held the top of the trunk some 30 feet off the ground. Those branches that were now on top shot upward a full 60 feet into the air above the trunk.

It was slow going but she soon reached a large limb which promised to take her up to the trunk if she got on top of it and climbed along its length. This she did and was soon faced with the huge trunk. From the limb, Diakrina had to climb about four feet up the side of the trunk to get onto the level top side.

Having reached it, she stood up and regained her perspective by finding the sun's rays coming through the thick foliage. She then walked along the topside of the trunk, climbing around large up-turned limbs. The trunk was so wide and round and the branches so near the size of small trees themselves, that it was like walking on a bark covered roadway with small trees to circumvent every few feet. Up ahead she saw an opening in the branches, beyond which the trunk stretched out uninterrupted. When she came out of the branches the warm sunshine struck her face—but at the same time, so did sudden panic.

The giant tree on which she stood stretched out across a gorge, 300 feet wide, which ran north and south in a westward turning arc as far as the eye could see. The gorge seemed to have no bottom and the loose dirt on its newly exposed sides was still falling away here and there into nothingness. But what brought the sudden chill up her spine and the yelp of shock from her throat was that in climbing along the tree trunk she had unwittingly walked out over the great chasm. Having come out of the leaves and limbs, she was standing in mid-air over a gaping canyon with only the tree trunk beneath her feet. Between the vast sky above and bottomless expanse below, the tree suddenly felt no bigger than a tightrope.

Diakrina stood frozen in place, too petrified to move. Then, after a few moments of numbing terror, she regained enough composure to slowly turn around and take calculated steps back toward the first strong limb. Upon reaching it, she hugged it tightly, maneuvering her way carefully around it until the limb stood between her and the naked trunk before her. From here, still holding on for her life, she gazed back out toward the chasm and surveyed the cataclysm before her as she gradually resumed normal breathing.

She saw a little off to her right, on the far side of the gorge, a waterfall had formed. Something about it struck her as strange. She realized it must be the water of the brook, its course now broken by the gorge. But what was it that seemed so unusual?

Then, instantly, it was plain. The waterfall was silent. The crystal ribbon plunged off the east side of the gorge into nothing but air. No roaring sound of falling water hitting a bottom echoed back up from the chasm. The water shot out into the abyss with slow-motion silence into what looked to be an infinite dive.

The air was now almost clear, and Diakrina could see the Garden on the other side of the gorge. There were signs of fallen trees in a few places, but most of those thrown into the air had evidently descended down into the hungry mouth of the abyss. All else looked beautiful as before—the turf was bright and green, the flowers swayed softly in the breeze and the squirrels were starting to poke their heads out to see if it was safe to resume their games.

Diakrina suddenly thought of Strateia. She turned around to call back behind her toward where she reasoned she had last seen him. The tree branches were so tall and thick she could see nothing at all. She called Strateia's name several times. The sound of her own voice echoing from the far wall of the gorge behind her was the only answer she received.

Diakrina continued to hug the tall branch, wondering what to do next. As she tried to gather her thoughts, something rather uncanny slowly penetrated her awareness. From the far side of the gorge she could hear the sound of birds beginning to sing again. As she turned toward the gorge, once more she noticed that the squirrels had resumed their games, chattering excitedly as they scampered from tree to tree. But on her side of the gorge, there was not a sound—all was deadly silent.

The contrast grew the longer she stood there hugging the branch. The sounds of life from across the gorge resonated with a beautiful symphony of living things. The silence around her was, by contrast, like an audible darkness, a silent dread, a gathering gloom. She turned back around and peered into the branches in the direction of this vacuum. Slowly, but definitely, a chilly breeze became discernible against the skin of her face. It was neither a strong nor very cold breeze, just slight and somewhat chilly with a growing dampness discernible both on her skin and in a subtle musty odor.

A swirling mist came crawling through the branches toward her, slowly rolling and gathering over and around limbs and trunk, with layered, creeping streams just thick enough to look like slowly approaching serpents, but not so thick that the branches disappeared completely. Diakrina watched as it slithered to the edge of the gorge. The unhurried swirling motion never stopped, and Diakrina expected the mist to slither its way along the tree trunk to where she stood out over the gorge. Instead, however, it rolled over the edge of the gorge and down into its depths without reaching her.

She gripped the tree branch even more tightly and slid around it to put it between her and the mist. The large branch blocked some of the chill from the breeze, while at the same time she noticed the warmth of the sunshine on her back. Behind her she could still hear the symphony of life. In front of her was a slowly writhing wall of silent mist holding her at bay.

She felt the tree under her feet give a slight shudder as a soft thud sounded behind her. She turned into the sun to see the sculptured eight-foot frame of Strateia standing a few feet away. "Strateia!" Diakrina gasped breathlessly. Momentarily forgetting about the chasm she turned loose her hold on the branch and ran toward him. She wanted to hug him in relief, but the impressive effect of his huge frame and brilliant countenance caused her to pull up short in a kind of self-conscious two-step just in front of him. He smiled warmly down at her but said nothing.

"What's happening?" Diakrina blurted out. Strateia's expression flushed serious as he lifted his head and peered at the swirling mist a few yards beyond Diakrina. "It has begun, as you were told, little one."

"But how could all this happen?" Diakrina persisted.

Strateia looked back down and, taking Diakrina's trembling face in his large bronze hands, looked deep into her frightened eyes. "You seek the wrong knowledge, little one. It is not yet for you to understand *how* all this can happen. You must first ask, 'Why?'"

As Diakrina looked back into Strateia's strong clear eyes, she felt a calm invade and surround her. The muscles of her body relaxed for the first time since the thunderous quake assaulted the quiet of the early morning. "Is this part of training and preparation?" asked Diakrina in a quieter and steadier voice.

"You must learn to believe what you are told, little one. Did I not inform you that when you awoke this morning your quest would have already begun?"

Diakrina dropped her eyes in acknowledgement. She had never imagined a quest beginning like this.

"Truth is best learned when you pay attention to what you are told," said Strateia. "Only then will you begin to hear again the Speaking Music and regain your place in the Great Dance."

"I'm sorry, Strateia. I will do better from now on."

"Ask the Living One to help you. He is your true Helper. You will find that in His Light all things become known."

A stab of intense longing and inexplicable joy flooded Diakrina's eyes with very different tears than she had been crying. The thought that the Living One could be her Teacher and Helper gave a new attraction to the possible trials ahead of her.

"I am ready to begin, Strateia. But I really want to know what this *quest* is that you keep speaking to me about."

"In due time, Diakrina. But first, we must give ourselves some working room."

Strateia unsheathed his crimson sword and turned toward the swirling mist, which was still slowly rolling over the edge of the chasm. Lifting his sword to the sky he raised his voice in a silver battle cry that caused the tree to tremble under their feet: "In the Name of the Living One, I order you to retreat!" A blast of warm, pleasant wind came suddenly from behind them from the far side of the chasm, and the swirling mist halted, then began rolling backwards into the branches of the great tree. Soon the chill of the writhing mist had faded like a bad dream.

"I'm so glad that is gone," whispered Diakrina with a shudder. She turned to look down into the gorge almost expecting it also to be gone, but it was still there unchanged.

"Will you make the awful chasm disappear, too," she asked with hope in her voice.

"No. Only One can do that, and I am not that One," said Strateia. "The Chasm is a most serious and stubborn reality, and as long as it is between you and the Garden, the mist will always return. The mist is not gone, little one, it is simply pushed back for the moment."

"What is that mist?" Diakrina asked as she motioned toward the silence.

"Do you not recognize it, little one?" asked Strateia.

"Recognize . . . ?" Diakrina was asking just as a memory flooded her mind and silenced her. Instantly her eyes widened in troubled recollection. "It's . . . it's the same dark cold that grasped at my heels as I ran toward the Door of the Rose," she said half under her breath.

"Yes, little one. It is what you have always known before being brought here."

Strateia paused as Diakrina's troubled face revealed she was processing what now seemed like ancient memories. She said nothing else but simply stared in the direction of the retreated mist.

"For now, little one, I have work to do. And the first thing I must do is to give you an expanded perspective."

Strateia picked Diakrina up in his arms and suddenly the tree-bridge, the gorge and the landscape of the Garden fell away at a blinding speed.

Diakrina gasped and grasped at the folds of his garment of light (though there was no need, for she could not make herself more secure).

Almost in the same instant they were motionless again. Only now the Garden and the gorge lay thousands of feet below. To the east, far up the valley, Diakrina could see great mountains rising into the clouds and the golden sunlight, their tops vanishing into the gentle blue of the heavens.

To the west, the valley stretched out in a slow descent to some smaller, more earth-sized mountains on the horizon. About 100 yards into the forest to the west of the tree-bridge, the mist still lay over the area like a gray blanket in slow swirling motion in and around the valleys.

The Garden below was vast, but did not fill the whole of the visible valley. The large ivy-covered stone wall formed a perfect square around the exterior of the Garden. Right in the center, on the highest plateau of the great Garden, spread the large lake. The waters were indeed boiling up, as though some deep geyser sprang up below the center of the lake spewing enormous quantities of water into the lakebed, and from there into four great rivers that flowed through the Garden.

As the rivers approached the stone perimeter of the Garden, they plunged into small lake-like depressions against the wall. Crystal clear water filled these four great pools, seemingly hundreds of feet deep. The outer stone wall of the Garden cut through the center of each pool, descending deep, deep below the surface, and the water, having finally made its journey under the wall, spilled out on the far side, filling the outer pools and continuing its prospective river course away from the Garden and on down the valley.

Diakrina could now see where she had been, slightly up the north side of the valley and above the four rivers. The small brook, which ran east and west, had gradually angled down toward the valley floor so that it joined the northern-most river just before it left the Garden.

The great gates of the Garden, where Strateia had first taken her, were on the east. When they had left the Great Dance, he had apparently taken her to this northwestern part of the Garden.

But what now commanded Diakrina's attention was the ugly, gaping chasm. It did not run all the way across the Garden from north to south as she would have concluded from her former vantage point. It was a circle, much too large to be fully seen, intruding into the Garden on this northern slope of the valley.

The chasm fell away into complete darkness, like a terrible scar that opened on a bottomless underworld where shadows reigned. It did not reach into the valley floor or intersect any of the rivers, because it turned west before it reached them. Only the brook, which had been near Diakrina, and a few other small tributaries on the northern side of the circle, were turned into silent waterfalls. However, beyond the Garden to the far north and west was another great river that seemed to disappear into a large canyon in the mountains.

Looking both north and south, Diakrina could see the enormous chasm arching back to the west. It covered an immense area of mountains, plains, forest and deserts. But it stretched too far for Diakrina to see the end of it, either to the north or west.

"Look carefully, little one, and remember what you see." Strateia cradled Diakrina into a sitting position in his left arm—as if she were nothing more than a toddler—freeing his right hand to gesture to the landscape below. "You see the area where you spent the night is now severed from the Garden by the great Chasm. No connection exists between the two, save the great tree which has formed the only bridge between them. You must now transverse this Severed Land."

"But why? What is the meaning?" inquired Diakrina, deeply troubled.

"Mere words cannot explain what must be experienced. It is a necessary journey in which you will be changed—transformed might be the better word." Strateia paused for a moment and then added, "The quest will not be safe. It will call for courage; more courage than you ever dreamed of needing."

"One thing more: the Couple's separation from the Great Dance caused this Severed Land to separate from the Garden. The Garden is forever part of the Great Dance. To separate from one is to separate from the other."

"Isn't the Severed Land connected to the Garden at the bottom of the gorge?" asked Diakrina.

"No created creature has ever found a bottom. It would take the Infinite One to reach its depths. So, as far as you and I are concerned, the Severed Land has no connection at all to anything at all, except by the tree-bridge."

With that the landscape suddenly began to rush at them and the mouth of the great gorge seemed to be opening ever wider to devour them. Strateia landed softly on the great tree-bridge and set Diakrina down in the same spot he had found her, standing out over the gorge. He took his sword in hand and with powerful swings of the crimson blade began cutting limbs from the tree.

Soon he had cleared the trunk of all its limbs but two, which he left attached about 30 feet in from the edge of the chasm. These two great limbs stretched out from the trunk along the ground opposite of each other from the trunk. From there the trunk continued another 120 feet into the Severed Land.

Diakrina watched as he cleared away the debris, many of the limbs as large as small trees, picking them up as if they were hollow sticks and casting them into a pile to the right of where the tree trunk rested on the west bank. Strateia even lifted the trunk slightly and began cutting away the broken limbs underneath so the trunk and the two outstretched limbs could lay flush on the earth. Then he lowered the tree gently. Diakrina felt suddenly dizzy, precariously perched over the great Chasm on the now limbless and moving trunk.

Diakrina looked inquiringly at the two outstretched limbs. Walking toward Strateia as he sheathed his sword, she pointed to either side of the great trunk with both hands and asked, "Why did you leave these two?"

"They will be needed," was his only reply. "From now on you may refer to this bridge as *the Tree Bridge.*"

The two walked along the top of the great tree and soon came to its most westward point. There on the ground, now visible from the end of the Tree Bridge, a path led into the forest of the Severed Land.

"You must now follow this path," instructed Strateia as he walked back a few steps to where Diakrina stood.

"You are not going with me?" The concerned face of Diakrina searched Strateia's eyes.

"I will always be with you, but for the moment it must be as before."

"I don't understand. As before what?"

"As I was with you before you came through the Door of the Rose," answered Strateia. "I will join you later. For now you must walk this path by yourself, though you will never actually be alone."

Strateia took her by the hand and led her to the very end of the Tree Bridge. He then turned her toward himself, facing her in the direction of the morning sun.

"When you step back onto the Severed Land, your quest will begin. But before you go I must inform you of what this quest is and of its utter importance. It is why you were brought here through the Door of the Rose. But even before I can tell you these things, I have a trust to give you."

"A *trust*?" queried Diakrina.

"A trust is something I am placing in your care which you must guard. This trust is for your protection and good, but not for yours only. If you keep it well it will become the protection and good of many because of you."

Strateia held out his sword toward Diakrina, seemingly offering it to her, yet pointing the blade toward her. Diakrina was puzzled.

"What are you doing, Strateia? I know you are not offering me *your* sword. You are a warrior, and a warrior never gives up his weapon unless conquered. Besides," she added quickly as she surveyed the huge blade, "I couldn't handle such a weapon; it is much too large for me."

"I am not giving you *my* sword," said Strateia, still holding the large weapon toward her, "I am offering you your own access to the only sword that exists."

Diakrina, who had been staring at the enormous, glowing crimson blade pointing toward her, looked back up at Strateia's face. "I don't understand," she said searching his countenance.

"It will be explained in full later. For now, what I am about to tell you will be sufficient. Listen carefully, Diakrina, to what I am about to say."

The tone of Strateia's voice had turned suddenly stately and serious. His earnestness enveloped Diakrina in a palpable atmosphere—like that of an elaborate and important ceremony in the court of a King. Her eyes were fixed on his noble face.

"In the Kingdom of the Living One there is only one Sword. That Sword is His Word. His Word is a consuming fire that creates, sustains or destroys. All things exist by His Word. To pledge allegiance to His Word is to embrace Reality, for His Sword pierces all illusions. If you pledge allegiance to His Word, you pledge allegiance to Him. In pledging allegiance to Him you must always honor His Word as truth; you must honor it as your sacred trust."

As Strateia spoke, the blade, still held out toward Diakrina, pulsed with crimson power. She could feel the heat of the blade on her face. Strateia continued.

"You must consider anything that contradicts Him and His Word to be a lie, even if you, yourself, are its source. The Sword cuts friend and foe alike. To its friends it brings surgery, healing and freedom. To foes it brings exposure, defeat and judgment.

"Diakrina, if you swear allegiance to the Living One, you surrender yourself willingly to the power of His Sword. To do this you must trust His love and wisdom above your own."

For the first time since Diakrina had come through the Door of the Rose, the stab of joy that always came with any thought or mention of the Living One had an accompanying sensation of panic, dread and alarm. The two sensations sprang up within her at the same moment. The stab of joy enveloped her in the deepest homesickness for anyone or anything she had ever known. It called her to throw caution to the wind and risk all for the joy of experiencing the Living One more fully.

Yet the panic, coming from somewhere deep within her—from an inner domain unknown to her until that moment—shouted warnings and pled with her to be cautious. "After all," it implored, "what *do* you really know about this Living One? It would be rash to move too quickly."

The inner surge of these two opposites crashed in on Diakrina like a tsunami. She groaned and wrapped her arms around herself as she slumped ever so slightly. Catching her breath she looked up again at the sword bearer before her. "Strateia, I want nothing more in life than to swear allegiance to Him with all my heart. But at this moment I am gripped by strange suspicions and a panic I do not understand."

"This suspicion, Diakrina, is the trait of all who have fallen in the Great Dance. Do not try to cure it yourself. That is a long road that spirals downward to defeat and bondage. Only the Living One can prove Himself to you and cure your unfounded suspicions. Swear allegiance with all the heart you can now command. He will liberate the rest."

Diakrina groaned once more as another surge of the opposing tidal waves crashed in on her.

"I am ashamed to offer Him so little, Strateia," she whispered between breaths. "He deserves full devotion; of that I am sure somewhere deep within. But every other part of my heart is manic and crazed, in fearful rebellion against the part that is eager to trust. How can I come, how can I swear allegiance, with only this small beachhead of sanity to offer?"

"Even this small beachhead of sanity is His gift to you, Diakrina," interrupted Strateia. "If He had not given it, you would have *nothing* to offer. Give back to Him this gift of grace and you will enter into the reality and mystery of Life."

As Strateia spoke the following words, golden and silver voices from all around them and above them joined in unison with him: "ALL FLOWS FROM HIM AND ALL FLOWS BACK TO HIM; THIS IS THE GREAT DANCE, THE ETERNAL DANCE OF LIFE. THERE IS NO OTHER. ALL GLORY TO HIM."

The great stab of joy and longing came over Diakrina as never before; it pierced like a lightning strike. She knew instantly what she most wanted and needed to do. She fell to her knees, clasped her hands together and looked up into the point of the sword, into the flaming eyes of Strateia and then beyond into the golden sunlight coming from the eastern sky. "Help me, Living One, to give myself to You," she whispered with all the strength she could find.

A shaft of light that made the morning sun seem dim fell like an anvil around Strateia and Diakrina. Instantly, she was aware of being in another place; a place without boundaries that made the vastness of the universe feel like an indoor affair. Her mouth dropped open and her eyes dilated in amazement as colors she had never seen and could not identify—colors beyond description and beauty—flooded her every sense. At the same moment the fragrance of flowers, maddeningly intoxicating, enveloped her upon the most delicious breeze.

When her eyes finally focused, she could see beautiful green mountains all around. Under her knees, instead of the wood of the Tree Bridge was a carpet of living green grass, so cool and sweet she felt as if she should dive and roll in it like a child in ecstasy. Music drenched her in majesty, lifting her soul to soar beyond any delight she had ever imagined.

Then, transcending all these wonders, her eyes caught a splendor beyond splendors. On a far horizon, shining brighter than the sun, gleamed a crystal city: The City. Diakrina never tried to describe it. At this point in her story her eyes would fill with delight and longing and all she could say was, "You'll see for yourself, someday. Then you will know."

It must truly be a City beyond words.

Strateia took a step toward Diakrina and, with great ceremony, lifted the blade of the sword in a salute before his face. Then lowering the sword just above her head, he said, "All who swear allegiance to the Living One embrace His death for them and die to themselves that they may live only for and in Him. Diakrina, will you so swear?"

From somewhere deep within, Diakrina could feel the old suspicion longing to speak: a suspicion obsessed with its own control, its own independence—a fearful dread of yielding authority to anyone. But in this place it could find no voice, and Diakrina was determined not to give it one. Even if it cost her life, she was determined. She knew now that she could not live without Him.

She gathered herself and spoke: "Whatever the cost, I give back to Him the life He gave. He may do with me whatever He must and whatever He will."

Strateia then tapped the tip of the sword onto Diakrina's head and she felt a surge of strength and warmth go through her all the way down to her feet. Then Strateia turned the pulsing sword upside down in his hand and hung the blade before Diakrina. It was both a threatening and beautiful sight. Looking deep into her eyes, he said, "All who reject His Sword reject Him, and die without cure. All who embrace His Sword willingly die His redemptive death and are by it healed. It is the door through death back into the Great Dance of Life."

Strateia then lifted the blade slightly toward Diakrina. "Embrace the crimson blade Diakrina. By it you will die to who you are and by it you will begin becoming the person the Living One created you to be."

The sword blazed up now with unremitting intensity until Diakrina was sure she could see crimson flames coming from its surface. With the singing beauty still all around her she reached out her arms and closed them slowly around the living blade.

When she finally embraced it, she closed her eyes tightly as again two opposite sensations surged into her. The first was the most searing pain she had ever known. The other was the sweetest embrace of peace and strength.

The pain burned through her until her whole body trembled as she clung to the blade. For just a moment she felt it would overcome her and she would not be able to continue her embrace. But then, with sudden terrifying intensity the pain burst through her and was gone. Only peace and strength were left.

Diakrina slumped to the ground in tranquil joy. Then she heard a voice beautiful beyond compare coming from everywhere. It addressed her in the most loving and personal manner.

"DIAKRINA, YOUR NAME HAS BEEN WRITTEN IN MY BOOK. IT IS THE BOOK OF THE LIVING."

She did not fully understand what all this meant, but peace flooded her total being. When finally she opened her eyes the light was gone and she and Strateia were once again alone on the Tree Bridge.

Strateia helped her to her feet. In his left hand was a sheath with noble engravings on its gold covered surface. The sheath was much smaller than his, but like it in every other way except one: the engravings on the smaller sheath were of a battle scene with a bright sun rising over a horizon of distant mountains. Strateia's had an engraving of what appeared to be the Crystal City with light flooding from it out over countless stars. The small sheath was attached to a wide, golden belt of very fine interlocking links. A bewildered look flashed across Diakrina's face, for the sheath was empty.

Then holding his sword in his right hand, about a foot in front of his chest, with the blade pointed to the sky, Strateia smiled and looked deep into Diakrina's eyes.

"Reach your right hand out and place it around mine, little one."

Diakrina reached out and placed her hand, as best she could, around the large muscular hand of Strateia as he held the mighty sword. Her hand looked like that of a child's on the warrior's bronze fist.

"Take the Sword of the Spirit, it is the creative Word of the Living One," said Strateia.

Diakrina watched intently as the sword began pulsing brightly and ever so slowly. After a moment she thought her eyes were losing focus. But no, what she was seeing was a second sword emerging from the first; identical to the first, though much smaller. She watched entranced as the emerging sword passed through Strateia's hand until she felt the red ruby handle push itself into her palm. As she closed her fingers around it, Strateia lowered his sword leaving Diakrina staring at the pulsing crimson saber in her uplifted hand.

"You are now in possession of the sword of the Living One. It is the same as my sword in every way that matters. Never abandon your sword and it will not abandon you. Trust what He tells you by means of it and never forget that every battle you fight is part of a war already won. The handle will glow crimson when danger is near. Learn to pay attention to its directions."

"I thought there is nothing here to fear," interrupted Diakrina, as she turned the sword over in her hands and examined it.

"While in a sense this is still true, in another it is not true in the Severed Land which lies ahead of you. But never forget what I will now tell you."

Strateia paused to be sure he had Diakrina's full attention. Then he said slowly and firmly, "One can be in battle and still have nothing to fear. None are safe from His Sword, not even you. But you are at peace with the Sword, for you do not wish to be safe from it. It is Life to you. It is judgment to all who oppose its truth."

"Diakrina, you are now empowered to embrace your transformation. Some of your enemies lie before you, some of them lie within you still. But go in confidence. Remember, as I told you, your personal battles are part of a war already won."

"Does that mean I will always win every battle?" asked Diakrina hopefully.

"Even in a war that is won, not all battles are victories," answered Strateia. "But if you never lose faith in Him and His Word, no battle is ever wasted. If you give your defeats to Him, He will harness them to a victory."

"Now, one last instruction," said Strateia becoming very serious. "Never surrender your sword to anyone—ever—no matter what it may cost you.

"There is only one exception to this rule. If I, or another brother or sister of the Light, ask for it in order to help you or ourselves, you may surrender it to them when you have asked them for the covenant vow of affirmation known only to the warriors of Uncreated Light.

"This vow I now entrust to you so you may both give it and require it when necessary. Commit it to memory and never willingly relinquish your sword without the confirmation of it."

Then pausing to fix her attention, Strateia quoted in a slow, stately silver voice that seemed to echo off unseen walls:

"I HAVE SWORN ETERNAL ALLEGIANCE TO HIM WHO ETERNALLY WAS, WHO ETERNALLY IS, WHO ETERNALLY IS TO COME. I BREATHE HIS LIFE, I AM EMBRACED BY HIS LOVE, I AM UNDER THE AUTHORITY OF HIS TRUTH, BY HIS LIGHT I SEE ALL THINGS."

With that said, Strateia looked very seriously at her and said, "Now, repeat the vow to me exactly, word for word, as I spoke it just now."

Diakrina was not sure she could remember it that perfectly. But when she began the first two words, "I HAVE . . ." she discovered she could hear Strateia's silver voice clearly in her mind as if recorded and being played back as a prompter. She continued, "SWORN ETERNAL ALLEGIANCE TO

HIM WHO ETERNALLY WAS, WHO ETERNALLY IS, WHO ETERNALLY IS TO COME. I BREATHE HIS LIFE, I AM EMBRACED BY HIS LOVE, I AM UNDER THE AUTHORITY OF HIS TRUTH, BY HIS LIGHT I SEE ALL THINGS."

"Very good, little one. Do not forget my instructions."Then reaching out his left hand, "Here, you will need this," he handed her the golden sheath and belt.

She put the sword into the sheath. But before she could put it around her waist Strateia motioned for her to step even closer to the edge of the Tree Bridge where it ended on the Severed Land.

"Now, I must reveal to you your quest and help you understand its meaning," said Strateia. "Sit here for a moment for I have some instructions for you, after which I must share with you a very ancient story. For unless you understand the history behind the quest, you will not be able to comprehend the part you have been called here to play in the present and in the future."

Diakrina sat down and hung her legs over the edge of the trunk of the Tree Bridge. Strateia sat down beside her.

"Diakrina, you were brought here for a reason. All that will, and must, happen *to* you and *in* you has a greater purpose. You have a very important role to play that affects not just reality here, but the other side of reality and the flow of time.

"You are about to step into the Severed Lands. This is the realm of Anomos. It is known as the kingdom of Parad. Parad is another name for Anomos, for it means *a severed self*. What lies before you is the kingdom severed from the Great Dance and ruled by the severed one.

"You and your race live in the kingdom of Parad. Here a great war must be fought for your own personal freedom and the freedom of many who will come after you. It will be fought incrementally, battle by battle, and the outcome for you personally is not yet written.

"In this war, you will write your chapter in the Great Story. If you write by trusting in the Living One, you will be led to write what can be woven into its unending plot and He will fight along with you and for you. But if you write in suspicion of the Living One, you will write in harmony with the kingdom of Parad, and all that is woven together with the attitudes and purposes of Parad have already been judged and condemned.

"Hear me closely, Diakrina. You are in no dream. This is all real, more real than you can now understand. You have been brought, in your perception, to the other side of reality—*this* side of reality—through the Door of the Rose. You have always lived here, but without direct perception of it. Previously, by the distortions of your race's fall from the Great Dance, your senses were tuned to perceive only the side of reality from which you came.

"What you perceive now is the deeper world of cause, the denser world of spirit. Since your kind has come into being, the world of spirit and cause has been combined with a new world of effect: the world of matter. In you and your kind, a new reality emerges. This new reality is called soul.

"The human soul is created by the Living One through the union of spirit and matter. And this union—soul—constitutes a third reality that encompasses both the realms of spirit and matter. This new blended reality cannot be reduced to either spirit or matter alone, and can be fully understood only when both are clearly perceived.

"This is an important truth for you to remember. You are not mere spirit. But you will war with some here that are only spirit.

"The world of spirit is stronger, denser, than the world of matter. You have always perceived it backwards: spirit has always seemed unclothed, vaporous and unsubstantial to you, for your perception has been clouded. You have seen the spirit world only through a nearly opaque window and have mistakenly concluded that the reality on the other side of the window must be ethereal and misty.

"When all is seen clearly, it is rather the material world that is flimsy and fragile by comparison. You will need to change the way you think of the spiritual, from metaphors and pictures of mist and smoke, twinkle and shadow, ghost and phantom, to that of iron and marble, steel and granite, rippling strength and bursting health.

"However, your *soulicalness* is not to be discounted. It has its own strengths and unique abilities and you will do well to remember it.

"But now, before I can explain to you the quest you have been called to execute, I must lift the veil on a most ancient story that most of your race has forgotten. Some of the details I am about to share with you, your race was never told. But it is a story in which you and your Great Parents have been swept up, and your destiny is forever determined by how you engage it.

And as they sat together on the Tree Bridge looking out over the Severed Lands, Strateia began a most amazing story.

———————— ✦ ————————

CHAPTER EIGHT

# The ANCIENT STORY

"Before your race came to be, Anomos broke with the Great Dance. And, as I told you yesterday, in doing so he gave birth to that creeping insanity, which we call *evil*. The act by which he broke with the Dance was not unlike what he tempted your race to do in severing itself.

"In those times he had not yet become Anomos. His name from the time of his creation was Heylel, and he was one of the greatest leaders among the host who served the Living One. In fact, the Kingdom of the Living One was composed of three realms, each ruled by a lord, and Heylel was one of those lords. Each lord carried the title, *Lord of the Realm*, and he ruled over one third of the host, as well as one third of the creation.

"When Heylel turned inward and severed himself from the Living One, a madness came over him. He believed he could become like the Living One, setting up his own realm—his own creation—to which he alone would give meaning and life. Needing the allegiance of the host under him, he wove a great deception designed to lure them into his delusion.

"In the center of every realm, the Living One had placed a great scepter—The Scepter of Kabod. As there were three realms, so there were three Scepters of Kabod. *Kabod*, Diakrina, means glory, weight, greatness and honor. It is the symbol of the Living One, Himself: the Source of all glory.

"The glory gives *weight* to all creation. By *weight* I mean significance, purpose and importance. Only He, the Source of all glory, can be the Center of creation, and only He can sing the Great Story of meaning and purpose.

"At the center of each realm lay a vast sea of solid crystal, filled and alive with swirling light of inexpressible colors. Brilliant glory flashed and moved within it. From the center of each crystal sea rose two great structures. The first was the Seat of Authority: a massive throne encircled by 49 great steps called the Steps of Ascent that led up to the summit of the throne. The second, which rested on the Seat of Authority and formed the back of the enormous chair, was the Great Crystal Spiral. The pinnacle of the Spiral, high above the throne and the crystal sea that surrounded it, held that realm's Scepter of Kabod, upright with its crown on its top.

"The crown of each Scepter was a diamond of moving, living light of infinite velocity, giving it a terrible density that makes all other substances in creation seem in comparison like vapor and mist. Radiating from this swirling, living crown came brilliant light that illuminated the whole realm and gave life to everything.

"Whenever the Lord of the Realm was called to the throne and to a gathering of his host, he would mount the 49 Steps of Ascent and approach the Seat of Authority. Then kneeling before the Great Scepter of Kabod, he would honor the Living One who had called him. Then from the crown of the Scepter a great shaft of light would flash down through the sky and come to rest upon the head of the Lord of the Realm.

"This light delegated the authority of the Living One upon the Lord, and he would rise with a small, but flaming crown of light shining on his head. This crown, while retaining its shape, swirled and flashed stunningly with a beautiful rainbow of colors, continually renewed by the shaft of infinite light descending from the crown of the Scepter. Only when thus crowned by the authority of the Living One ruling over him, could the Lord of the Realm approach the Seat of Authority and conduct the business of the realm.

"For glorious ages the Kingdom grew and prospered under the three Lords of the Realm and all worshipped and served the Living One.

"At the beginning of each age, the Living One called the whole Kingdom together. This is difficult to describe for you to understand, Diakrina. Try to imagine each Lord of the Realm taking his place on his Seat of Authority with his one-third of the host gathered before him. Then, above the three seas, the Living One's great Throne would appear, and the three crystal seas—each with its host, its Lord, its Seat of Authority and its Great Crystal Spiral with its Scepter of Kabod—would all be drawn up before the Throne of the Living One, until the three seas were one Great Crystal Sea with no boundaries.

"There the three Seats of Authority would receive places of honor before the Throne of the Living One, though infinitely dwarfed in His Presence. The Elders around the Throne would rise and welcome the three Lords of the Realm, and the combined throng would celebrate the birth of a new age of creation and beauty, as the Living One unfolded the next great ascent of the Kingdom.

"This Great Dance of Life around the Throne was so glorious that the words of creatures cannot describe its wonder and beauty. Only the Living Word can sing its glory into the minds and hearts of created ones."

Strateia paused for a long moment, leaning back and looking into the sky as though relishing the scene he had just described. Then his eyes darkened as he turned once again toward Diakrina and continued his narrative.

"When Heylel plunged into his insanity and the great corruption was born, he envisaged himself becoming equal to the Living One. In this madness, he, of his own accord, called together the host under his command, and they assembled around the Seat of Authority and its Great Spiral. Then, to the stunned amazement of the gathered host, he proceeded to mount the 49 Steps of Ascent to the summit of the throne, without being summoned by the Living One.

"In the scene of belligerence that followed, Heylel defied three distinct boundaries that were innately understood by every creature of the realm, committing a series of insane acts forbidden by the law of Reality. First, he ascended to the throne without being called by the Living One. Second, he dared to sit upon the Seat of Authority without first bowing before the Scepter and receiving the crown of light upon his head. And third, in an act unthinkable to anyone with any remnant of sanity, he climbed the Great Spiral to seize the Scepter of Kabod for himself. But I am getting ahead of myself.

"I must tell you something more about the Great Spiral and how the Living One designed it. From the throne area—just in front and to the left of the Lord of the Realm as he sat on the Seat of Authority—an enormous staircase circled back and wrapped around the Great Spiral, ascending all the way to the top. All creatures knew they must not climb the staircase, yet they also knew that it was possible to do so. This possibility was their freedom.

"This freedom made love possible. For love of the Living One, each creature willingly refrained from ascending the Great Spiral. By this act of honor, each *self* chose to embrace the Great Dance with all its beauty and purpose, and to bow before the Living One, the Source of all Life and all delight.

"Every self in the Kingdom inherently knew and honored the great unfolding design of Life and reveled in the overflowing joy that continually drenched them. To any sane creature—and there had never before been any form of insanity—the thought of ascending the Great Spiral was unthinkable, an intolerable blasphemy against all that they cherished.

"But Heylel was no longer sane. Yet who could diagnose this madness? It had never before existed. Such madness was inconceivable. So, as the host watched Heylel mount the Steps of Ascent uncalled, they assumed the Living One was doing a new thing through Heylel and waited in great anticipation to hear the strains of this new theme of the Speaking Music.

"When Heylel reached the summit of the throne, he turned and began to sing. Now you must understand that a Lord of the Realm, like Heylel, did not sing with a voice of a single note as humans do in your material world. No, an orchestra of 10,000 instruments of perfect pitch and power played by the greatest musicians of all time in your world could not reproduce the music Heylel was capable of creating. And being one of the most ancient of the Living One's creatures, he knew haunting melodies from the most distant reaches of eternity.

"He began to weave them together into a mesmerizing thousand-dimensional melody that echoed back to the great moments when the Living One created the host and all that exist. And upon its glorious, haunting strains came forth the first seeds of the great lie that had taken root in him.

"Slowly, ever so slowly, he sang of a deep and glorious mystery locked away in the potential of created beings—a mystery instilled from the very beginning that held the key to a new and glorious age yet to come. This mystery, he sang, waited for the creatures to grow to the point they could embrace it for themselves through a great deed of self-actualization.

"And here, from his cunning deception, flowed a deadly twisting of truth that would poison those who heard him. This *great deed*, this act of ultimate courage by which the great mystery could be realized, had to originate *within* the creature. For only when the creature could find within his own *self* the will to consider the great deed, had he evolved enough to actually perform it.

"What is more, according to Heylel's mad song, the Living One wished the great deed to be done. He longed for His creatures to uncover the hidden mystery He had planted in them from creation. Yet He could not command it, for the unfolding of the mystery demanded the maturation of a tiny *seed* He had placed in them, a seed that must grow on its own and finally come to light by self-discovery and self-actualization, resulting in a new power in each self that seized it. This power must be released by the self upon the self.

"'This great unfolding ensures the proper timing,' he sang. 'When we become aware of the deeper possibilities of freedom, we have grown up into those who can release the deeper mystery planted within us. And since we now know we can, because He planted it there within, are we not obligated to find it and unfold it?'

"'Here lies the deepest magic of creation,' he sang. 'For though the Great King wishes it, He cannot will it. His creatures must do it for Him. Each creature must do it for himself. For in this great deed, serving the self is the profound secret to serving the King as He wishes!'

"Then he called on each member of the host to serve their King by turning inward. They must look within to see if they could detect in themselves the *seed* of the great mystery: *'It is your duty,'* he insisted with a crescendo. If they could find this *seed* within they would be granted the necessary courage to perform the great deed.

"'This is what the Great King wishes from you,' he repeatedly sang. 'By the very fact that He created this potential within you, He lays a hand of obligation on your shoulder. He cannot command the great deed, but He waits longingly for you to embrace it of your own free will. Do not disappoint Him.' Little by little he pushed them—and they unaware—toward the very edge of the abyss of his madness.

"But not fully unaware. For deep within they knew this song did not come from the Speaking Music, but challenged it, even defied it. But the skill of Heylel was so great and his song so captivatingly haunting, that few could bring themselves to turn away.

"So, on and on he sang for what would be in your world, days. For perfect creatures do not grow weary. And little by little he watered the seeds of his lie by his hypnotic song. And all the while he called for their service to the great and ancient mystery whose time to unfold had arrived. He sang:

*'Look within and find the key,*
*For the Living One longs for this to be;*
*As He planted the seed beyond the Great Sea*
*And timed the unfolding from antiquity.*

*'Look within, He placed it there;*
*He wants you to find it and choose to dare*
*To actualize the great deed with care:*
*Did He not, Himself, create the Spiral's circuiting stairs?'*

"Tirelessly he sang. Again and again he returned to the theme of the Great Spiral and its winding stairs, hinting over and over to what none had ever dared to think: *that the Living One actually longed for them to climb the stairs and seize the Scepter of Kabod.*

"Heylel agreed that a deep magic of love had hitherto kept creatures from climbing the Spiral. 'But,' he insisted, 'the King has embedded in us an even deeper magic—a magic of Aseity, of self-existence and self-sufficiency. The great mystery,' he sang with haunting strains, 'holds a never-before imagined secret: it calls for us to ascend to Him.'

"Then bursting suddenly out in a panorama of crescendos that shook the realm, he declared that he had looked within; he had found the seed—the key—within himself. Surely the time had come! This plan, which began unfolding before their creation, was near its zenith.

"'Look within! You too will find the key!' he roared. Then, with sudden and astonishing impact, the realm fell silent.

"Heylel allowed the pregnant stillness to hang in the air for a long moment. Then, he whispered a whisper that echoed like a trumpet over the crystal sea: *'I will do the great deed. I now see that He wishes me to ascend, to defy His uniqueness. Can it be that Trinity is to become a Pannity?'*

"Then just as abruptly, with a great swell of ascending and spiraling musical themes, 'RISE! It can never be unless you ascend by your own will. He has provided the steps. By His law He made it possible for us to ascend—to actualize our self.

"'Can't you see?' he shrieked, 'He must forbid the great deed—the great step—or it would not be available to us. It is made possible by the forbidding! For in the great deed self throws off all forbidding and rises to become like Him, a law unto its self. Becoming like the Maker is our created purpose. This is the great step. And now I know He planned it from the beginning!'

"Heylel's madness enflamed a persuasive power that swayed even him, for he had actually begun to believe his own lie. He was not only the creator of the delusion, but also its first victim.

"'Look within! Look within!' he sang over and over. And slowly, one by one, the members of the host began to turn inward. Those closest to the throne turned first. And as they did, a donut shaped ring of distorted light—if seen from the sky—encircled the throne and began to move outward over the host. As it swept out from Heylel, the expanding wave grew in force with the addition of each subjugated will, slowly subduing each member of the host.

"Seeing what was happening, a small few came to themselves and cried out in great alarm. But it was too late. The distorting light had become an awful expanding and unstoppable force. Only a small remnant who were on the outer edges of the host managed just in time to recognize the danger and flee into the skies, crying for the protection of the Living One.

"A hideous distorting sickness infected the host. Each victim filled up with empty reflections of *self* as they collapsed inward into an endless abyss of mirrors, locked into an infinite reciprocation between the self and a myth of self. Selfism was born.

"Slowly rising, they joined with Heylel in singing the great lie, their song culminating in a manic chant: 'Do the great deed! The mystery is ours! Do the great deed! The mystery is ours!'

"Heylel turned and approached the Seat of Authority and, without kneeling to the Scepter of Kabod, he sat down. A great roar of ecstasy swelled until it shook the crystal sea beneath their feet.

"Then Heylel raised his hand and all became quiet. 'Bow before me and vest me with your power and will, so I may do the great deed on behalf of us all. Worship me! For in me the great mystery is about to be realized. By your worship it can be realized in you, too! You will ascend with me and in me!' Then he sang a defiant song of dark passion:

'I will ascend to Heaven;
I will raise my throne
Above the stars of the Living One;
I will sit enthroned on the Mount of Assembly,
On the utmost heights of the sacred mountain.
I will ascend above the highest reaches of the clouds of glory;
I will make myself like the Most High!'

"'Bow!' he bellowed. 'We will morph the Trinity into a P A N N I T Y !'

"In that dreadful moment, the original act of idolatry—Heylel's self-worship—spawned the first act of collective idolatry. The great host fell to the crystal sea in passionate, raging thirst. But each self's eye looked inward to *his* myth—his own great rising—even as he bowed in submission to Heylel.

"Heylel rose, stepped left and mounted the stairs that circuited the Great Spiral. Up, up he ascended, unhindered and unchallenged, with every infected eye now fixed upon him.

"When he finally reached the zenith of the Great Spiral, he reached out his hand and paused for only a moment, as a terrifying silence filled the crystal sea. Each distorted mind stared hungrily into the myth of the deeper magic of freedom.

"Slowly he touched the Scepter of Kabod, lifted it from its base and held it high into the air. From the great sea far below him every eye stared in utter silence at the spectacle: the great deed was done. Then the horde burst into a thunder of celebration, sending shivers resonating through the crystal sea beneath their feet.

"Heylel began to rise as the Scepter lifted him from the Great Spiral toward the sky. In his madness, and theirs, it seemed his lie was actualizing: the myth of the deeper magic of freedom was unfolding. Heylel was rising to take his place and become like the Most High. Up, up the Scepter of Kabod lifted him.

"With every eye focused upward on their ascending lord, no one noticed the change taking place beneath their feet. The brilliant living colors within the crystal sea began to die and fade, until the sea beneath them was darkened like a piece of coal.

"Suddenly, a blast of golden light exploded from the crown of the Scepter and burst into an expanding ring of fire across the sky. The infinite light fled from the Scepter of Kabod, and its crown turned black like the sea beneath their feet.

"Like slivers of metal responding to a magnet, all the infinite light in the realm shot up into the fiery golden ring that bulged to fill the whole sky above them. With every passing second, the realm of Heylel grew darker and darker until everything below was dim as dusk, with the ring of fire blazing high above. Then instantly, the light above vanished.

"Against the black sky—shooting like a falling star—fell Heylel. Violently, like a meteor crashing toward the surface of the crystal sea, he was thrown down, down with terrible speed.

"He smashed into the summit of the throne with dreadful force, sending a shudder, then a quake, rippling through the throne. The quaking intensified, splintering the throne into great shards of crystal, and the now-darkened crystal sea began to crumble from the center outward, sending the panicked horde scrambling to the land surrounding the sea.

"Then the Great Spiral toppled and fell. As it struck the crumbling crystal sea, they both shattered into trillions upon trillions of pieces.

"The shaking finally stopped and silence settled over the realm. From the land surrounding what had been the sea of living light, the horde stood staring into darkened ruins of crystal shards. A field of gaping crystal crevasses descended deep into the very essence of the realm.

"Heylel climbed out of the rubble and onto the highest point of what was left of the throne. The sky filled, as Michael, Lord of one of the other two realms, hovered in the sky above with a great host of warriors under his command, all arrayed for battle. Though no battle had ever before been fought, the Living One who knows all things in advance had prepared Michael and his host with the art and weapons of war.

"And war there was. A great conflict raged throughout the heavens of Heylel's realm, and one-third of the creation was devastated. The great lie corrupted the realm. In the end, Heylel and his hordes were defeated and brought before the throne of the Living One for judgment. (Nothing is done in the Living One's Kingdom without the highest kind of justice and fair play being observed at every point. For He is Light and in Him there is no darkness at all.)

"Heylel was allowed to make his case before the Living One and all of Heaven. He harnessed all his great talents to spin his illusion and plead his case. But it was to no avail. Lies shrivel and vanish in the blazing actuality of the Maker.

"Yet Heylel, in his cunning, made a startling accusation before the Court. He claimed he was indeed unfolding a great mystery and none could prove him wrong as none, save he and his followers, had ever experienced this mystery from the inside. He claimed all the Court's evidence was based in their military victory, not in true justice.

"'You, Living One, have never been inside my mystery by experience,' he challenged. 'How can You prove it false only from without? Now that it has come into being, the only ones capable of judging its true value and worth are those who have experienced it from within. Yes, You have the power to vanquish me, but might does not make right.

"'You rule in power, but I appeal to justice. I challenge you to lay aside your power and confront my mystery on its merits alone. Anything less cannot be justice, but only tyranny. Or are you afraid of justice? Does the potential of your creatures make you hide behind your power?'

"Then the Living One spoke. 'Your challenge is well made, Heylel. I indeed gave you great gifts. I see already to the end of this challenge, and I know its outcome: you will not prevail. However, I accept your challenge, for your slander must be answered. My creatures shall be relieved from any doubts regarding the justice of your condemnation, and your hideous 'mystery' of evil shall be exposed for what it is.

"'You are condemned. That is My verdict. But I will withhold your sentence for a time until this appeal is answered. However, from this moment forward, you shall no longer be Heylel for you have abandoned your first station. You shall have many names: the endless duplicity of what you have become will give you many lying faces. You shall be known as Anomos Poneros, for you are now diseased with lawlessness. But until your accusation and slander is answered, you shall also be known as Slanderer, Accuser and Adversary, for so shall you be to all the living.'

"The Living One continued, 'Your title, Lord of the Realm, is stripped from you. Though you will still lead your realm, it is now the Realm of Darkness, the Realm of Death, and you shall be known as the Prince of Darkness and the Prince of Death. The kingdom you will insist on trying to create will be called Parad, for you have severed yourself from the Source of Life and Light.

"'You and your realm will continue to exist during this time of the appeal, so that your mystery of *selfism* will have every opportunity to be validated. But you and your realm are confined to isolation, to safeguard the other realms from your deadly infection.'"

"And with that Anomos Poneros and his horde were cast out."

Diakrina sat speechless for some moments before her tutor began again in a most earnest manner.

"Diakrina, another story, which I cannot take time to unveil to you now, holds vital significance to you and your race. It concerns how the Living One took up the challenge to overcome evil on the merits of truth alone— without using His power, only his *weakness*. You and your race find your place in that story, for you are the Living One's instrument of weakness. In you—that is in the weakness of your race—He has chosen to defeat evil. Though weak, yet by becoming His instrument, you will be made great."

Diakrina had little time to marvel at these cryptic words, for Strateia hastened on with his instructions. "For now, you need to know several important facts that will enable you to understand the nature and objectives of the battles ahead of you.

"Your race was created in the realms of Anomos as a beachhead to deal with his slander. You were given the power of a great truth, held in trust through your direct relationship with the Living One. As long as you held that truth in trust, it protected you against Anomos' power, for his only power is lies.

"But, as you know, Anomos succeeded in deluding your Great Parents. They exchanged the truth of the Living One for the lie, and followed Anomos in severing themselves from the Great Dance. They forfeited the great trust and its privileges, and humankind fell under the power of the lie and were absorbed into the kingdom of Parad.

"As a result, the defeat of evil and the rescue of your race have become coterminous. The Living One knew this from the beginning and planned the rescue of your race to be the final answer to Anomos' slander and power.

"Another fact you need to know, Diakrina, is that you were brought through the Door of the Rose into a different point in time on this side of reality. What you are experiencing now does not parallel the time period you knew before. *This*," Strateia motioned in a vague sweeping circle around them, "is what you would call *the past*. Your passage through the Door brought you to the days shortly following your Great Parents' severing from the Dance.

"The Severed Lands before you are antediluvian—the age between Eden and the great flood. In many ways, this world is superior to what you have known. It is also much more dangerous, filled with beings and beasts that have long since been banished from the world as you know it.

"You have been brought here for a great task. Your success or failure will reap consequences that will flow down through the centuries, even to the time you consider your own.

"But why me?" interrupted Diakrina. "Why not some great warrior, if there are battles to be fought? Why not some great genius, if there are riddles to be solved? I am only a young woman with little strength or experience. I don't understand this, Strateia!"

"It is true, Diakrina, that you have not been chosen for your strength or wisdom, nor for your lack of them. No human strength or wisdom is adequate for the quest before you. Anomos is far too clever an adversary for that. The Living One has chosen you for reasons known only to Him.

"But take heart, little one. Even if you are the least of your race, the Living One has chosen you as His weapon, and His strength and wisdom *flowing through you* is more than adequate to subdue all the cunning of Anomos, if . . ." and here Strateia paused for effect, "*if* you choose to trust Him.

"This battle is not of mere weapons against weapons or warriors against warriors, but of wills against wills. You are a weapon of the Living One, but you possess your own will. The proper and highest use of that will is to choose to be one with His will, but yours is the freedom to choose, at every moment, whether to do so or not. He will not take that freedom from you.

"This freedom is the prime directive of all creation. Only then is the highest expression possible to you—the expression of love.

"You are not free *not* to choose. Freedom *from* choice does not exist for rational creatures. And this necessity of choice opens before you a dark abyss of terrible possibilities. This is a necessary risk, without which no meaning or purpose could exist. Your freedom is both your strength and your weakness, depending on whom or what you choose to trust.

"And now, Diakrina, regarding your quest . . . I have saved one part of the story for this moment. It is the key to understanding what you must do.

"Before Anomos seduced your Great Parents to sever themselves from the Dance, he planned and executed a daring heist. Under Anomos' orders, one of his principalities stole into the Garden by night and picked one of the golden fruits from the Tree of Life planted there by the Living One, and carried it back to Anomos. This Tree of Life was created specifically for your race, Diakrina. One bite of its fruit renders a human immortal. My kind has no need of it, for we are already immortal.

"Imagine the devastation if this fruit were to be eaten by fallen humankind, severed from the Life of the Great Dance. It would seal him forever in his diseased and tortured condition: dead but unable to die, an immortal soul with no hope of restoration to the Source of Life.

"Anomos entrusted the golden fruit to another of his principalities: Thanatos, lord over the realms of death. He ordered him to hide it away in his realm where no mortal can touch it until Anomos calls for it to be brought forth.

"Anomos has laid a most diabolical scheme. He knows mankind is precious to the Living One, and that they are part of the Living One's plan to expose his lies and defeat his slander. Furthermore, he harbors insane jealousy toward them for their dominion over the material world. And so he fears and loathes your kind, Diakrina. Having succeeded at severing mankind from the Great Dance, he hopes to finally pervert some of them into irredeemably corrupted and immortal creatures who will serve him and bring much of the material universe under his control.

"His scheme is to accomplish all this by giving a single bite of the Golden Fruit to each member of a select human family, trans-morphing them into immortals with great physical power and cunning. He would then breed this corrupted strain, forming a host of indestructible humans to make war on and exterminate all other humans.

"If he succeeds, humanity will no longer be an instrument in the hand of the Living One, but will instead be an increasingly corrupt and cruel weapon in his own hand. By this he hopes to sabotage the Living One's case against him and satisfy his own mad and insatiable thirst for self-actualization.

"Diakrina, this must be stopped. But only a member of the human race can retrieve this Golden Fruit. And yet, no mere human can enter into the realms of Thanatos and recover it.

"Then it sounds hopeless," interrupted Diakrina. "What can I possibly do?"

"More than you, know, little one," responded Strateia. "Because you are from a far later time, you are a daughter of those who live under privileges purchased by the Living One when he joined the Great Dance as one of your race. You have freedom and power under a Covenant unknown and unimagined by this ancient world before the Advent of the Living One into the Great Dance. Through the Covenant, the Person and Power of the Living One's Spirit actually lives in and through you. I said 'no mere human' could accomplish this task. By right of the Covenant, Diakrina, you are no mere human.

"The Living One has brought you through the Door of the Rose from your own age—the age of access to the Covenant of Life by which He will win the final victory over evil and redeem the whole of creation to Himself. In your time, the Covenant is already an accomplished fact, though all the implications have not yet been finally seen.

"Your quest, commissioned by the Living One Himself, is to journey into the realms of Thanatos, retrieve the Golden Fruit stolen from the Tree of Life and bring it back to this Tree Bridge. In the Severed Lands, the Fruit is deadly. In the Garden where it belongs, it is beauty and life."

Diakrina's eyes widened in disbelief.

"When you return, this Tree Bridge will be a very different place to you than it is now. Once you have stepped into the Severed Lands, many things will change. Yet, because you can be under the power and possibilities of the Covenant of Life accomplished in your time, you can enter Thanatos' realm and return here again safely. The Living One will walk with you and work through you, giving you His aid and protection in this great quest. If you learn to continually accept His direction and fully rely upon Him, you can succeed."

"Strateia, with His help is it possible for me to fail?" asked Diakrina with strains of panic in her voice.

"Yes. It is possible for you to fail. But it is not necessary. All will depend on your choices of trust. And for those choices, you will be given great help. You will be equipped to trust. You will face other battles before confronting Thanatos, battles that will prepare you for the realms of death and build in you the trust necessary to succeed once you are there."

"Strateia, will you be with me?"

"Not within Thanatos' realms. I cannot enter there, for death is not a place I can know. However, it is for the best. Relying on my presence would hinder the deepening of your own trust in the Living One, which is the key to your success. But I promise you, Diakrina, you will never be alone."

Diakrina's mind was racing. "Will this Golden Fruit still be there? Won't it be spoiled and rotten by now?"

"Immortal Fruit never spoils, Diakrina." Strateia used a tone that made it clear he knew she was merely dredging up any objection she could think of. "For now, your first test is to make your way west, through the Mist, into the Severed Lands. Start by following this path and the dry stream bed."

Strateia took Diakrina's downcast chin in his giant hand and gently turned her face up toward his until she was looking into his eyes. "The Living One has chosen you, Diakrina, and He makes no mistakes. Never surrender your sword, and keep it at the ready. With His help you can do this. Much, so very very much, hangs in the balance."

Strateia then stood and Diakrina did the same. Placing his hand on her head and looking up to the sky, the bronze warrior spoke with kind conviction. "The blessing, wisdom and protection of the Living One be on you."

And suddenly, he was gone.

Diakrina stood for some time looking toward the west. Then she wrapped the golden belt with its golden sheath around the waist of her grass tunic. The crimson handle of the sword sparkled in the morning sun as it hung on her left side. With a deep, long breath she steadied herself and prepared to leave the Tree Bridge.

CHAPTER NINE

# The MIST

Diakrina, buried deep in thought about many things Strateia had said to her, climbed down off the end of the Tree Bridge onto the Severed Lands and began her hike along the footpath that led into the trees. She soon came to what had been the brook, the well-worn and smooth rocks now parched where they had once glistened through the flowing crystal water. She shook her head sadly at the loss.

The path appeared to end, so Diakrina turned to her right and followed the gently winding dry bed through the forest. Every few hundred yards or so, she came upon small depressions where deep pools of water had once teemed with life. Each depression now held a shallow pond, just a few feet deep.

She stopped at one of these ponds to look. Hundreds of fish filled the tiny basin, their gaping gills desperately begging for more oxygen than the leftover pool of water could offer. Some of the larger fish had already rolled onto their sides, one gill panting above the surface. Diakrina recognized the brightly colored fish as being just like the ones she had played with the day before. Her heart ached as she watched them struggle, but there was nothing she could do.

She avoided going too close to the other pools as she passed them. She couldn't bear the sights and felt sickened by the inaudible cries from the gentle fish. This was all so out of place from the Garden she had known the day before. The Great Severing had changed everything.

Deliberately circumventing one of the pools, Diakrina strayed some distance from the streambed into the thickness of the forest, where overhanging branches of large, rough-barked trees partially blocked the sun. She had paused in the shade to survey the landscape and plot her best course forward, when she suddenly felt like she was being watched, as if someone or something were stalking her.

A deep uneasiness swept over her. Every shadow took a crouched and threatening pose, as a foreboding eeriness haunted the forest around her, creeping toward her from every direction. She struggled, without success, to dislodge from her mind the tormenting images of gasping fish. Their desperate fear and despair seemed to fill the air around her.

Now on high alert, she turned and stepped warily back toward the streambed and the promising sunlight, but the prospect of confronting another pool of dying fish stopped her in her tracks. Diakrina felt trapped, loathing her options. The haunting atmosphere of the forest where every shadow looked threatening pushed her toward the streambed and the sunshine, while the silent screams of dying fish pushed her away. Yet she could not shake the sense of some kind of crouching and creeping presence circling her from behind the tree trunks and glaring at her from every shadow.

She had stood for a long moment, frustrated with her choices, when the words of Strateia crept back into her mind. He had promised that she would never really be alone, and had even said he would be with her himself, though she wouldn't see him. "Oh I hope so," she said, almost aloud.

The thought calmed her rising fear just a bit, but the feeling persisted of being helpless prey walking into an ambush. She reminded herself to take courage. After all, this really was something like the kind of adventure she had imagined, and so far she had managed to stay one step ahead of whatever might be stalking her.

Her need to get back into the sunlight broke her paralysis, and she determined to make her way back to the streambed, steeling herself to avoid the visage of tormented fish.

Then she saw it.

From the direction of the streambed, moving with the same slithering motion she had seen before, came the dark mist that had earlier retreated at Strateia's command. Slowly it curled in and out, around every trunk and limb in its path. As Diakrina watched, swatches of dry forest turned damp, slippery and clammy as they fell captive to the grey mist. The invading wall advanced, blocking the sun and leaving only the palest grey light illuminating everything it conquered.

The streambed—Diakrina's mental refuge—had already fallen, engulfed in the advancing mist. Frantically, she turned back toward the dense forest. There, from less than 20 yards away, the wet, grey blanket slithered toward her. Retreating toward the Tree Bridge seemed to be the only route left to her, so she turned and ran in the direction from which she had come. But it was too late. She had only run a few yards when she nearly fell into a stream of slithering dampness that stretched across the path. The mist, like a clever pack of predators, had outflanked her.

She glanced quickly around for any possible escape, and noticed a small hill to her left. The hill was bare, without any foliage except one lone tree near its top. The mist had not climbed the hill. Perhaps it could not, thought Diakrina. Up she ran as hard as she could push herself.

Reaching nearly the top, she turned around to look down over the forest. She was wrong. The front edge of the mist had left the tree line below and, like a ghastly long serpent winding its way back and forth on itself, was pursuing her up the side of the hill.

Diakrina turned and ran past the lone tree and across the crest of the hill to get a look at the other side. "Just maybe," she thought, "the other side of the hill will be clear." But she was disappointed. Here, too, the mist slithered back and forth as it crept toward her and the hill's summit.

She ran back past the tree, only to run nearly into the mist. Turning again and stepping to the crest of the hilltop, she spun in all directions to see the grey serpent slithering toward her from every side. She stared helplessly as the noose tightened, and shifted her position this way and that to stay in the center of the ever-shrinking circle of sunlight.

Ever closer the mist curled and swirled. Diakrina felt its cold sucking at the warmth of the sunlight around her. A strong odor of mold and mildew filled the air as a damp and clammy condensation settled on her face and arms.

Then she heard the voices—dark and cruel voices—whispering endless chants in a panoramic hiss from within the swirling mist.

From her left, in slow, breathy, depressive, mournful tones, the voices murmured over and over:

"This is all there is.

There is no more.

This is all there is.

There is no more."

From her right, bitter, hard, resentful cries hissed relentlessly:

"It is all up to you.

You are on your own.

It is all up to you.

You are on your own."

Behind her, fearful, frightened, panic-possessed voices shouted coarse and guttural whispers:

"Trust no one.

Protect yourself.

Trust no one.

Protect yourself."

In front of her a single angry, snarling chant demanded:

"Take control!

Take control!

Take control!

Take control!"

Like the shrinking eye of a grey hurricane, with its eye-wall reaching from the ground to some 30 feet in the air, the mist crawled closer and closer, choking ever smaller the circle of sunlight. Instead of howling winds, the confusing roar of the malevolent, demanding, obsessed voices swirled around her.

She covered her ears hoping to deafen the chaotic chants. But it was of no use. The voices were not merely coming through the air. They were in her head. Covering her ears only amplified the sound, like the roar inside a 55 gallon metal drum—echoing and rolling in all directions.

When the tightening circle of light on the hilltop was only about 20 feet in diameter, a new, now-visual, horror began to grip Diakrina. Just discernable in the mist, hundreds of distorted faces and gaunt, twisted bodies appeared, moving within the grey wall. She tried to look away, but the images seized her attention against her will.

They wore the expressions of the damned. Seemingly, they swam in the muck of some stench-filled swamp, body on top of body, each struggling hopelessly to extricate himself, only to sink ever deeper.

A few of the desperate condemned rose above the ooze and slime by climbing on top of others and pushing them down below the dark surface. Once on top, these masters of the moment would soon fall victim to the clawing, grasping panic of another temporary victor.

All the while, they chanted: writhing and chanting, chanting and writhing. Their eyes, empty and colorless, pled in utter hopelessness to no one in particular. They appeared hypnotized and mechanical in their chanting, almost unaware of their tortured mantra. Yet their frantic expressions and helpless thrashing betrayed a conscious inner terror.

Suddenly, out of the sea of anonymous tortured specters, a familiar face caught Diakrina's eyes—then two, then three. Family members, classmates, childhood friends . . . materialized before her one by one, reaching out to her, their empty eyes pleading with her to do something to help them. Diakrina's eyes widened in horror. The writhing grey terror she loathed with everything in her was reaching to her with the very hands of those she loved.

Among the familiar faces, one riveted Diakrina's attention and she stepped toward the mist for a closer look. From within the swirling grey, her little sister peered back at her. A year before, while they were swimming together in a river, Alice had been caught in a swirling current and pulled under. Diakrina had reached out for her little sister and tried to pull her to safety, but the current was too swift and strong, and Alice had drowned. The memory was excruciating.

Now, here, from out of the mist, Alice was reaching out for Diakrina's help. Maybe Diakrina was getting a second chance. Maybe this time she could reach through the clammy wall and save her little sister.

Just then several hands, drenched and grasping, shot out of the grey prison toward her. She leaped backwards as one of the hands almost caught her. A sharp pain shot through her wrist and up her arm. Though the hand had not gripped her, a deep gash, like that left by a large claw, gaped at her from the top of her wrist. She stared in astonishment at the blood that began to fill the gash in her arm and didn't notice the wall of mist quickly tightening the circle around her, bringing her again within its reach.

She looked up just in time to see Alice—or what appeared to be Alice—reaching out of the wall toward her. The empty eyes, yet frantic face of her sister froze Diakrina. Suddenly, her left wrist was grasped as by a vise and she was being dragged into the grey wall.

Diakrina dug in her heels and pulled back with all her might. What alleged to be the small hand of her sister was clearly nothing of the sort. The hand—if you could call it a hand—was so large its grip consumed Diakrina's entire forearm. Hard claw-like fingernails dug into her skin. Strength her little sister clearly did not possess was pulling hard at her.

Now other hands were reaching for her. If they succeeded in grasping her, she knew she would not have the strength to resist their pull. She would be lost to the grey, cold swamp.

She ducked and scrambled back and forth with all her strength and agility, trying to keep out of reach of the damp appendages lunging for her. But she knew she was losing the battle.

Grasping the claw-like hand with her right hand, she tried to peel it from her left arm. Sharp, razor-like nails dug deep into her arm as it tightened its grip in violent desperation. Diakrina screamed in pain.

At the same moment, a red glow rising from her left side caught her eye and she glanced down at her forgotten sword. Its ruby red handle throbbed with bright crimson light. Instantly, she twisted her body to the left, maneuvering the golden sheath as far as she could away from the grey wall and its grasping claws. She turned loose her hold on the clammy hand and made a frantic grasp at the crystal handle of the sword.

She missed. The scaly hand pulled her left arm so close to the grey wall she felt the stinging, wet cold slap her forearm. Once more she twisted and grasped at the sword. This time her hand found the glowing handle.

A lightning bolt of strength shot through Diakrina's right arm and into her whole body. She had never felt such strength. With a great tug she pulled away from the swirling wall until the arm that held her was fully extended. Then with a quick slash of the crimson blade she came down hard on the ghastly arm.

An ear shattering, animal-like scream drowned the hissing chants as the arm, still clinging to Diakrina's forearm, fell severed from the wall of mist and its vaporous impersonator. Diakrina lifted her arm and watched as a huge, dragon-like appendage became visible for only a moment and then dissolved away as vapor and cold water drops falling to the ground.

But the battle was still on her. The wall of mist closed within a few feet of her on all sides. Wasting no time, Diakrina began swinging the crimson sword in every direction. As the blade cut into the grey mist, numerous screams like the former one shattered the dark, chanting mantras.

The mist began to retreat. Driven by a claustrophobic need for air and light, Diakrina kept swinging at the grey prison around her, running first to one side and then another, cutting and chopping at the swirling poison. The mist continued to retreat until she stood in a circle some 70 feet across with sunlight pouring down around her.

Exhausted, she staggered to the center of the sunlight and, breathing heavily, looked up into the welcomed warmth. The hissing stopped. Diakrina slowly lowered her sword and watched as the mist slithered down the sides of the hill in all directions, seeking refuge in the trees at the bottom. There, with deliberate writhing movements, it formed an unbroken wall around the base of the hill.

A deadly silence hung in the air: no chanting, no screaming. Only the fast rhythm of Diakrina's panting breaths could be heard. All around the mist swirled and dripped, but it did not close in.

The ordeal left Diakrina shaken. Was that really her little sister in the mist? The thing that had tried to drag her into the grey swamp certainly wasn't Alice. What *was* it? No. There could be no doubt: it was *not* Alice.

Diakrina shuddered at the image of her little sister reaching out for help. "Please, God," she found herself praying, "don't let it be true that she is in such a place."

After a few moments, Diakrina's attention shifted to her surroundings. She stood in a circle of light, while all around her oozed an ever-moving blanket of grey. At the top of the hill stood the only tree not shrouded in mist.

Unlike most of the trees she had seen since leaving the Tree Bridge, this one had smooth, grey bark. It was not large or small but medium in size. It was obviously a fruit tree of some kind, as she could now see red and yellow fruit hanging from its branches.

The fruit looked somehow familiar to Diakrina, and slowly and cautiously she stepped closer to examine it. She was within a few feet of the tree when the silence, which had now lasted for several minutes, was broken ever so faintly.

From one side of the circle a low whispering chant began again. It was so soft that Diakrina had trouble discerning the words at first. It was slow, with long pauses between syllables, uttered again in that breathy, hissing manner. It sounded like hundreds of voices asking a single question over and over. Eventually, she began to make out the words:

"Should . . . I . . . trust . . . Him?

Should . . . I . . . trust . . . Him?

Should . . . I . . . trust . . . Him?

Should . . . I . . . trust . . . Him?"

The chant did not become louder, but just continued. Diakrina found the question curious. What did it mean? Trust whom?

The question carried a tone and inflection that implied a negative answer: more accusing than questioning. The last word, "Him," dripped with contempt. What was really being said, in bitter sarcasm disguised as a question, was, "I . . . can't . . . trust . . . *Him*."

The renewed chanting put Diakrina back on full alert. But the mist did not seem to be closing in. After several minutes, another chant slowly penetrated her consciousness, rising up from the opposite side of the hill. She had not noticed it at first, because it was so soft and she was paying such close attention to the first chant. It, too, hissed in slow, pausing syllables, just audible:

"Who . . . am . . . I?

Who . . . am . . . I?

Who . . . am . . . I?

Who . . . am . . . I?"

This was even more confusing. Was the mist asking her who *they* were? Were they asking *themselves* who they were? She wasn't sure. The question echoed in her head like an annoying song you wish you could forget but can't stop humming. The mantra soon lodged itself in her own mind, and the question became hers: "Who . . . am . . . I?" Over and over it whispered. Over and over she pondered it without an answer, "Who . . . am . . . I?"

The haunting refrain went on and on. Was she still hearing it from the mist around her, or was it now only inside her head? She wasn't sure. A growing discontent gnawed at her. She tried to shake the unsettling words from her mind, reminding herself that its source was some hideous monster that intended her harm. But she couldn't shake it.

It was like walking through a waist-high bur patch. Soon thousands of burs cover your clothes, and no matter how you try to remove them, they cling to you. The words, like unyielding burs, fastened themselves to her mind. The mist, though visibly constrained at the foot of the hill, seemed to have taken audible form and settled like a heavy fog in her thoughts. She could not muster even the slightest breeze of resistance to disturb it. Deeper and deeper it settled, finding the deepest crevices of her mind. "Who . . . am . . . I?"

Then a third chant ascended the hill from her right:

"If they lose, I win!

If they lose, I win!

If they lose, I win!

If they lose, I win!"

Thankful for the distraction, Diakrina forced her attention to this third, fascinating whisper. It posed no direct question, but an assertion. Yet it swarmed with unspoken queries. What could it mean? Who must lose? Who would win? Why must someone lose for someone else to win? Who must lose in order for *her* to win? At least the idea of winning was a welcomed thought.

Might the chants explain or interpret one another? "Can I trust Him?" "Who am I?" "If they lose, I win!" Is this a code, or a riddle?

As she wondered about this, repeating the words to herself in search of some clue, a fourth chant joined in, rising up the hill from her left:

"I am right if they are wrong!

I am right if they are wrong!

I am right if they are wrong!

I am right if they are wrong!"

"Right?" Diakrina repeated thoughtfully to no one. Who has to be wrong for me to be right?

On and on the whispering chants continued in a chaotic but mesmerizing chorus. "Should . . . I . . . trust . . . Him? Who . . . am . . . I? If they lose, I win! I am right if they are wrong!"

A rhythmic pattern—difficult to describe in mere words—began to pound in Diakrina's head in an unrelenting synchronized incantation. The pauses in the slowly beating questions were accented with the statements. "**SHOULD** . . . If they lose, I win . . . I . . . I am right if they are wrong . . . **TRUST** . . . If they lose, I win . . . **HIM** . . . I am right if they are wrong." And, "**WHO** . . . If they lose, I win . . . **AM** . . . I am right if they are wrong . . . I . . . If they lose, I win."

Over and over this repeated as the minutes passed. Diakrina felt her head would explode from the drumming. She tried to cover her ears but, again, it was useless. The voices rolled like hissing thunder in her mind.

She heard herself screaming, "STOP! STOP! STOP!" and wondered how long she had screamed.

But her screams went unheeded. Like madmen in an insane asylum chanting a taunting limerick that has obsessed their tortured minds, the piercing whispers jeered on and on. Diakrina, still holding her sword, fell to her knees with her arms wrapped around her head and pressed her forehead into the grass and dirt.

Then, suddenly, it stopped.

A split second of relief—had she not begged for silence?—immediately gave way to alarm. She jumped to her feet, expecting to find the mist closing in on her. But it still kept its dark vigil at the edge of the trees below.

The silence had lingered for several long seconds, perhaps minutes, when a sneering whisper swept up the hill in front of her:

"SHOULD?"

It was followed by mocking, hissed staccatos from behind, then right, then left:

"WHO?"

"WIN!"

"R...I...G...H...T!"

The last word came in a drawn out sneer that lasted a full five seconds.

It had begun again, only now each phrase was reduced to a single word intoned like a vile blaspheme.

SHOULD? WHO? WIN! R...I...G...H...T!

SHOULD? WHO? WIN! R...I...G...H...T!

SHOULD? WHO? WIN! R...I...G...H...T!

Each word triggered a maddening repetition of its entire phrase in Diakrina's mind. But the single word now gave each chant a focus that cut like a dagger.

Diakrina closed her eyes in painful frustration and sank once more to her knees. As she did, the warmth of the sword's handle against her skin pulled at her attention. Opening her eyes, she saw that the crimson handle, still glowing, was pulsing brightly with the rhythm of the hissing voices, as if reacting to each word.

Could the sword push back this audible attack?

Instantly, a firm yet gentle answers spoke into her mind with a clarity that pierced through the mocking chant: "Yes, if you speak in the name of the One to whom the sword belongs."

Diakrina's mind whirled. "To whom the sword belongs?" she asked aloud to herself.

"Of course!" she nearly shouted as she jumped to her feet. Strateia had commanded the mist back by raising his sword and shouting, "In the Name of the Living One, I order you to retreat!" Could she do the same?

Her heart raced with new hope. Lifting the sword in the air high above her head, she gathered all her remaining strength and shouted as loud as she could against the hissing chants, "In the Name of the Living One, I order you to be still!"

Crimson light flashed from the sword in every direction for several seconds as Diakrina held its pulsing handle. As the light pierced the mist below, the grey wall shuddered. Shrieks, hisses and snarling yelps sliced through the chant in mid syllable. Then, silence.

Slowly the mist retreated a few more yards away from the base of the hill. After slinking some distance into the trees, it stopped, hiding in the forest just out of sight.

If ever the words, "Silence is golden," had meaning for someone, it was Diakrina at this moment. The welcomed silence that fell over the woods and the hilltop was met with an even more blessed stillness that hushed the haunting voices in her head.

She walked a few paces and, slumping down to the green grass, leaned back against the fruit tree and turned her face up toward the warm sunshine. The peace was delicious. She sat there for several moments drinking in the stillness.

The contrast only highlighted her dilemma. She was still surrounded—a prisoner in this last little stronghold of light and warmth, besieged by the dreary swirling cold. She tried not to think of it, at least for the moment, wishing instead to bask in the idyllic stillness.

Just then, a slight disruption to the perfect stillness arrested her attention. From behind her, on the far side of the tree, an ever-so-subtle sound betrayed the crushing of crisp, green blades of grass beneath slow and deliberate footsteps. Every muscle in Diakrina's body tightened. Moving her right hand stealthily onto the handle of her sword, which lay on the ground by her right leg, she shifted her weight and prepared to pounce. She was about to spring to her feet swinging her blade when the sound of a single pair of hands clapping announced the presence of the intruder.

Spring she did. Turning swiftly in the direction of the applause, she saw the lower half of a man dressed in a grey tunic, still somewhat hidden by the tree.

"Very good, my dear; quite excellent. You have impressed me more than you know," came his voice. He continued clapping as he circled the tree and ducked under one of its lower limbs.

Diakrina crouched into a fighting stance with her sword swaying threateningly in front of her. When he saw the sword, the smile he had worn as he spoke faded, and he turned quite sober. He stopped short and held his place. All was still for a quick moment, the space between them charged with tension.

Then he spoke again. "Now, now, you will not need *that!*" he said as he clasped his hands together and pointed slightly toward the sword blade with the index finger of his right hand. Then opening his hands out wide to his sides, with the palms up, "As you can see, I am unarmed."

Diakrina kept the sword swaying in front of her and continued to crouch like a cat ready to strike. She said nothing. She had experienced enough of the mist's deception to suspect this was only some new trick. She was not about to lower her guard for a moment.

He held her gaze momentarily. Then realizing she was not going to lower her weapon, he raised one eyebrow at her with a look of resignation and stepped toward the fruit tree. Diakrina moved in a circular fashion, keeping the sword between them as he turned and sat down where she had been seated.

Leaning back against the tree, he said, "Come now, we don't need that thing. I'm not going to harm you."

Diakrina held her place without relaxing a single muscle.

"It seems you have been badly frightened," he said in a concerned voice. "Is there something I can do to help?"

Diakrina took about two steps back from the man and stood up straight keeping the sword held across her body with the blade slightly elevated. "I doubt that very much," she said in her sternest voice. She wanted to add, "I have very deep suspicions of you," but didn't.

He turned his hands, which lay in his lap, slightly upward in a quick gesture, shrugging his shoulders in a kind of mock helplessness. He then folded his right hand over his left fist and held them just above his waist. Leaning back against the tree, he simply stared at Diakrina and said nothing more.

Diakrina continued to eye him with concern. She walked around to one side, keeping her distance from the man and the tree, to gain a better vantage point. She had no intentions of being surprised by a second or third intruder.

Now that she had a moment, she studied his countenance searching for any clue to who or what he might be. He had a dark head of hair that was full and thick. His sideburns continued uninterrupted into a very close-cut and neatly trimmed beard and mustache. His eyes were a cold steel grey. Nothing in his face or countenance was either frightening or welcoming— he was a blank.

"Where did you come from?" she finally asked.

He stared down at his hands and pursed his lips slightly as if trying to think how to answer. "I came from where I was before I was here," he finally offered.

"That's no answer at all," snapped Diakrina. "That obviously goes without saying."

"But I did say it," countered the stranger. Diakrina wrinkled her forehead a little, but recovered her sternness.

"That too could go without saying," she countered.

The stranger pursed his lips again and smiled down at the ground as he nodded thoughtfully to himself. "I can see you like to argue."

Diakrina said nothing. He looked up at her. "Am I *right?*" he asked. Before Diakrina could respond, a low hissing cry from the forest at the far side of the hill echoed, "RIGHT!"

Diakrina instinctively crouched back into her fighting stance with the crimson blade swaying in the air. The stranger looked at her as if puzzled by her reaction.

"Does that question somehow frighten you?" he asked.

"It's not your question," snapped Diakrina. "It's those infernal voices."

"Voices?" said the stranger as if confused. "What voices are you talking about?"

"I'm talking about those . . . hissing . . . shouting . . ." she struggled for words, "seething whispers."

"Whispers?" came his reply as he looked around. "I'm not sure what you mean."

"Are you deaf?" exploded Diakrina. "Those voices have been chanting here for hours. They only stopped just before *you* showed up."

The stranger stood up. Diakrina stepped back, crouched at the ready. He looked around momentarily and then shrugged his shoulders. "I . . . hear nothing."

"They're not chanting now. But didn't you just hear that hissing whisper shout, 'Right!' a moment ago?" Once again the forest hissed loudly, "RIGHT!"

"See, there it is again!" Diakrina said as she gestured with her sword toward the forest behind and beyond him.

"I'm sorry, but I hear nothing. Are you okay?"

"No, I'm NOT okay!" screamed Diakrina back at him. "These hellish voices have been chanting for hours, and some kind of beast tried to drag me into that mist at the foot of the hill. Then you show up out of nowhere and claim you can't hear these voices. NO! I'm not okay!"

"There, there, Miss, you need to calm down," said the stranger taking a step in her direction.

"Don't you come another step," shrieked Diakrina, pointing her sword straight out toward him. The stranger stopped short and retreated a step back to where he had been.

"We just need to talk about this, Miss. I'm sure there is some explanation." He seemed shaken by her intensity.

"Okay, mister, you start the explaining," demanded Diakrina. "Who are you?"

Instantly, from the forest to her left came a shrill whisper, "WHO?" Diakrina couldn't help swinging her sword wildly at the voice. The stranger simply began his answer as if nothing had happened except her erratic behavior.

"Well," said the stranger cautiously eyeing Diakrina with increasing concern, "who do you want me to be?"

"That's not an answer," shouted Diakrina in quick retort. "I asked you to tell me who you are."

"WHO?" hissed the mist.

This only made Diakrina more frightened and angry. "Now, answer me! If I don't get an answer soon, I will dispense with you like I did that scaly hand!" Her fear and anger animated her into action. She surprised herself with her boldness. Just to make her intention perfectly clear, she took a couple of rapid steps toward the stranger.

Quickly he retreated behind the fruit tree. Then, cautiously, he poked out his head. "Okay, lady. Just calm down."

Diakrina stepped back a single step, her eyes still wild. "Well, out with it," she demanded.

Slowly the stranger came from behind the tree. He stood up straight and looked Diakrina in the eyes. "My name is Tuphoo" (Too-FAH-oh).

Diakrina, due to the classical education of her younger years, recognized the name to be Greek, with the spelling, tufow.

She quickly searched her memory of Greek vocabulary. "I am familiar with the word, *tuphos*. It means to be wrapped in smoke. And if I am not mistaken, your name means, *high-minded and puffed up with pride*."

Tuphoo shrugged his shoulders again. "Who can control how he is named?" he quipped. "Names mean nothing to me. Do they to you?"

"I'm not sure," said Diakrina. "They seem to mean quite a lot since I came through the Door of the Rose."

"Door of the Rose?" said Tuphoo. "Are you saying you came through such a door?"

"Yes," answered Diakrina.

Tuphoo looked puzzled for a moment. "I have heard strange stories about such a door, but I thought they were just old myths—stories and nothing more. However, the door in those stories was called the Door of the Road."

"It is no mere story," retorted Diakrina. "I came to this Garden through a door, but it is known as the Door of the *Rose*, not *Road*."

Tuphoo looked puzzled again. "Garden? What garden? There is nothing all around but the dark forest."

Diakrina heard the hissing whisper, "This is all there is, there is no more!" It unnerved her and she gripped her sword even more tightly.

"The Garden is real. In fact, we are in . . ." Diakrina's voice trailed off as she realized how outrageous she was about to sound, given their present surroundings.

"Were you about to say that we are in this *Garden* right now?" asked Tuphoo quickly.

"Well . . . yes, in a sense we are," Diakrina confessed.

"Does this look like a garden to you?" asked Tuphoo. "There is nothing but gnarly old trees and slimy, stagnant pools along dry streambeds. I don't think this is anything like the fabled Garden."

"Fabled Garden?" repeated Diakrina, picking up on his expression. "Are you saying the Garden is only a fable to you?"

"What else could it be? I have never seen it or met anyone who claims to have seen it, until now. All I have heard is old stories, and no one takes them seriously."

"What stories have you heard?" she asked, with guarded, though genuine interest.

"Well, you know how they always go: stories of a beautiful, golden-lit land where streams of water flow abundantly and sunlight streams from the sky by day and beautiful patterns of starlight fill the night sky with moving stories. Soft green grass covers the earth and the air is kissed with cool warmth. And they speak of a door called the Door of the Road, through which some have found their way to this unspoiled paradise. In fact, one of the oldest stories speaks of a young lady, much like you, who is called through the Door into the golden land by a tall, powerful guardian."

"Are you saying you have heard about what is happening to me?" said Diakrina, now startled that Tuphoo might know anything at all about her. "What do you know about *me*?"

"I'm not sure I know anything about *you*, Miss. As I said, they are just old stories that no one takes seriously."

"But perhaps they are not just old stories," Diakrina pressed. "Maybe they are something more."

Tuphoo moved back to his place in front of the fruit tree, sat down and looked up at Diakrina. "It is a long story and I do not remember it. I have not heard it since I was a very young child."

Tuphoo was quiet for a moment looking at Diakrina as if he were trying to remember something. "Miss, tell me your name and perhaps you will have your answer."

"My name? What does it matter?"

"You are the one who thinks names matter, not me," shot back Tuphoo. "I gave you mine, perhaps you could just return the favor. It *is* rather awkward calling you *Miss* all the time."

Diakrina had no desire to be on a first name basis with this man, but then, she could see no reason to withhold her name. "My name is," she hesitated, "Diakrina."

"Diakrina," he intoned slowly. "I know a bit of Greek, too. Doesn't your name come from the word, *diakrino*?" Diakrina only nodded.

Tuphoo continued. "If I remember correctly, it has several meanings. *Dia* means asunder, to divide. *Krino* means to judge, to distinguish, to decide. Together, it can mean to contend with or to separate oneself.

It can also mean to discern between issues and make judgments. In certain uses it can mean to doubt, by being *un*able to judge between things."

He focused his gaze into Diakrina's eyes. "So, which is it, *Diakrina*? Are you the contender, the discerner or the doubter . . . or *all three*?" When he said, "all three," his demeanor changed for the smallest part of a second. His eyes narrowed and his voice trailed off as if resisting a smirk.

The question burned into Diakrina's forehead. She had been the contender and the doubter all her life. But discernment? Of that, she was not so sure. She said nothing.

Responding himself to the question hanging in the air, he said, "I think you are *all three*."

It felt like an accusation, but Diakrina had no idea how to defend herself. She had no answer.

"WHO?" whispered the mist.

"Who am I?" echoed back from within her head, and it did not stop. Louder and louder it crescendoed. Then dying away, it began again, and then again. Diakrina, still holding her sword, tried to put her hands over her ears, but that only turned her head into a canyon of echoing, hissing whispers.

She saw Tuphoo take a step toward her. "Can I help you?" his lips said, but she could hear nothing but the rolling, roiling taunt, "Who am I?" Surely her head would burst.

She backed away while swinging her sword toward him as a threat to come no closer. He stopped but looked puzzled. She saw his lips form the question, "Is it those voices again? Maybe I can help."

With that Tuphoo raised his finger to his pursed lips and gave a long, "Shhhhhhhhhh!" All went quiet. Diakrina fell to one knee still trying to hold up her sword in front of her.

He turned back to her. "Is that better?"

Diakrina didn't answer. She just stared at Tuphoo.

"It seems I *can* help you," said Tuphoo, taking her relaxing silence for a positive response.

"I don't think you can," seethed Diakrina, shaking herself out of her stunned silence. "I think you *are* the problem. I know now that you *can* hear those hellish voices."

"I don't hear *your* voices," retorted Tuphoo.

"Don't mock me!" screamed Diakrina swinging her sword at the ground between them to drive home her demand. The earth in front of her erupted in an explosion of grass and earth as the crimson blade struck the ground. Tuphoo fell backward toward the fruit tree and nearly hit his head on the tree trunk.

"You heard the voices, I know you did! And what is more, they obeyed you." Diakrina was now standing nearly over Tuphoo with the blade tip swinging back and forth over his chest.

"Then doesn't that make me on your side," yelled Tuphoo as he scrambled on his back up against the tree trying to get away from the sword tip. "Why else would I try to stop them?"

Diakrina pressed him with the sword even closer to the tree. "I can think of other reasons," she said through clenched teeth. "You claimed not to hear any voices and now I find you controlling them. I think you are playing with me."

A boiling anger rose inside of her. This had to stop. She was sure Tuphoo was in league with the grey mist.

She pushed the tip of the blade so close to his face that the crimson glow turned his cheek red. Tuphoo, now visibly afraid, pressed against the tree as hard as he could, trying to keep the blade from touching his skin.

Diakrina looked sternly into his steel grey eyes and said in her most determined voice, "You have just a few seconds to say something to me that I can believe. If I don't hear something to make sense of your being here, you die."

Tuphoo's steel grey eyes searched Diakrina's face frantically. He seemed to be assessing her resolve; weighing his options. For a long moment nothing happened, and Diakrina poised to strike.

Just then, for a bare fraction of a second, all expression—all sign of life—slipped from his eyes, and just as quickly they refocused and narrowed, as a sinister sneer spread across his face. The transition was eerie. Suddenly, a totally different person was looking at Diakrina out of those steel grey eyes, now cold and cruel—the color of the grey mist.

"Okay, we'll do it your way," came a chilling hiss from Tuphoo's snarling lips.

Now certain of the threat before her and what she must do, Diakrina quickly stepped back with her right leg to give herself room to swing the crimson blade with maximum force. As her right foot landed firmly behind her, a cold, wet chill with a sudden vise-like grip closed around her ankle. The last thing she remembered was being wrenched off the ground, high into the air, as Tuphoo's face twisted in sardonic delight below her.

All went dark.

CHAPTER TEN

# The CAVE

Diakrina had no idea how long she had been unconscious. Slowly, a terrible sensation of wet and cold crept into her awareness.

When she finally opened her eyes, she could make little sense of the dim greyness around her. The only apparent point of illumination came from straight in front of her, like a light at the end of a dark tunnel.

Between her and this flickering glimmer, the air shifted and writhed mysteriously. She stared through the mist for several minutes, trying to make sense of the light and the motions that appeared to surround it. Gradually, the distant images began to take shape in her mind and form the silhouette of a man moving from side to side in the dim glow of the light.

Of course! It was a campfire. Diakrina appeared to be about 100 feet back inside some mist-filled cavern, with a campfire blazing just outside the mouth of the cave.

Diakrina, now fully awake, drew her attention back to her own immediate surroundings. Even in the relative darkness, she could see large iron bands around her ankles and just above her knees, fastening her tightly against a cold, wet rock wall behind her. Looking from side to side confirmed that her arms suffered the same fate. Thick iron bands, clasped just above and below her elbows, pinned her outstretched arms snuggly to the wall.

At the same moment she both saw and felt the handle of her sword, still clutched tightly in her right hand. The crimson blade glowed faintly in the swirling mist around her. Knowing she still held the sword comforted Diakrina, though she could do nothing with it. She could not move her arm at all. She wondered why the sword had not been taken from her.

As she thought about this and tried to remember what had happened to her, new patterns of movement from the campfire caught her attention. Someone had lit a small torch in the fire and was making his way into the cave toward her. The mist swirled around the flame as it and its bearer came closer, step-by-step.

The man's face remained hidden in shadows until he was just a few feet in front of Diakrina. Then he lifted the torch up over his head slightly in order to illuminate her face. It was Tuphoo.

"I see you are back with us," he said as the torch flickered between them. Diakrina said nothing. Their eyes fixed on each other, each studying the face of the other.

"Nothing to say?"

Diakrina only stared at him with her sternest expression. Tuphoo turned and walked a few steps back and sat down facing Diakrina on a rock in the middle of the cave floor.

"Now, I see you are clearly upset," began Tuphoo. "But things are not as bad as you might think."

"You say that, and yet I am pinned to this cave wall."

"Yes, you are—and that for everyone's protection, I assure you," responded Tuphoo. "You are a bit dangerous with that sword, young lady," he said as he nodded toward Diakrina's right hand. "Your hand seems welded to that handle. We could not get you to turn it loose." Then adding in a softer voice, "Sorry for having to take such extreme measures, but you really left us little choice."

"Us?" repeated Diakrina back to him, "You and who else?"

Tuphoo looked down for a moment and then back up at Diakrina. "There are as many of us as necessary."

"Necessary for *what?*" pressed Diakrina in her hardest voice.

"Necessary for you," came the cold, bloodless answer. A slight smirk escaped from the right corner of his mouth as he answered her. The sense of veiled evil that came through that expression made Diakrina's flesh crawl with a shudder up and down her spine.

But just as quickly, the expression was gone. "Now, I have a little proposition for you, Diakrina. Are you interested?"

"That would of course depend on the proposition."

"Well, it is very simple. If you would be willing to turn loose of that sword and drop it to the ground, I would be willing to set you free from the iron bands that are holding you to the rock."

Diakrina looked at the sword in her right hand almost as if she had forgotten it. Tuphoo's request puzzled her. She looked back at him and then again to her right hand.

"Why haven't you already taken it from me?"

Tuphoo looked down at the cave floor again. "Let's just say it would be best if you dropped it willingly."

"Never!" stated Diakrina firmly.

Tuphoo kept his head down. "I really think you should reconsider," came a voice, clearly from him, but sounding more like one of the voices of the mist.

"You are afraid of the sword, aren't you? You can't touch it, can you?" challenged Diakrina.

There was a long silence.

In those few moments while she waited for a response, Diakrina grew certain that the sword was her last line of protection, even in her immobilized hand. If *they*—whoever *they* were—could get her to surrender it, she would be truly helpless. Without her sword, they would have no need to fasten her to the cave wall, for she would succumb to the mist like those writhing helpless horrors she had seen earlier. Whether they were real people or not she wasn't sure, but she knew they represented what this revolting Mist wished to do to her. (From this point on, Diakrina capitalized *Mist* in her mind, for she now knew for sure that it was no mere cloud of water vapor, but a vile, living, evil thing.)

Tuphoo stood up slowly and took a few steps toward Diakrina, being sure to move to her left. Diakrina took this as confirmation that he feared the sword in her right hand. Approaching her left arm, he held the torch so close to her face that she could feel its heat against her cheek and ear, and looked sternly and steadily into her eyes. The blank coldness of his grey eyes made Diakrina want to turn her face away, but she steeled her resolve not to flinch and held his cruel stare, pouring into her expression all the determination she could marshal.

Tuphoo studied her for several seconds, until it was clearly uncomfortable for them both. Then he stepped back a single step.

"Your stubbornness will not help you," he announced solemnly. There was a cold, machine-like clip to his words. "We will leave you on that wall to rot, if we have to. And a lot of good that sword will do you then," he hissed with a sneer.

Diakrina did not consider this an empty threat. His cruel voice, cold eyes and obvious fear of the sword all spoke in unison. He would leave her here to die if she didn't give in.

But she couldn't give in. Surrendering to the Mist was unthinkable, though rotting away strapped to a cold cave wall carried no appeal, either. Eventually she'd weaken to the point of collapse and drop the sword anyway. But no. She would not do so willingly. Never.

Tuphoo's voice suddenly and unexpectedly changed to a warm and concerned, almost soft, entreaty. "I'm sure neither of us wants that, now do we? Surely you can see we need to talk about this. There seems to be little benefit to you continuing to hold on to the sword, now does there?"

Tuphoo sounded almost father-like. "It just keeps me from setting you free. But once you drop that sword, we both will be done with a very sticky situation. I will not have to worry about the sword, and you won't have to be pinned to this cold, wet wall. Sounds like a win-win to me." He let his last words hang in the air in order to elicit agreement from Diakrina.

"There is nothing to talk about," said Diakrina, raising her head to look at him. "I will not drop the sword even if you leave me here to rot."

She hoped she sounded more courageous than she felt.

"Well," Tuphoo countered, "in that case, some of your friends are waiting to speak with you." Diakrina was taken aback by this statement, for she remembered seeing her little sister, Alice, trapped in the grey Mist.

"You will not fool me again with those illusions, Tuphoo. I know now that it is only your filthy Mist trying to manipulate me by impersonating those I love. I will not fall for it again. Don't waste your time."

Tuphoo, who had turned as if to leave, paused. Without turning around he retorted, "I was not referring to anyone other than you, yourself. It can be rather enlightening, let us say, to meet the more hidden aspects of one's *self*. Very enlightening indeed," he sneered. And with that Tuphoo simply vanished as the torch fell with a thud to the cave floor.

If Diakrina had any lingering doubts that Tuphoo was anything other than some hideous incarnation of the evil Mist, they evaporated in that instant. The sudden silence chilled her. She was alone. The torch burning slowly on the floor about 10 feet in front of her cast the only light visible in the dank cave. The distant, untended campfire had retreated into a few low flames limping tentatively among a mound of glowing embers. Several minutes passed in grey silence.

Suddenly, a deep shadow blocked her view of the dying campfire as a dark presence fell between them. Squinting her eyes to see into the darkness beyond the torch, she could just discern a boiling wall of seething Mist rolling down the cave toward her.

An uncontrolled fear crawled, almost literally, up Diakrina's spine. She struggled with all her might at the iron bands that held her to the wall, but the more she struggled the more deeply each band cut into her limbs and the rough rock of the wall scraped her skin raw.

Images filled her mind of the clawed appendage that had nearly dragged her into the cold slime of the Mist. If such claws attacked her now, they would easily shred and disembowel her defenseless body. Panic seized her as the dark terror rolled steadily closer and closer.

Creeping forward, it devoured the spot just 10 feet away where the torch lay burning on the floor, and slowly smothered the flame. Diakrina stared in helpless horror as the last of the light sizzled into smoky ash.

The slight crimson glow of the sword, clutched helplessly in her shackled hand, shed the only light remaining in this cavern of palpable darkness. She turned her face and stared longingly at the glow of the sword, forcing her eyes away from the menacing Mist that bore down on her. Just then, she heard a hissing whisper and felt cold breath on the side of her face.

"This is all there is! There is no more!"

Diakrina tried to force the sword blade toward the Mist by maneuvering her wrist what little she could, but the iron band was too tight. As she strained to reposition the weapon in her hand, being careful not to loosen her grip, suddenly a crimson light blazed up from the blade. In a flash, Diakrina saw several faces floating only a few feet in front of her, bathed in a crimson aura. The faces gasped at the glowing sword and retreated hastily back to about where the dead torch lay, as an involuntary scream of mixed fear and anger escaped Diakrina's own lips.

The faces—Diakrina counted eight of them—turned and stared coldly at her, the light from the sword holding them at bay. After a standoff that lasted only a few moments, though it felt much longer to Diakrina, all but one of the faces withdrew into the shadows. The one remaining face glared scornfully at Diakrina, but said nothing for several minutes. When finally it spoke, the words came in that loathsome hissing whisper.

"Diakrina, it is time you understood your situation. Look closely at me. Do you not notice something familiar?"

Diakrina, letting curiosity triumph over repulsion, forced herself to look. The face before her revealed the countenance of an older woman, not elderly but clearly aged enough to have several grandchildren. A few deep-set wrinkles betrayed the passage of time, but otherwise her skin appeared smooth and resistant to old age—almost youthful.

Diakrina instantly noted something hauntingly familiar about the face, but she could not place it. For a split second she caught an expression that reminded her of her mother, but just as quickly the resemblance vanished. No, it was clearly not her mother.

Diakrina was still studying the face, trying to make some connection with people she had known, when the hissing voice interrupted. "Just by adding a few years it seems that your own face has become a stranger to you."

Diakrina's eyes widened in disbelief as her forehead furled under the shock of the implications. "Can't be!" she heard her mind object. But at almost the same moment, an acknowledgement of recognition flooded over her. It *was* her face . . . just older! She had often been told she had certain facial expressions that reminded people of her mother. Seeing it in her own age-worn face was uncanny.

Diakrina always struggled to explain what she felt at that moment. "I expected almost anything—a demon or monster perhaps. Instead I found my own face staring back at me. Yes, it was my face, but also not my face. I saw my face as I had never seen it before. It took my breath away."

The astonishment she helplessly conveyed brought a sly smile and subtle sneer to the confronting visage. "So, now you know," it hissed. "I am you as you will be. Look deeply into my eyes and behold your future. It is here in the Mist. *This is all there is. There is no more!*" The last two lines became a unison of hissing voices.

For a moment that seemed an eternity, Diakrina could not move or speak, like a bird hypnotized by a serpent. She longed to look away, to scream, "Never!" but no sound would come. Some morbid fascination drew her toward this specter, this professed window on her own future. Who is not curious about the unseen tomorrows? It pulled her in, against the futile warnings of her better instincts.

The Mist closed in. She felt consumed by it. Only her right hand and a small pocket of air around the sword resisted the piercing dampness.

"Release it!" hissed the specter.

"This is all there is. There is no more!" muttered the soft chants.

This demand and its echoed pronouncement merged into a metered incantation, replaying itself again and again as Diakrina—helplessly transfixed—stared into the time-warped mirror of her own face. The cold, grey Mist drenched her body and numbed her limbs, sucking away her strength.

A wave of weakness poured over her and she dropped her chin onto her breast. As she did so, a slight crackle announced the forming of an icy film on her skin.

The rhythmic chanting continued.

Forcing her thoughts toward her only remaining vestige of hope—the sword—Diakrina realized she could no longer feel her right hand. The numbing cold had done its work. Had she dropped the sword? Was it really all over? Was this all that was left? Would there never be anything more?

The possibility of having dropped her sword hit her like the terror of a plummeting guillotine and snapped her instantly out of any Mist-induced lethargy. Jerking her head up and to the right, she frantically searched for any sign of the sword in her hand. A heavy curtain of Mist had fallen around her face, blinding her to anything beyond just a few inches. Stubbornly she fixed her gaze on where she knew her right hand must be and stared desperately into the darkness, begging her eyes to focus. There, for just a split second as the Mist swirled and folded, an ever-so-faint crimson glow showed itself and then vanished. Afraid she had imagined it, she blinked fiercely and then fixed her eyes on that spot, praying it would happen again.

There! This time there was no doubt. The sword had not fallen. Her hand, though numb and invisible, had not betrayed her. Or perhaps the sword itself had not betrayed her weakened grasp.

An indescribable elation flooded Diakrina's mind. Just a glimpse of that crimson flicker in the cold and dark of the Mist-filled cave triggered a surge of sweet hope from deep within her spirit. Visions of the Garden, The City, Strateia—all framed with green grass, lush roses and bubbling brooks—paraded like a victory procession through her mind.

"There *is* more!" The confident assertion swelled from that faint glow of unquenched light. Diakrina rallied all her thoughts and centered them on that blissful assurance. "Yes, there is more."

The cold and the Mist pressed her to the wall, sucking the last bit of strength from her body. She could barely breathe. But something inside her had shifted. Knowing the sword still rested in her hand sent a wave of hope through her that refused to surrender to the frigid darkness. Diakrina willed her unseen, unfelt hand to grip the sword even more tightly, though the numb extremity offered no feedback, no hint that it intended to obey.

With her last bit of strength, she gasped in all the cold, wet air she could. It stung her throat and stabbed her lungs, but she forced aside the pain and sucked an even deeper breath. Then, marshalling this hoard of foul and frigid air, she shouted with forceful defiance against the entombing Mist, "There *is* more! This is all a lie!"

The chanting halted and gave way to a low angry growl. For about two seconds, Diakrina felt the pressure pull back off of her face and chest. Pressing her momentary advantage, she quickly snatched another deep breath and shouted even more loudly, "I KNOW there is more! I KNOW this is a lie!"

A violent and ear-shattering scream—a "G R O A A A A A A H!" like that of an unearthly beast in torment—shook the cave and echoed down its black mouth. The specter of Diakrina's age-rendered face disappeared.

Behind the roar came an eerie and bizarre howl, like a trapped timber wolf. Starting on a high piercing note held for about five seconds, the cry descended into the most agonizing vibrato Diakrina had ever heard.

As the tortured howl dropped in pitch, Diakrina felt the damp and cold retreat from her. The darkness receded enough for her to see clearly the glow of crimson light radiating from the sword in her hand. The murky Mist had withdrawn about three feet from her face. She drank in the comfort of the light and gulped several pants of air as the howling continued for half a minute or more.

When it finally stopped, Diakrina heard deep, pained breathing. A breathy growl—almost a bray—punctuated each exhale. For several minutes, no sounds other than the disquieted breathing passed between them. Diakrina spoke first.

"Truth is too potent for you. You cannot endure it. You are nothing more than a lying illusion and truth is your undoing."

The breathy growl continued without an answer. Slowly, the visage of Diakrina's aged face materialized at the edge of the Mist.

"You are a lie, too," Diakrina said through clenched teeth, still shivering from the cold. "Go away!"

But it did not go away. It glared at her coldly for several seconds and then replied with a hiss, "I hold enough truth that *you* cannot banish me."

The emphasis on *"you"* did not escape Diakrina. The statement hung in the air with a cold certainty that hit Diakrina like the hard edges of an inconvenient truth. She knew the statement reeked of manipulated truth, but an unsettling taint of plausibility accompanied it.

"*I* may not be able to banish you, but I know One who can," countered Diakrina.

"I will concede," sneered the face, "that there is *One* who *could* banish me, but you would never consent to it."

"And why is that?" queried Diakrina.

The face smirked slightly and then answered, "Because what *is* true about me, is also true about *you*."

Diakrina winced. This statement had landed a painful blow, though she did not fully know why.

The face added, "I may not be a flattering mirror, but I am a mirror all the same."

"You are a distorting mirror and, thus, a lie," shot back Diakrina.

With a smug smile, the face retorted sarcastically, "A distortion relies on a reality. All the best lies carry a little truth in them."

Diakrina recoiled at this cruel candor. Gathering herself, she engaged the face again.

"You may say there is truth in your lies, but truth that is distorted ceases to be truth, just as something straight made crooked ceases to be straight."

"Or maybe," answered the face, "it becomes a new kind of truth."

Diakrina leveled her eyes at the specter, "There are no *versions* of truth; there is only truth. And lies are not a *'new kind of truth,'*" she protested.

"Lies have no content of their own; they are parasites on the truth. They are the discordant note in any melody, the broken part in any machine. They are useless or destructive departures from right and good. Strateia taught me that!"

The face started to interject a reply, but Diakrina gave it no chance and hurried to continue.

"Truth stands alone. It doesn't need anything. But a lie cannot exist without truth, for it needs some piece of the true and the real, something actual on which to feed. The very truth you hate and distort is your life force. You can't exist without it. You are a diseased lie, feeding on the healthy. You are nothing in yourself, but a malfunction, a failure, a breakdown, an error, a fault and a glitch. You are a nuisance generating zero!"

The face did not flinch. "I accept your evaluation, for with it you have accused yourself. What is true of me is true of you."

Diakrina's eyes flash angrily. "I am not you! And you are not me!" she yelled in passionate protest.

The specter smirked again and moved ever so slightly closer to Diakrina. "That is a statement the sword will not defend, my dear. For what is true of me, *is* true of you. And what is true of *you*, is not true."

Diakrina's mind raced as she sorted the possible meanings of these words.

"What could that possibly mean?" she shot back, trying to project a confidence she did not quite feel, for she was not sure she wanted to hear the answer.

"It means," responded the face, "that I am that something about you that is true *of* you, but is, itself, a lie."

Diakrina most definitely did not like the sounds of this, but determined to hide her alarm. In her most condescending tone, she parried, "And what about me are you suggesting is a lie?"

The eyes of the face danced with evil delight. "Fear, my dear, fear! All improper fears are built on some lie. You, Diakrina, are full of fears, and every one of them is grounded in a lie and hidden behind more lies. Just now, you tried to cover your fear with a false boldness. It is your nature. You lie about your fears and then fear that your lies will be discovered."

Diakrina could not speak. She was exposed. The face knew. Sensing its advantage, the specter pressed her quickly.

"I am not an imposter. I am you. My face is your face—your fears—reflected. My words are your own fearful thoughts externalized. The chants that haunt you are merely the static of your own heart, the background noise of your daily existence, amplified so you can hear them for what they are. Nothing you have seen or heard here is new to you, for they are but echoes of what your fearful heart whispers night and day. Others around you have seen and heard beyond your pathetic pretenses, but you are blind and deaf to your own fearful insecurities until I show you yourself."

If Diakrina could have moved her arms, she would have covered her ears. But she could not. Instead she began to scream uncontrollably, "Damn you! Damn you! Damn you!"

The face went silent, but moved a few inches closer and to her left. "Truth hurts doesn't it?" sneered the specter. "I think you will find your lies more comfortable, more convenient. Believe what you want to, it is easier. And here, in my realm, the realm of *altered truth*, I can teach you how to make the best of what you have left. So, it is in your best interest to turn loose of that useless sword."

"What makes you think I would ever settle for your filth?" retorted Diakrina.

"Settle or not, my *filth* is *your* filth, and *it is all there is*. Everything decays and degenerates. In time, it all descends to me. And you, Diakrina, are no exception. You have my lies within you and they *will* do their work. My masterpiece is in your veins. You will never be healthy. The spiritual *bacteria* of suspicion infect your every perception in ways you still cannot perceive. You have a cancer eating away at your ability to trust. And without trust, you are a prisoner of lies and fears. Already you are my prisoner in more ways than you know. Your bondage to this wall is but a physical manifestation of your inner condition—a caricature of the lies that enslave you."

Diakrina, who had been silent since her last frantic outburst, suddenly came to life. "Did you say, *caricature*?" The specter held its peace and glared back as Diakrina continued, "You have already admitted that you distort everything you reflect. I know there is double meaning in nearly everything you say. Like a caricature, you amplify certain aspects of truth in order to hide other aspects. And I suspect that what you are trying to hide would cancel the false conclusions you are flinging at me. I may be infected with your lies and fears, but that cannot be the whole truth. For if it were, this battle would not be possible—you would not have to contend with me. You would simply take charge of me completely. But the truth is, you haven't."

The specter winced and drew back a foot, emitting a low rumbling growl. Diakrina pressed her point.

"I am sure that you are the most skillful of liars. You bend and weave the truth in and around your illusions with great cunning until your lies mix and mingle so convincingly with the truth, and your victim falls so completely under the power of your fears, that every perception is filtered through *your* twisted interpretation. If you achieve this, you can then march truth out unvarnished right in front of your victim and it will not be recognized or welcomed. This, I am sure, is to your pride the crowning moment of success. And I must confess, you are skillful at what you do, but I think you just revealed your hand too soon."

"You're no match for me, so quit stalling," snarled the face moving once again toward Diakrina. "Drop that sword now, or I will suck the life out of you until you do!"

Diakrina straightened herself as best she could onto her feet and yelled back at the face, "So, you are a victim of your own fears. And to quote you, *'Every one of them is grounded in a lie and hidden behind more lies. Just now, you tried to cover your fear with a false boldness.'*"

In that touché moment, the low growl all around her confirmed that Diakrina's words had landed a heavy blow.

"You will not suck the life out of me, you freakish distortion! If these iron shackles are but caricatures of the lies within me, then they are themselves but extensions of illusions. And no illusion is going to hold me in this dark dungeon!"

With that Diakrina began flailing with all her might against the iron bands as she screamed, "Damn these lies! Damn these lies!"

The sardonic face wailed with cruel laughter. "*Knowing* that something is an illusion is not the same as defeating the illusion, you foolish child. You cannot renounce your faith in the iron bands; that I promise you," shrieked the face. "Go ahead, trrrrrrrrryyyyyyyyy!"

Diakrina screamed and fought with reserves of strength she did not know she still possessed until her rage had set it free. "They're a lie! They're a lie! They're a lie!" Over and over she screamed as she fought against the iron bands with frantic abandonment. The shackles cut deeply into her arms and shins until the pain was excruciating. Yet she was determined. Louder and louder she screamed, thrashing back and forth against the cave wall like a crazed madman.

Diakrina focused her manic rage against her cruel restraints for nearly a full minute. All the time the specter howled like a wolf over fallen prey. When her strength gave out, Diakrina's blood streamed from under every iron band. But the shackles had not budged.

Her screams descended into cries of fear and panic. Tears burst from her eyes and a sense of helplessness swept her up in its grip. The howling face morphed into derisive laughter, and then faded into the shadows of the swirling Mist.

In its place, Tuphoo stepped out of the grey toward Diakrina. He walked slowly to her left, staying well clear of the sword still clutched in her right hand. She took little notice of him. Her body shook with sobs and cold exhaustion as she hung helplessly limp in the shackles. Ice once again began to glaze her battered skin.

"Now, my dear, can we dispense with all this?" he asked with a cold, controlled sternness that felt like a dagger to Diakrina's heart. "I can remove those iron bands immediately, if only *you drop that sword!*"

All fell silent for a few moments, except for Diakrina's heavy breathing and low, shivering sobs. Tuphoo stepped closer until his mouth was almost touching her left ear. Then with a voice stingingly sweet and breathy with a façade of concern, he whispered in her ear as if sharing a secret he wanted only her to hear. "We both will be so relieved when that sword is finally gone. And when it is gone, so will be these awful, torturous restraints. They will . . . just go away."

Diakrina slowly turned her hanging head to look into Tuphoo's cold grey eyes. She searched them for only a moment. Then between her shivers she gathered herself and answered through clenched teeth, "To be replaced, I'm sure, with something even more torturous?"

Tuphoo stepped back a little and with mock concern replied, "I guess that is just a chance you will have to take, now isn't it?"

Diakrina dropped her head and stared at the cave floor. Then slowly, she turned her head toward the sword, still glowing slightly with soft crimson light, and her mind began to recall what seemed like an ancient memory. Standing on the Tree Bridge at the great Chasm, Strateia had given her this sword, forged out of his own sword, for, he had said, there is only one sword in the Kingdom of the Living One. What she now held was her own form of that one sword, fashioned personally for her and entrusted into her keeping.

Her memory shifted once again to images of the beautiful City, the warm sunshine, the soft green turf and brilliantly colored flowers she had beheld. She recalled the moment when she was faced with the decision to embrace the sword and swear allegiance to the Living One, and the feelings of suspicion that had risen up in her and mingled with the thrill of joy that always came when the Living One was mentioned.

Then, as if hearing Strateia's voice again, his words came rushing back to her: *"This suspicion, Diakrina, is the trait of all who have fallen in the Great Dance. Do not try to cure it yourself. That is a long road that spirals downward to defeat and bondage. Only the Living One can prove Himself to you and cure your unfounded suspicions. Swear allegiance with all the heart you can now command. It is He who will liberate the rest."*

*"Do not try to cure it yourself. That is a long road that spirals downward to defeat and bondage."* Those words leaped into her mind like a burst of light. Of course, she had been trying to cure these fears herself. Then rushing powerfully into her mind came again the words that had followed, *"Only the Living One can prove Himself to you and cure your unfounded suspicions. Swear allegiance with all the heart you can now command. It is He who will liberate the rest."*

Diakrina's eyes widened with realization as she continued staring into the crimson light of the sword. In that moment, she knew she would never turn loose of its ruby red handle. If necessary, she would rot on this wall with it clutched in her frozen hand. She heard Tuphoo, who now seemed far away, speak again.

"Well, what's it going to be, my dear?"

She was too immersed in her thoughts to even answer him. He no longer mattered, though he did not yet realize it. From deep within her, a prayer came rising up: a plea as well as a resignation. With the last of her strength, she looked deeply into the light coming from the crimson sword and whispered, "Living One, please prove yourself to my heart and kill these unfounded suspicions and fears. I cannot. I am again ashamed to offer You so little, and even that so sick and polluted. Yet, with all the heart You enable me still to command, I trust You to do what I cannot do."

At first, it seemed nothing happened. But then, a new warmth brought the fingers of her right hand to life and began flowing through her hand and along her arm. When it reached her shoulder, it shot straight into her heart and then exploded into her head. It flowed rapidly down her left shoulder, out her left arm and to the extremities of her fingers. Diakrina felt delicious life pulsing through her! Then, with a sensation she could only describe as the explosive burst of a supernova, warmth and life surged down her torso and legs. She was revived.

A look of terror gripped Tuphoo's face as Diakrina's whole body began to glow crimson red. The glow—at first subtle—grew with astounding intensity. Tuphoo fell backward with a blood-curdling scream.

Diakrina felt the layer of frost breaking loose all over her body and heard it shattering on the rocks at her feet like delicate china hitting the floor of her grandmother's kitchen. An unbelievable rush of power came over her as crimson light flooded the cave with a blinding flash.

Instantly, the cold Mist sizzled, turned to steam and vanished. The hissing of seared vapor filled the cavern, along with the screams and howls of tortured specters. Diakrina could see absolutely nothing except the blinding light, but the audio drama that surrounded her told a descriptive tale.

For nearly a full minute, beastly voices brayed, pled, growled and gurgled in desperate hatred and despair. Fragmented chants halted mid-sentence and scattered into meaningless shrieks. Finally, the frantic screams faded and gave way to distressed whimpers.

Then, as abruptly as it had started, the crimson light that had been bursting from every pore in Diakrina's body withdrew and centered once again in the sword itself. Diakrina blinked her eyes trying to focus. When finally her eyes came right, she could see that the Mist was gone. The mouth of the cave about 100 feet away now revealed a rising sun just peaking its head over a distant horizon. Warm sunlight flooded the cavern and turned everything golden as it mixed with the crimson light from the sword.

CHAPTER ELEVEN

# The RELEASE

Renewed strength filled Diakrina's limbs as she drew the cleared air into her lungs and welcomed the morning sun. She discovered with astonishment, however, that the iron bands still held her fixed against the cave wall in that same crucified position in which she had spent the horrible night.

Crumpled in the middle of the cavern floor lay further evidence that her ordeal had not been a bad dream. For there, clutching himself in a fetal position, whimpered Tuphoo.

Diakrina was about to push against her restraints when a beautiful silver voice spoke from her right. Looking quickly toward the voice, her eyes met the most welcoming sight she could have imagined. Standing a few feet away, with sword in hand, beamed Strateia in all eight feet of his bronze, chiseled strength.

"Strateia!" she screamed with delight.

Strateia smiled warmly at her, "Good morning, little one."

Then turning, he walked slowly toward Tuphoo and, towering over the whimpering heap, brought his sword close to the trembling head. Tuphoo snarled like a wounded beast and slid several feet back. Strateia then pointed his sword straight at the quivering mass and looked back at Diakrina. "You have done well. I am glad you held out until I could get here. It is time to set you free, little one. Are you ready?"

"Yes!" cried Diakrina with anticipation.

"Then," said Strateia, "we must make this pretender give up his claims."

Tuphoo looked up with bitter, baying rage at Strateia. "You want to set *that* free?" He sneered as he glared at Diakrina with a cold contempt that would have frozen a waterfall.

"*She*—'*that,*' as you refer to her—is already free, as you perfectly know," answered Strateia. "That is why you can no longer keep your shackles on her. So, no more of your twistings and distortions! You will hold your deceitful tongue!"

Tuphoo snarled and curled again into a tight fetal position.

"How many bands hold you to the wall, Diakrina?" asked Strateia in an instructor's best rhetorical teaching voice.

Diakrina looked quickly at her limbs. "There are two on each limb, Strateia. So eight in all," she answered.

"Then we shall unlock all eight, each in its turn," Strateia remarked.

He walked to Diakrina and smiled down into her questioning face. "It is okay, little one. It will soon be over," he said with the demeanor of a very kind doctor reassuring his patient who is about to undergo a procedure.

"I don't understand, Strateia. Why are these shackles still holding me?"

"That is about to change, little one," he answered confidently. "But this is not magic. We don't just wish them away. Their power must be unwound, their lies undone. Only then can the truth freely manifest."

Unexpectedly, perhaps triggered by the trauma of her surreal night, a philosophical musing flooded over Diakrina in that moment. As she looked into Strateia's clear, determined eyes, she *knew*—she *felt*—that life is a real and valuable risk. No freedom is won cheaply. Reality consists of sterner stuff than men often recognize. Life is dear. Living is precious. Every story matters. The adventure is real, the risks are actual, and everything is at stake in every chapter of the Forever Story.

"Do you trust me, Diakrina?" Strateia's pointed question brought her back to the tangible present.

"Yes, with all my heart, Strateia."

He then turned and walked to Diakrina's right hand. "Then I ask you to entrust your sword to me for the purpose of cutting your bonds."

Diakrina's questioning face filled the few silent moments between them.

"Of course, I will trust you with my sword," she finally answered. "But why can you not use your own? After all, are they not really one and the same sword?"

Strateia smiled at her last question. "Yes, Diakrina. It is true that only one sword—one truth—exists in His Kingdom. We have each, however, been created unique, and He, in His infinite uniqueness, relates to each of us individually. No one-size-fits-all relationship with Him exists, for we each reflect some aspect of His infinite glory in ways that no other creature can. Our relationship with Him is intensely personal as well as corporate. While all truth is His truth and never contradicts itself, your sword represents His personal application of that single truth *to you*. These bonds hold you uniquely and call for your sword to cut them."

Strateia paused waiting for Diakrina to respond.

"I will wish to learn more of this later, Strateia. But for now, I am content to trust you with my sword."

"Very good, little one," Strateia answered. "But you must understand, before I take it, that I am acting on behalf of the Living One, who will be acting through me. Therefore, you must trust whatever I do with the sword . . ." he then paused for emphasis, ". . . no matter what."

The words certainly carried a sober, even warning tone, and Diakrina searched Strateia's warm and love-filled face for some clue to their meaning. Almost instantly, however, she came to herself and realized it did not matter what he meant. Distrusting Strateia was unfeasible. What is more, she had vowed to trust the Living One, *no matter what*. There was no alternative, whatsoever: nothing to think about or consider.

Sensing her resolve, Strateia put his left hand under Diakrina's right hand. Instead of releasing her sword, however, a sudden flash of memory compelled her to tighten her grip. "Strateia," she said holding his gaze, "the Mist wields the art of illusion with cunning skill. Perhaps even you are such an illusion, though I know in my heart you are not. I must, as you instructed me, hear you declare the Covenant Vow before I will release my sword to you."

Strateia smiled with the air of a pleased teacher. "I was wondering if I would need to remind you. Very good, little one."

Strateia nimbly bent his massive frame and leaned down until his face almost touched Diakrina's right ear. Then in a stately, silver whisper that could only be heard by Diakrina, he said:

"I HAVE SWORN ETERNAL ALLEGIANCE TO HIM WHO ETERNALLY WAS, WHO ETERNALLY IS, WHO ETERNALLY IS TO COME. I BREATHE HIS LIFE, I AM EMBRACED BY HIS LOVE, I AM UNDER THE AUTHORITY OF HIS TRUTH, I SEE ALL THINGS BY HIS LIGHT."

The words filled Diakrina's soul with peace, and for the first time since the battle at the fruit tree, she relaxed her grip. The sword handle dropped into Strateia's large palm.

Strateia sheathed his own sword, transferred Diakrina's sword to his right hand and stepped in front of her. Diakrina noticed how small her own sword looked in his giant hand. Then, lifting one eyebrow he asked, "Are you ready?" Diakrina nodded an affirmative, having no idea what her consent might mean.

Strateia, without even turning around, raised his silver voice as his eyes narrowed and his eyebrows dropped in determination. "Tuphoo! It is time!"

The temporarily forgotten clump on the cave floor snarled and looked up fearfully. Strateia turned quickly and stepped toward, and then over, Tuphoo's trembling body. He then stood behind him, turned around and, pressing the tip of Diakrina's sword against Tuphoo's head, prodded the miserable creature toward her.

Tuphoo yelped and slid in Diakrina's direction, just far enough to be beyond the sword's reach. Strateia took a step forward and prodded again, eliciting another yelp and slide. This scene replayed itself until the sniveling specter lay crumpled at Diakrina's feet.

Diakrina, not knowing what to expect next, cringed as Strateia raised the crimson blade and brought it forcibly down, piercing the top of Tuphoo's head. Without a sound, Tuphoo sat up straight, his eyes wildly dilated.

"What is your name?" asked Strateia firmly. Tuphoo began to speak but his eyes never blinked, nor did his face change expression.

"My name is Tuphoo. I am the Mist. I am the smoke of blindness that my master blows into the minds of humankind so they cannot see truth."

"Confess your master!" Strateia demanded.

"My master has many names. He is the Deceiver, the Serpent, the Accuser, the Adversary, the Intruder, the Enemy and many others. He is called Anomos. He is light turned inward, giving birth to darkness. He is life severed from its source, giving birth to death. He is truth turned wrong-side-out, giving birth to lies. He is identity imprisoned in the self, giving birth to pride, rebellion and emptiness. He is reality twisted into illusion, giving birth to ignorance and fear. He is the Prince of Darkness, the Lord of Death, the Slayer of Men."

"And do not forget," added Strateia, "he is the forever defeated one!"

For a moment Tuphoo did not reply. Then he said quietly and slowly through clenched teeth, "Yes. There is that, too."

"Relinquish your first lies!" demanded Strateia.

"The first four lies pertain to the worldly kingdom," said Tuphoo. "By means of the first lie, *'This is all there is! There is no more!'* we fixate mankind on what they perceive to be physically tangible and reduce them to an earth-bound existence, cutting them off from the Forever Story."

"Renounce your claim!" demanded Strateia.

"I do now renounce it."

In one deft motion, quicker than the eye could follow, Strateia drew the sword upward, swung it through Diakrina's torso and returned it to its place in Tuphoo's head, all with such lightning speed that Diakrina didn't even flinch. A moment later she felt a deep burning spasm race through her whole body. Then, just as suddenly, the iron band on her left wrist simply dissolved and fell away.

"The next one," came Strateia's command.

The Mist began, "By means of the second lie, *'It is all up to you. You are on your own,'* we isolate men even in the midst of their friendships."

"Renounce your claim!" demanded Strateia again.

"I do now renounce it," came the voice of Tuphoo.

Diakrina knew what was coming this time, but again it happened so quickly that she could not even gasp in a breath. The sword did its work, followed by a burning pain, and the band on her right wrist fell away.

"The next one," charged Strateia.

"By means of the third lie," replied the Mist, "'*Trust no one! Protect yourself!*' we turn men one against the other and turn each man inward."

"Renounce your claim!" demanded Strateia again.

"I do now renounce it," came the voice of the Mist.

The sword flashed, the burning followed, and the band on her left upper arm vanished.

"The next one," Strateia commanded.

"By means of the fourth lie, '*Take control!*' we put men on the endless treadmill of futility, the fearful attempts to master the circumstances of their lives by manipulating others to serve their passions and fears."

"Renounce your claim!"

"I do now renounce it."

The sword, the pain, the dissolving iron band . . . and Diakrina's right arm was free. She moved both arms back and forth, each in turn, thinking how good it felt to move them. Her wounds—self-inflicted from her violent struggle to free herself—stung a bit, but mattered little in the delight of being able to bend her arms and rub them.

"Diakrina, there are four to go. These will cut more deeply. Will you trust me?" asked Strateia.

Diakrina took in a deep breath and answered resolutely, "Gladly!"

"Relinquish your next four lies!" demanded Strateia of Tuphoo.

"The second four lies concern trust and identity, and they bind men with fears," said Tuphoo. "By means of the first of these, '*Should I trust Him?*' we cast suspicion on Him who is their only hope."

"Renounce your claim!" demanded Strateia.

"I do now renounce it," came the slow, but forced words of the Mist.

Diakrina expected the lightning fast swish of the sword. But it didn't come.

"Here, little one," said Strateia, "these you must extract yourself. You cannot walk with Him unless you trust Him for your whole identity. Take the sword and drive the blade into your leg just above one of the iron bands."

Diakrina took the sword slowly from Strateia. Standing passively and letting him wield the sword was one thing, but this was different. This was harder; much harder. She had come too far, however, to shrink back now.

Determined to see this through, Diakrina extended her arm out to her side and turned the sword toward her leg until the tip almost touched her right thigh just above the iron band. She felt the crimson heat radiating from the blade.

Just as she was about to thrust the blade into her leg with a quick stab, a voice from deep inside rose up and took over her tongue. Before she could stop herself, she heard her own voice say in begging, pathetic tones, *"Should I trust Him?"* The voice—*her* voice—appalled her. She nearly dropped the sword.

Strateia caught her hand and helped steady it. "Continue, little one. The lie is deep within you, but the cure of His Word will go deeper!" Strateia then unsheathed his own sword and pierced the tip into Tuphoo's head as he had done with Diakrina's sword.

Diakrina looked into Strateia's dancing eyes and confidence surged through her. She felt the voice try to rise again, but this time she was ready for it. She took control of her tongue and shouted as she drove the blade home, "Yes! I trust Him!"

Sickening pain swept through her whole body, deep into her bones. Her whole being shuddered violently as a deep, blunt, pervasive sickness racked her body. A grotesque parade of freakish and deformed fears stumbled through her—fears regarding God and her reluctance to release her life to Him, fears she had lived with from her youngest memories, fears that for years had protested every attempt she had made to trust Him. They staggered and grasped frantically at her inner spirit. But dying, they lost their hold and fell away. Then it was over.

Diakrina pulled the sword from her thigh as the iron shackle dissolved. To her surprise, the sword left no wound.

Strateia smiled at her and said, "To those who embrace the wounds of truth, the sword becomes a bloodless healer."

Diakrina suddenly noticed that Tuphoo had shrunk in size. Whether this had just begun or she only now began to notice, she never knew for sure. But clearly, he was shrinking.

Strateia looked at Diakrina and smiled again. He then nodded to her that they would continue. "The next!" he commanded Tuphoo.

The slightly shriveled specter spoke. "By means of the second of these lies, *'Who am I?'* we turn men inward, duping them into pursuing their identity through self-actualization. We divert them from the truth that they can never know themselves by themselves, and we poison them with suspicion toward the only One who can provide them with true identity."

"Renounce your claim!" came the silver voice of Strateia.

"I . . . do . . . now . . . renounce . . . it."

The voice of the Mist sounded forced and broken, as if tormented by a secret inner battle. But Strateia held the blade of truth steady until the renouncement was complete.

Diakrina transferred the sword to her left hand and, as before, reached up and out to her side so that the point of the blade hovered just above the iron band on her left thigh. Once again the inner voice rose up in protest. *"Who a . . ."* it began, but this time Diakrina caught the words in her mouth and stopped them. In defiance of every rising fear or rebel dissent, she forced her lips to speak what her heart knew to be true: "I am who the Living One created me to be!"

She took a deep breath and plunged the sword into her leg. Once again the dull, blunt, pervasive sickness poured through her body, and she shuddered violently. She heard her voice screaming "WHO? WHO? Who?" over and over. But like a receding echo, each cry diminished until the lying screams fell finally silent.

She pulled the sword from her thigh and the iron band dissolved. "Only two bands left," she encouraged herself, looking down at her ankles. She could hardly wait to be done with this ordeal.

Strateia apparently shared the sentiment, for he was *not* waiting.

The moment her screams faded, he pushed ahead with a commanding, "The next!"

Diakrina looked at Tuphoo's shriveled form, now a mere dwarf of his former self. A thin, small voice escaped the dwarf.

"By means of the third of these lies, *'If they lose, I win,'* we instill competitive jealousy in the hearts of men. We persuade them to pursue superiority by putting others down and to seek identity in comparing themselves with each other. We occupy them with vain self-aggrandizement, like passengers on a sinking ship bickering over the most comfortable cabin spaces while the ship goes down beneath them."

"Renounce your claim!"

"I . . . do . . . now . . ." The voice trailed off, but Strateia twisted his sword inside the shriveled head, and the tormented voice continued, ". . . re . . . nounce . . . it."

This time Diakrina was ready. The split second the words escaped from Tuphoo's mouth, she thrust the sword into her right ankle just above the iron shackle. Pain shot up her leg, went through her body and hit like a sledgehammer in the top of her head. As her body shuddered, she heard her voice crying, "WIN! WIN! Win!" in a desperate reprise, but she knew it was only the death throes of a long-pampered lie, now exposed and powerless.

When the shuddering stopped, Diakrina pulled the blade from her ankle and watched as the iron fetter fell away. Then she heard Strateia's firm voice command, "The last!"

What was left of Tuphoo reminded Diakrina of a rodent impaled on the end of Strateia's massive sword, as a weak, raspy voice began to squeak out a final confession.

"By means of the fourth of these lies, *'I am right if they are wrong!'* we fuel men's pride and ego by teaching them to condemn others and to obsess over being right at the expense of others. By judging others—even by use of the Living One's own commands—they foolishly think they are deflecting and appeasing their own guilt. They try to feed themselves by consuming others. Instead, they merely convict themselves further, unaware that judging, itself, is a self-condemning act that produces many false paths of righteousness; paths we decorated with religious ambitions to make them seem noble. It is so easy for there are many wrong paths to decorate, but only one right path we have to camouflage."

"Renounce your claim!" commanded Strateia.

"I . . . do . . . now . . ." there was a long pause. The hesitation this time seemed more from weakness than resistance. Strateia twisted his sword in the shrunken knot at the end of his glowing blade. It then finished, ". . . renounce . . . it."

Diakrina, now eager, plunged the blade into her left leg, just above the one remaining ankle restraint. As before, pain ricocheted up her leg, through her body and slammed into the top of her head, ripping through her with violent convulsions. Her shouts betrayed her shattered allegiance to the cherished lie—"RIGHT! RIGHT! Right!"—until they trailed off into silence.

The seizures finally stilled. Diakrina looked into Strateia's warm and smiling face, pulled the sword from her ankle, and stepped away from the cave wall.

## CHAPTER TWELVE

# THROUGH the CAVE

Strateia wiped the last smudge of the Mist from his sword. Together he and Diakrina walked down the long tunnel of the cave and out into the morning sunlight. There, just ahead, lay the hill with the fruit tree at its top. The warmth of the sunlight streamed down and flooded Diakrina with an overwhelming sense of joy.

She wanted nothing more than to put some distance between her and the vile cave. Sensing her desire, Strateia stepped out ahead of her and led up the hill until they reached the top. They sat down on the green grass next to the fruit tree, and Diakrina leaned back against its trunk and drank in the delicious sunshine.

Presently, Strateia spoke. "There is no time for lengthy instruction, Diakrina, though I am sure you have many questions. Events are unfolding rapidly in the Severed Lands. We must let you rest and renew your strength, and then we must press on. This all-out attack by the Mist suggests that Tuphoo operated under orders from Anomos. He does not yet know of your quest, but your presence has raised his suspicion. Before his interest becomes too piqued, we must move quickly to accomplish the first phase of the quest: gain the Immortal Fruit.

"You have experienced a powerful principle at work in the lies the Mist used against you: it drew its power through an inversion of your weaknesses. Lies and the fears they generate are parasites with no power of their own. They pretend to have power by feeding on weakness."

"I need no commentary on this principle, Strateia. This terrible night has driven the point home to me beyond words."

"Enough then, since we have little time," said Strateia. "For now you need rest and refreshment. Sit here and I will return shortly."

With that, Strateia was gone. Diakrina, weary and bruised by her ordeal, gladly rested her head back against the fruit tree and fell fast asleep.

Several hours later—in fact, by now the sun had started its decent in the afternoon sky—Strateia gently shook her awake. As she rubbed the sleep from her eyes, Strateia busied himself on the soft turf in front of her, laying out a meal of fruit and vegetables that looked so delicious that Diakrina knew they must have come from the Garden beyond the Chasm. When she was sufficiently awake, he removed a crystal-clear canteen of water that hung on a strap over his shoulder and offered it to her. Her eyes widened with delight at the first sip of the cold refreshing water. Then, with an eager smile, she drank deeply.

"It is time to eat, little one," said Strateia. "You need strength and healing."

As Diakrina stretched to reach the closest fruit, she muttered an involuntary groan. Her whole body ached, stiff and sore from the night's trauma. More hungry than sore, however, she continued reaching and picked up the fruit—a deep reddish purple specimen—and examined it. The color reminded her of a cross between an apple and a grape. It was the size of a very large apple, and felt firm to the touch. When she bit into it, expecting the resistance of an apple, sweet juice splashed her face as if she had chomped forcefully into a very ripe peach in its prime.

Once again, as in the Garden after the Great Dance, something awakened and stirred in her that she had never felt in her previous life on the other side of the Door of the Rose. Her whole being burst to life and embraced the experience of eating this luscious fruit. Not only did the fruit give itself to her, it somehow brought all of her senses into precise harmony with itself, making her a perfect receptor of all the flavor and delicious pleasure it had to offer. In the act of devouring the fruit, she felt mastered by it in a give and take of ecstatic equality.

Strateia had invited her to eat, and eat she did! This banquet of delights surpassed anything she had ever experienced. As she ate, palpable strength surged through her veins infusing health and energy into her muscles and, even deeper, into her bones. By the time she finished, every ache was gone. Her bruises had disappeared and her wounds from the shackles looked like they had been healing nicely for several days. She felt as though her body could respond to whatever feat she asked of it.

Having eaten to the point of perfect satisfaction, Diakrina laid her head back against the fruit tree once again and looked in Strateia's direction. He sat with a kind of relaxed attention, keeping his eyes trained on the Mist that swirled just beyond the edge of the forest at the bottom of the hill.

"Strateia, what *is* this awful Mist?" she asked.

Without diverting his gaze from the forest's edge, he answered in firm, but soft tones. "It is a defeated foe that rapes and burns as it is forced to retreat. We've no time now for prolonged explanation; that will come later. For now, think of it as a matrix of mirrors, *millions* of them, cunningly placed to hide reality and truth. It reflects a false picture of one's self by multiplying lies into delusions, delusions into fears, and fears into paranoia.

"This cycle of endless skepticism feeds on the victim until he questions everything except his own suspicion. Ultimately, it rapes the soul, transmuting it into a perplexed, echoing question mark that rejects all possible answers. In the end, the Mist binds the conquered soul of its victim to another and greater enemy: Thanatos."

Diakrina said that one can hardly imagine the impact Strateia's words and somber demeanor had on her, fresh as she was from being impaled by the soul-torturing skill of that cold, damp obscenity. She now knew more deeply than ever that she must not dismiss this foe lightly. By its parasitic power, it could suck all reality, all life, all hope from its victim. In place of a valid self, it would leave only a hollow illusion, a vacant stain, a foul blemish.

Diakrina's mind filled with dark images and profane word pictures of what the Mist intended for its hapless prey.

Strateia felt Diakrina's repulsion and understood the impact his words had made, and he approved of it. Taking his eyes off the Mist for a moment, he walked over to Diakrina and reached out his hand toward her. She took hold of it and he helped her, like a small child, to her feet.

"To defeat the Mist," he said, holding her gaze steadily with his intense eyes, "always look beyond it and beyond yourself. Focus on truth—almost any truth or piece of reality—and you will weaken the Mist's hold on you. Thrust that truth into its face again and again, and it will retreat. It cannot endure truth, for truth dissolves the lie that perpetuates the Mist's very existence. As light dispels darkness, truth dispels lies. While you were bound in the cave last night, your sword anchored you to truth. It was your only defense, and your survival depended on your refusal to relinquish it."

"I will *never* relinquish it," added Diakrina with deep conviction.

"I will hold you to that boast, little one," said Strateia seriously, with a hint of a twinkle in his eye.

"Strateia, you spoke of a greater enemy called *Thanatos*. Who is he? I believe his name means *death* in Greek."

Strateia's brow wrinkled and his somber expression deepened visibly. His muscles appeared to tighten and the distinct look of a warrior prepared for battle came over him. The shift in his body language was so palpable that Diakrina hurriedly glanced around her, expecting to see some new threat assailing them, but nothing tangible had changed.

"He is the curse that flows from Anomos' very first act of evil and the cause of all subsequent evil," replied Strateia. "He is not an entity or thing in himself, but a negation—the absence of life; the severance of things from the Source of Life. For death, as you correctly identified him, is the separation of things from their rightful place.

"Sever a branch from a tree, Diakrina, and that act of severance brings death to the branch. Cut off from its life source, it slowly withers and decays, falling into a progressive corruption of death. Death begins at the moment of severance but is actualized in stages of subsequent decay. This holds true of any living thing severed from its source. The more complex the entity, the more complex become the stages of its corruption.

"Thanatos *is* this severance and all its corruption. He is the resulting dysfunction when anything is cut off from Life.

"All life, Diakrina, flows from the Living One and all vitality springs from a proper connection and alignment with His order and design. Death feeds on rebellion against, and displacement from, that order and design. Death reigns anywhere the authority of the Living One is disregarded or defied.

"Some in your world say death is 'natural,' but it is not. Death is a hostile intruder. It defies the natural life-giving dependence and interdependence the Creator intended. By severing its victim from the Source of Life, it ravages and destroys the natural order.

"Thanatos' very existence, if you can call it that, depends on this. He is the vacuum that remains when Life is gone.

"He even infects Anomos. When Anomos defied the Living One and severed himself from Life, death rushed in to fill the vacuum. Death may appear to dance at Anomos' command like a trained bear at the circus, but in time it will turn and devour Anomos, himself. Anomos wields death as a weapon against the Living One's creation, but he also hates and fears death, for he knows he will ultimately fall prey to its destructive force. In his prideful rebellion, he only hopes to inflict as much damage on creation as he can with what time he has.

"Thanatos—this death-curse—makes war against Life with two weapons. You have met them already in the Mist. As Anomos' traitorous warrior, death devours its prey with two great and gruesome claws: the weapons of lies and fears. By these he assaults all living, rational beings."

As Strateia spoke, Diakrina sensed that he had first-hand experience with this enemy, for he spoke like a soldier remembering former battles.

"Will I have to face this great enemy?" Diakrina asked with concern in her voice.

"Yes, but not alone," came the answer.

Diakrina was relieved. "Then you will be with me," she assumed.

"Oh, no, not I," answered Strateia. "Only the Living One can help you when you face Thanatos. And your victory is assured—you will have no need to fight—*if* you entrust yourself to the Living One, for He has already fought and forever defeated Thanatos. Death is no longer a weapon in the hand of Anomos against any who are united to the Living One in covenant trust, for the Living One's victory becomes theirs. Thanatos may roar and posture when you face him—remember, his two weapons are lies and fears—but if you are united to the Living One and obediently entrust yourself to His victory, trusting not in any strength or virtue of your own, in the end Thanatos must bow and retreat from you."

"When will I face Thanatos?" asked Diakrina, feeling more resigned than anxious.

"Soon," said Strateia looking her straight in the eyes. "It is necessary in the quest. However, your first meeting with him will not be your last. You will have to die before you die. Do not worry yourself about it now. He will, for you, be one of your first battles and also your last battle and there will be many between.

"It is to this first battle you must now give your attention. For though you will encounter Thanatos in this first battle—as you must enter his realm to retrieve the Fruit of Immortality—you will not fight him face to face this time.

"However, as with the Mist, he will be present and aiding every enemy you encounter in the days ahead. For his name is not only Thanatos, but also Phobos Thanatou—*Fear of Death*.

"Thanatos—that terrible beast with many faces and forms—rules as the greatest of the evil lords, save for Anomos himself, and in the end he will devour even Anomos. But there is One he cannot devour, though he will try. And it will be his eternal undoing."

Strateia seemed to shake himself awake from his memories and came back to the present moment. "It is time for you to continue. I will accompany you as far as Nekus Canyon, where I will give you your necessary instructions. There the quest will truly begin."

Strateia walked up to Diakrina and laid his large right hand gently on the top of her head. "The blessing of the Living One will accompany you on your quest. Take courage. The journey shall not be easy, but it will be worth it."

Strateia picked up the water canteen and pulled its strap over his shoulder. Then, smiling at Diakrina and motioning for her to follow him, he strode past the fruit tree and headed down the hill toward the cave. As it became apparent they were on a trajectory toward the mouth of the cave, Diakrina stopped and stood staring after him. Before she could say anything, Strateia paused for only a moment and, without looking back at her, said, "Yes, we enter the cave again. Come." And with that, he resumed his former gait.

Diakrina, not enthusiastic about re-entering the cave, nevertheless quickened her pace in order to be near her powerful warrior-friend as they approached the gaping tunnel. They continued down the hill and then up the slight rise that led to the cave's mouth.

At the entrance, Strateia stopped and turned to Diakrina. "This cave branches off in many directions to the left and right of the wall to which you were shackled. The cave is part of a great mountain—hidden by the Mist—through which we must pass in order to reach the valley on the other side. The valley narrows until it empties into a great, high-walled canyon, known as *Nekus*.

"There, at the canyon, I will give you your necessary instructions for the first part of your quest. Following my instructions, you will pass through the canyon, obtain the Immortal Fruit and then battle your way out of Nekus, taking the Fruit with you. Beyond Nekus to the west, not far from Sapient Castle, lies a spring where you must meet me the following day. For now, I will be your guide through this cave to the valley beyond."

"Sapient Castle?" questioned Diakrina. "What is this place and must I go there?"

"Not immediately," answered Strateia. "Once you have obtained the Fruit of Immortality you must engage in a partial conquest of Sapient Castle. But we will not speak of it now, for it depends first on your success in Nekus. For now, stay focused on the great task before you: secure the Immortal Fruit and bring it with you to the spring. From there we will discuss Sapient Castle and ventures that lie ahead.

"We must be on our way. I will tell you more tonight before you enter the canyon of Nekus."

Strateia's words raised many more questions in Diakrina. But before she could speak, Strateia placed his finger over his pursed lips in a silent hush.

"The day is far spent and we must pass through the cave before the sun sets in the west. You will have to ask your questions as we journey through the cave, or else forgo them." Strateia then turned and motioned for Diakrina to fall in step as he entered the cave.

Diakrina hurried to keep close to the giant, striding warrior. Yet in her burned one question she would not forgo. But before she could put voice to her query, they came to the wall to which she had been fastened the night before.

She had been quietly dreading this encounter, shuddering at the vivid images of the terrible fears and horrors of that night. But as she looked at the actual spot—her very own place of torment—she felt strangely disappointed. The place appeared completely unremarkable: no bloodstains, no remnants of broken shackles, no hint of violence, nor, for that matter, *anything* out of the ordinary. There stood a grey, common, cool-to-the-touch cave wall, and nothing more.

Strateia turned to the left into a branch of the cave that disappeared into shadows, out of reach from the light reflecting through the mouth of the cave. As she passed close to the place of her imprisonment, Diakrina ran her hand lightly across the wall then quickened her pace to keep close to Strateia as they entered the darkness.

Strateia unsheathed his sword and held it out before them as they passed into the blackness of the deeper cave. The sword began to pulse with a bright crimson light that filled the darkness ahead of them.

Though the winding passageway itself offered ample width and height for them to walk side by side without Strateia needing to crouch, the constant intrusion of rocky outcroppings and generously scattered piles of boulders made their progress slow and tedious. A few times they came upon deep holes that required cautious maneuvering. Clearly, this was an ancient underground riverbed. At first, navigating through the labyrinth of rocks and crevices required nearly all of Diakrina's concentration.

Eventually, as she grew more accustomed to this underground terrain, her conscious mind returned to that question she was not willing to forgo.

"Strateia," she finally asked, "what does *Nekus* mean?"

When Strateia did not answer immediately, Diakrina started dreading what he might say. After a long pause, he answered slowly. "Nekus means *corpse*, for that is the fate of most who enter, and they will never exit until the great Day."

Neither of them spoke again while they were in the cave. Diakrina felt that she needed to apply all her attention on calming and focusing her resolve.

They walked for about an hour into the unrelenting darkness, illuminated only by the crimson, pulsing brilliance of Strateia's sword. Then, as they turned a corner in the cave, Diakrina detected the faint glow of daylight coming from somewhere up ahead. At last their winding course brought them around a bend that revealed an opening ahead, emptying into a green valley.

As they exited the cave, Diakrina looked around to take in the landscape. Their trek had landed them in a mountain-rimmed valley. The last of the day's sunshine poured over a mountain on the far side of the valley, casting long shadows over the entire basin.

Strateia did not pause to admire the scenery, but rather quickened his pace, as though resolute to make some prearranged deadline. At times, Diakrina had to almost run to keep pace with his generous and determined stride.

They had turned to the right, north as she reckoned it by the setting sun, and began a slight ascent up the sloping valley. At first, green vegetation carpeted the valley floor, creating a sharp contrast to the bare rocky walls in the distance. But as Strateia and Diakrina continued their gradual climb, the flora slowly gave way to craggy clearings and rugged slabs of rock.

With every step, the rising walls of rock crept nearer until it became apparent to Diakrina that the valley was closing in on them like a gigantic funnel that would inevitably deposit them at the mouth of a narrow and deep canyon. Also, to their left in the west, another canyon broke through the mountain toward them. From its direction came the sound of rushing water, like the roar of a mighty and swift river.

The walls of the canyon ahead of them rose several thousand feet. The canyon appeared so narrow that the rocky cliffs on either side seemed, from a distance, almost to touch high above the canyon floor. Diakrina knew without asking that this looming crevice was Nekus.

The valley terrain leading up the canyon grew increasingly rugged and difficult. With every bit of attention she could spare from simply finding her next footing, Diakrina studied the dark canyon ahead. If someone were to describe Nekus as "haunted," she would have readily agreed. An imposing dread fell more heavily on her with every step. She tried to shake it off as only "nerves," but the feeling only grew into a settled conviction.

This heaviness would not be dismissed as mere nerves. An actual, tangible atmosphere of malevolence pressed unmistakably on her, and it clearly came from the direction of the canyon.

Strateia suddenly halted and indicated that Diakrina could stop on some nearby boulders and rest. While she watched, deep in thought, Strateia gathered wood to make a fire. When he had formed a stack high enough to make a small bonfire by our standards, he unsheathed his sword and with it struck the base of the pile of wood. A small flame blazed from the tip of his sword and began to lick its way up the stack. Soon a pyramid of flames danced brightly against the deepening dusk.

Strateia then walked briskly away and disappeared over a small rise to the west of the fire. Diakrina felt a bit unsettled to be left alone so abruptly, but her need to rest and the welcoming glow of the fire kept her seated on the boulder.

As she tuned in to her surroundings, she noticed the sound of rushing water seemed quite close and came from the direction Strateia had ventured. A breeze wafted over the ridge, carrying the unmistakable aroma of a swiftly flowing river—the scent of spray, wet stones and river vegetation.

After about 10 minutes, Strateia came striding back over the rise and into view, as the last of the light turned the sky bright red and gold.

She later learned that the river flowed from the western canyon, turned north, and ran along the west edge of the valley until it dumped into Nekus Canyon.

Strapped over Strateia's shoulder hung the crystal-clear canteen, which he had filled with water for Diakrina. In one hand he carried, to Diakrina's great surprise, three fish, each about 18 inches long, strung on a thin vine. Several plants and small branches with leaves filled his other hand.

With the skill of a master chef, he laid the fish out on a rock near the fire and cleaned them with the tip of his sword. He then raked a few coals away from the base of the fire with his sword and stacked rocks on either side of them. Using a small branch, he erected a spit on which to roast the fish.

Diakrina watched as Strateia selected the plants and leaves he had collected, tore them into small pieces and mixed them together. He then took the mixture and rubbed it vigorously between the palms of his powerful hands, crushing it into small flakes and powder, and finally sprinkled the medley over the skewered fish as they began to cook.

Soon the tantalizing aroma of roasting fish and spices prodded Diakrina's hunger fully alert. Since entering the Door of the Rose, she had eaten nothing but fruit and vegetables. Her last meal, just before their long trek under the mountain and through the valley, had clearly been from the Garden beyond the Severed Lands. Though she was certainly eager to enjoy the roasted fish, this meal before her seemed somehow strange—a reminder that even the very best of this land carried constant reminders of its severed condition.

The hot coals soon did their work, and Strateia handed the makeshift skewer to Diakrina. The fish were truly delicious: exceptional in both taste and texture. Whatever herbs Strateia had used seasoned the meat with captivating flavor. Grateful for the nourishment and scrumptious taste, Diakrina could not help but notice the lack of that inner awakening and explosive pleasure she had found in eating the fruit of the Garden. Nonetheless, this was indeed a welcomed meal.

THE OTHER SIDE OF REALITY: Book One

When she had finished the three fish—Diakrina once again wondered to herself exactly what *did* Strateia eat?—he handed her the crystal container and she drank deeply of the cool water.

"Thank you, Strateia," she said as she found a seat on a rock just the right distance from the fire. Leaning back, she continued, "That was exactly what I needed."

Diakrina looked up. The night had now fully fallen, and tiny stars dotted the dome of the sky above them. The moon—only a small silver sliver—peeped over the rim of the valley. Being the first night after a new moon, the tiny reflective arc offered little hope of illumination, leaving the sky, valley and canyon all deeply dark.

"Yes, deeply dark," Diakrina thought, almost aloud. The canyon exuded a palpable darkness; a darkness spawned by something more than merely an absence of light. A heavy, ominous, menacing presence poured out from the canyon and pressed down on Diakrina's spirit. With the distractions of the meal removed, Diakrina had little else to occupy her mind.

Strateia noticed the change in her demeanor as she glanced nervously toward the canyon's mouth. "I see you are quite aware of the dark powers of this place. They are brooding about our presence," he said rather matter-of-factly.

Diakrina looked toward the dark, towering canyon walls, visible only as black silhouettes against the stars. "Whatever it . . . or they are . . . gives me the creeps," she finally answered.

Strateia took a deep breath and looked toward the canyon himself. "Nekus certainly reeks of evil and danger, little one," he said slowly, "but do not lose sight of who you are and who you are becoming. A powerful stronghold within you—the old suspicion that resisted your union with the Living One—has fallen. Tonight you shall have occasion to exercise your newfound capacity for trust, and in so doing you will actualize it."

He then walked around the fire and sat down on a larger rock next to Diakrina. They both sat, now to the left of the fire and slightly behind it as they faced toward the canyon's mouth, which was beyond and to the right of their camp. "It is time for me to prepare you for the quest, Diakrina. Listen carefully. My words are life to you."

Diakrina sensed a depth of seriousness in him she had not felt before. All her senses went on alert and she riveted her full attention on every word.

"Tonight, Diakrina, you must pass through the first part of Nekus before the sun rises on the morrow. Getting through before the light of dawn is essential. Otherwise you will never pass through, for great beasts live within the canyon that you must not perceive by sight. You are not yet ready to withstand the terror of seeing them. You will remain safe from them *if* you do exactly as I instruct you."

"How will I see to make my way? What shall light my path?" asked Diakrina, frightened at the prospect of entering Nekus on such a dark and nearly-moonless night.

"You may use your sword," answered Strateia. "It will cast just enough light to illuminate your next step. It will give you no more light than that until you pass the threat of the terror beasts. Once you reach the stairs into the inner realms of Thanatos, your sword will give you more light as needed."

Strateia paused, then continued. "As you journey, point the tip of your sword toward the ground just in front of your feet. I must warn you sternly against trying to find your own way through the darkness. Once you enter Nekus, your sword is *your only guide* for your steps. Follow where it leads you, no matter how fearful may seem the path, and you will be safe. Trust—a trust greater than your fears—is the only weapon that will bring you through this canyon. You must surrender control and entrust yourself to One greater than you."

An overwhelming fear suddenly gripped Diakrina. But before she could identify and face it, it morphed into a rage. The injustice of being forced, completely against her will, to endure such terrifying possibilities appalled her. Ugly and desperate emotions surged through her in uncontrolled waves.

"But why? Why must I do this?" she found herself almost shouting. "I don't understand. I don't understand!"

Strateia stood and stepped close to Diakrina. Taking her trembling head in his large, steady hand, he turned her face up toward his. Her eyes flashed with fright and searched his face for some hope of a way out.

"You have touched the heart of your quest, little one," he said softly, like a kind counselor. "This is the time for trust: now, when you don't have the answers. Trust must be chosen, based on what you *know* about the character of the One being trusted, in spite of your feelings or lack of understanding. This is your quest reduced to its simplest terms."

His words hit home. Strength flowed from his voice and the light from his eyes infused Diakrina with new peace and confidence. She drank in his gaze for only a moment and then, taking a deep breath, said, "Thank you, Strateia . . . Thank you. But, I must confess, I still do not understand." Then after a pause and another deep breath she confessed, "You know, I am quite terrified."

"Yes, I know, Diakrina. Time will heal it if you face it. And concerning why you must face this valley there *is* one answer that may go deeper than you realize. In addition to recovering the Fruit of Immortality—a matter that is external to you, though vitally important to you and your kind—something lies within you that only this quest can fully heal.

"This quest will unleash in you fuller and deeper purposes than you could ever otherwise know. It will allow you to become what you were created to be. This is no arbitrary test from which you could walk away, if only the Living One allowed it. This canyon and every aspect of the quest before you are necessary to your own journey from who you were to who you need to be. In the end, the Living One intends to lead you Home—to The City. You are on that journey. This canyon lies between you and the path that will take you Home. You *must* pass through it."

"But, Strateia," Diakrina interrupted, "I know you could simply carry me over this canyon like you carried me high into the sky above the Chasm. Why won't you, and let me forgo this vile place?"

"Because," answered Strateia, placing his hand on her shoulder reassuringly, "your journey is more than a mere physical passage from one place to another. It leads through paths of change and growth that you can only know through personal experience. You must engage what lies ahead in order to actualize the transformations and joys the Living One has in mind for you. If I were to whisk you away and land you gently beyond the canyon, I would deprive you of the necessary—even *precious*—arrival that transcends any geographic destination. Instead of being closer to your purpose or to The City, you would be farther from them both.

"As you pass through Nekus physically tonight, Diakrina, you will also travel terrain in a different realm: terrain no physical sun can illuminate. Conquering Nekus will change you. If you follow my instructions, you will step into the sunlight of a new day, in many ways a new person. You will have taken a necessary step in your becoming the person the Living One created you to be.

"In one sense, you are already that person because of what He has secured for you. But in another sense, you are still becoming, for you must embrace and internalize your identity in Him. All He has secured *for* you must be realized *in* you. His purposes for you can only find fulfillment as you willingly walk in them. Only then can you realize the full benefits of all that is yours in Him. This is the path to the Eternal City. Your right to dwell there is His gift—already yours. Your ability to dwell there is His provision, realized through the process of obedient trust.

"As you walk with Him in trust, he continually provides all that you need for the next step. You mature with each step, and you mature the most with those steps which require the most trust. The full realization of all He has given you unfolds with each grace-empowered choice."

Then Strateia's countenance lightened and he added with a slight twinkle in his eye, "Besides, the Immortal Fruit lies within the canyon. Flying over it would accomplish nothing."

Diakrina stared into the fire thoughtfully and warmed her hands against the slight chill of the evening air. She was beginning to understand something of the true nature of the quest before her.

"Diakrina," said Strateia, "the spring on the other side of the canyon is a pleasant and wonderful place. To you, it will be all the more wonderful because of the journey you must take to get there."

"So," interjected Diakrina, "my journey entails more than I have yet understood. I am traveling stranger worlds than I could ever have imagined."

Strateia smiled at her, Yes, little one, that is one way to put it. And, perhaps, for you, the best way.

"You must remember, Diakrina, to follow the path the sword reveals. It will lead you to the secret place where Anomos has hidden the Immortal Fruit. It will take all your resolve to remember to *follow*, and *only* follow, without searching on your own throughout this night. This quest does not demand your cunning or cleverness, but your trust and courage."

Strateia looked up at the sliver of a moon, and noted its position. "It is time, little one. I have three things more to tell you.

"First, throughout the night you must hold your sword just in front of you and follow the slightly glowing footprints it will illuminate. It will take courage, but you must follow these footprints wherever they lead, for they are your *only* way through the canyon. Do not allow anything to lure you away from them. You must follow or be lost."

"Will the footprints be yours, Strateia?" Diakrina interjected hopefully.

"No, little one," he answered. "They are much more precious. They are footprints of the only man who has ever passed through Nekus by his own power and wisdom. And his footprints are ever fresh, for every place he has trodden he treads still."

Strateia turned and took a few steps toward Nekus Canyon. With his back still to Diakrina he added, "I would gladly be by your side throughout this night if I could, little one. But I cannot. My kind cannot enter Nekus.

"Besides, my presence would hinder you, for you would look to me for strength and direction. To reach your destination, you must learn to trust One stronger and wiser than I, even when you have but a faint and indirect glimpse of His presence."

Turning back toward Diakrina, he continued his three-part send off. "Second, as you enter the canyon you will pass a great Altar. Behind the Altar stands a large rock on which you will find engraved the words of one of the Living One's servants: a prophet of the ancient Scriptures, which you call the Old Testament. His name is Isaiah. Read his words carefully for they contain the key to what you *must not* do as you pass through Nekus.

"Before you begin your night's journey, I will make a torch for you from this fire. This torch will illuminate the message in the rock, but you must not take the torch with you beyond the Altar into the canyon. Only your sword can light your way by illuminating the footprints on your path."

Strateia then fell silent as he turned and once again stared into the blackness of the canyon's mouth. Diakrina stood, adjusted her belt and sword, and walked up beside him. Together they peered into the darkness. After taking a deep breath and exhaling with a sense of determined resignation, she said, "I understand, Strateia. It is okay."

For a moment no one spoke. Then Diakrina took two steps toward the canyon and turned around to face Strateia. "Will I succeed? Will I come out of Nekus?"

Strateia turned his gaze down onto her face, which was just visible in the light from the fire. "It is certain that you *can*," he answered. "That has been provided for. Whether or not you *will* cannot be seen from where we stand. Only the Living One, who dwells in all points of time at once, can see the results of your quest. Soon we shall know."

Strateia turned toward a nearby fallen tree and broke off a three-foot length of a large limb that snapped like a twig in his powerful hands. He silently held up a finger indicating that Diakrina should wait while he completed an errand, and then he walked over a small rise in the direction of the canyon.

In a few moments, he returned with the limb; one end wrapped tightly in dry vines covered in a black pitch. He lowered its pitched end into the fire and it burst into flames. He then walked over to Diakrina and handed her the burning torch.

"This will burn all night," he said, looking into her face by its light.

"But you said I must not take it with me into the canyon," responded Diakrina a little confused.

"That is correct—you must *not* take it into the canyon."

Diakrina was puzzled. "Then, why does it matter that the torch should burn all night?"

"For two reasons, little one. The first is that you must *choose* not to take the torch into the canyon. If I gave you a torch that would burn out in an hour, the choice would have been made for you.

"The second reason is the third of the three things I said I must share with you before you go. In the center of the Altar, which lies in front of the prophet's inscription, you will find a hole just large enough for this torch. If you choose the obedience that comes of trust, drop the torch—flame-side up—into the hole. There it will burn all night, and while it burns, you must pass through the canyon of Nekus."

Handing her the crystal water container, he continued, "Diakrina, take this container. When you reach the Immortal Fruit, you must open the cap of this container and drink the last of its water. Then place the mouth of this container next to the Fruit and speak the word carved here on its side. When you do so, the Fruit will pass into the container." He then took her hand and lifted the container into the glow of the firelight so she could see carved, not on its outside, but on its inside, the Greek letters, πεποιθώς.

Diakrina read haltingly, *"Peh . . . poi . . . thos."* She started to say she did not remember the word when suddenly its meaning seemed to push itself into her mind. "Does it mean, *trusting?"* she said, more of a statement than a question.

"Yes, little one, it does. You even recognized the tense of the verb. Being in the present tense, it emphasizes the continual act of trust*ing*, for trusting is a continual choice. Once you choose to trust, it always remains in your power to reverse that choice. By saying the word backwards, *Sothiopep,* the Fruit of Immortality will come back out of the container into your hand.

"Listen closely, Diakrina. You need protection from the power of the Immortal Fruit. It was created for your race to consume and you were created to consume it. You cannot resist its allure once you expose yourself to its pull. Your being cries out for it, for in your natural state it is life to you.

"But you and your kind have not yet been fully restored to your natural state. In your present condition, the Immortal Fruit can only bring eternal death. It is the ultimate poison! Do not, under any duress—even to the point of death—take a single bite from this Fruit. For if you do, the curse will forever be on you. For untold millennia you will exist in the ravages of a death that never dies. Place the mouth of this container on the Fruit the instant you reach it. Do not delay! Speak the word, *Pepoithos*, and the fruit will pass inside the container. Once you have done this, only you can undo the protection, no one else. *Only the one who enacts the trust can undo the trust.*

"I warn you sternly, do not trust yourself! Rather, entrust yourself to this necessary provision. Immediately entrust the Fruit to this container and do not take it out again for any reason until you give it to the Living One at the end of the quest."

"Why would you even tell me how to reverse the trust commitment, Strateia?" Diakrina genuinely wished she had not been give this bit of knowledge.

"Much like with the torch," he answered, "you must continually choose to trust. Trust begins in the decision of a moment and then lives in the continual honoring of that decision. Your relationship of trust in the Living One never inhibits your freedom. He gives you the help you need every moment to succeed, but He never coerces.

"This container is grace to you. It is a provision by which you can carry the Fruit and succeed, *if* you entrust the Immortal Fruit to it as you have been told."

Strateia then placed his hand on her shoulder. "Be courageous, little one. Face the fears you will meet. Expose the lies that seek to mislead you. Trust!"

And, suddenly, he was gone.

## CHAPTER THIRTEEN

# The ALTAR

Everything suddenly changed. The gaping canyon seemed to drool hungrily and mock Diakrina's vulnerability, now that her protector had vanished. Terror—like cold, murky, rising water—oozed from the direction of the canyon's mouth. It lapped at her feet, then slowly crawled up her legs. Before she could take a step, she already felt knee-deep in a clammy soup of rapacious, malevolent fear.

Diakrina shuddered and forced her first stride toward the canyon. As she did, a scream like that of an enraged cougar shattered the dark silence just to her left.

She instinctively reacted. Drawing her sword with lightning speed, she crouched into a fighting stance and raised the torch in her left hand high above her head in order to illuminate the night around her. She held this position for nearly 30 seconds, peering into the darkness. The sounds of panting betrayed the presence of something beastly in the nearby rocks just beyond the reach of the torch, but she could see nothing.

Her legs and arms began to shake and weaken, making it impossible to hold her position much longer. Satisfied that the threat was keeping its distance, she slowly straightened her legs and stood. Lowering the torch in front of her, she once again resumed cautious steps toward the canyon.

A second scream pierced the night, this one to her immediate right. Again she turned and crouched with torch held high and sword swaying in front of her in the direction of the audible assault. Almost immediately, another scream tore the night behind her. It sounded no more than 20 feet away. Diakrina turned, and then turned again. Pivoting on the balls of her feet in wary circles and swinging her sword from side to side, she braced to fend off whatever unseen terrors could possibly make such a hideous cry.

Though the torchlight failed to reveal any visible threat, Diakrina clearly heard breathing, now on both sides of her path. The binaural rhythms of the unseen panting jowls held a terror all their own. "I'm not even to the canyon and I'm already petrified," she heard her thoughts whisper as she noticed the quivering flames from the torch in her trembling hand.

With every sense on high alert, she once again took a step toward the canyon, and then another, and another, with torch held high and sword swaying back and forth as though slicing thin ribbons through the air in front of her. Her ears wrestled with the night sounds, straining for the slightest noise and, at the same time, bracing themselves against the anticipated shrieks of the lurking beasts. The heavy breaths kept pace with her on either side as the stalking predators—whatever they were—matched her cautious stride.

She suddenly stopped. The sound of a dull splash at her feet had demanded her attention. Looking down, she realized that her right foot had stepped into something wet, thick and sticky. She lowered the torch slightly, just enough to dispel her own shadow that had shrouded her feet, and recognized a small puddle—if it could be called that—of black pitch, smooth and sleek like a dark mirror. "How did Strateia find this so quickly in the dark?" some corner of her brain wondered.

The swath of pitch was only a few feet wide, and a path veered around its left edge and on toward the canyon. Diakrina pulled her foot from the goo and continued her swaying, defensive gait down a slight decline toward where the path narrowed between several large boulders.

Taking a deep breath, she passed quickly between the boulders, feeling dangerously vulnerable as she did so. The moment the path widened again, a sound spun Diakrina around in her tracks: the unmistakable thuds and clicks of clawed feet landing on the tops of the boulders on both sides of the trail. Raising her sword overhead, alongside the torch, she backed away as two piercing screams from atop the rocks nearly shattered her ears.

Though the glow from the torch lightly brushed the tops of the boulders, still she could see nothing of the hideous creatures snarling down at her. A sense of peril gripped her. With two vicious beasts perched just above her ready to pounce, her fight or flight instinct turned fully in one direction and all she could think to do was to turn and run. And run she did, with all her might, toward the mouth of the canyon.

Only a few steps into her desperate run, Diakrina heard two heavy thumps behind her, followed instantly by a crescendo of pounding feet speeding after her in what sounded like an all-out charge. Carelessly strewn boulders forced a sharp zig-zag bend in the path, which Diakrina barely noticed. With adrenaline-enhanced agility, she raced through the turns as the deep, grunting breaths of her predators grew louder with every step.

As the path straightened out before her, Diakrina frantically scanned the darkness ahead for any possible escape from the jaws now snapping almost at her heels. The dim outline of the canyon wall before her offered little promise and was still a frightful distance away. She noticed, however, a smaller outcropping of rock much closer. In the glowing torchlight, it appeared to be a ledge about six feet off the ground, jutting out toward her from the canyon wall.

Diakrina wasn't sure she could leap high enough to scurry onto the top of the ledge, and she had no reason to hope it would offer any real protection, but it appeared to be her only option. By the time she processed this information, only six or seven strides remained between her and the ledge. Dropping both hands with sword and torch at her sides, she leaned forward like an Olympic sprinter and strained to maximum speed.

Just then, a hot, vile breath on the back of her neck and the swipe of a claw nicking her left heel triggered a surge of adrenaline like she had never experienced. In a flash, before she realized what she had done, she gave a blood-curdling scream and threw herself headfirst into the air toward the top of the oncoming ledge.

In retelling the story later, Diakrina would muse over the impact the adrenaline must have had on her in those frantic moments. She jumped so high and far that she landed on her feet atop the ledge some three or four steps beyond its edge. The momentum of her jump pulled her with such velocity that she fell forward and began to roll. With agility that amazed her on reflection, she tucked her right shoulder under her and tightened her grip on her sword and torch, rolled several times, and then sprang to her feet and turned back toward the edge, with her weapons at the ready. (She had begun thinking of the torch as not only a source of light, but a weapon.) She fully expected to encounter snarling fangs and gnawing claws in her face as she righted herself.

Instead, she stood in silent stillness, except for her own panting breaths and the slight flutter of torch flames in the nighttime breeze. Her eyes and ears on full alert, she searched the darkness for any sign of the vicious beasts. For what must have been several minutes, she stood frozen in a warrior's crouch with all her senses straining to penetrate the night.

Gradually and cautiously, she began to relax her muscles and straighten her legs and back, still keenly tuned to any possible scent, sound or flicker in the blackness around her that might betray a stalking predator. Nothing.

Finally, she found the nerve to turn—ever so slowly—and look behind her. There, only about four feet away, stood an enormous white stone structure with seven large steps leading up to its top. This had to be the Altar Strateia had mentioned.

Still shaking from her ordeal and fearful that the beasts might at any moment leap from the shadows, the steps—ascending away from the edge of the ledge and toward safer, higher ground—seemed inviting. She waved her torch and looked carefully up the stairs to assure herself that nothing lurked on them, and then suddenly ran to the top as fast as her legs would carry her.

Diakrina quickly surveyed the top of the Altar. It was large and flat—some 20 feet across—and made of white stone that looked like marble, but with a hint of translucency that reminded her of crystal. The best she could determine by the light of the torch left her with the dominant impression that the Alter was *very* white.

A raised stone slab marked the center of the Altar. About seven feet long, three feet wide and one foot high, it gave the appearance of a stone lid to a burial crypt. Beyond the slab stood a white wall of the same kind of stone that comprised the Altar itself. Its face, like an impressive monument, was carved with seven lines of text in six-inch high capital letters. Surely these were the words of the prophet of which Strateia had spoken.

Diakrina walked around the slab and raised the torch over her head as she paced back and forth in the darkness reading the text. This is what she read:

*"Who among you fears the Lord and obeys the word of His servant?*
*Let him who walks in the dark, who has no light,*
*trust in the Name of the Lord and rely on his God.*
*But now, all you who light fires and provide yourselves*
*with flaming torches, go, walk in the light of the fires and of*
*the torches you have set ablaze.*
*This is what you shall receive from My hand:*
*You will lie down in torment."*

The sober words weighed heavily on Diakrina. She felt deeply the warning of a curse on those who rely on their own torches and do not trust the Living One in the face of this sovereignly-decreed darkness: this darkness with a purpose, as Strateia had described it. She had every intention of obeying the command to leave the torch at the Altar, but having already experienced terrors of the night, she blanched at the thoughts of facing even greater horrors in Nekus without the aid of the torch.

Why this forbidding of torchlight in the canyon? What was the point of Strateia's warnings and these somber etchings in the stone? Could it be that darkness itself, when decreed by the Living One, offers a form of protection? That seemed somehow unreasonable in this cold, malevolent place where fearful, invisible beasts haunt the darkness right up to the skin on one's face. Yet, Strateia had given a severe and stern warning, and the inscription in the stone confirmed his words and promised dire consequences for trusting one's own perceptions.

Diakrina's will had decided to give up the torch, yet she talked to herself for several minutes, hoping to convince her emotions to *feel* like doing what she knew she must do. But none of her reasoning helped. She was truly and deeply afraid.

Diakrina then interrupted her own inner discussion as she remembered Strateia's sense of urgency about the importance of getting through the first part of the canyon before daybreak. She quickly read once again the words of the prophet and then turned and walked back to the raised slab in the center of the Altar.

As she approached the slab and held out her torch to study it, she noticed on its top an opening that formed the shape of a cross. Once again she felt impressed by how much the slab looked like the lid of a grave.

Having maneuvered to the end of the slab farthest from the inscribed wall, she stepped up on top of it, stood at the foot of the cross-shaped opening and looked down into it. Though she turned the torch at different angles, she could not see the bottom of the opening.

She did notice several lines of small, carved letters at her feet, just beneath the cross-shaped hole. Getting on her knees, she lowered the torch and read the following words:

*"For You are the fountain of life; in Your Light we see light."*

*"Send forth Your Light and Your Truth, let them guide me;*
*Let them bring me to Your holy mountain, to the place where You dwell."*

*"What You have spoken is a lamp to guide my feet*
*and a light for my path."*

*"Trust in the Lord with all your heart;*
*do not depend on your own understanding.*
*In all your ways acknowledge Him and His ways,*
*and He will show you which path to take."*

Diakrina read the lines over and over again. She had learned some of them as a young child, but never before had their meaning leaped into her mind with such force as they did in this place.

The power of the words triggered something deep in her heart. Tears rolled down her face and her body began to tremble. Soon the tears gave way to sobs and her body collapsed over the hallowed inscriptions. With her face pressed against the cool white stone, she wept like a child. She knew what she must do, but now she was struck with a new fear. The darkness and the beasts it hid still held her in a grip of terror, but an even greater fear was now one of self-doubt: would she be able to let go of the torch? Could she master her panic enough to act on what she knew she must do?

Oh, how she longed to go to His holy mountain, to see light in His light, to have Him light her path. But could she trust Him enough in this dark, terror-haunted place?

Lifting her face just a few inches off the stone, with her sword still in hand, she traced the etched letters with the tip of her index finger: "Trust in the Lord with all your heart . . ." That's what she wanted more than anything! Her finger continued as she silently mouthed the words, ". . . do not depend on your own understanding."

"Help me, Living One! I have no courage! Please be courageous through me!" she cried in a desperate whisper. She wondered how she could have been through so much already—her night in the cave, her battle with the Mist, her being set free from the shackles of the cave wall—and still feel so paralyzed in this place.

Yet, this was different. This fear was more external and pressed on her from without. It was trying to force open the doors to her mind and heart in order to infect her. In the cave the terror that surrounded her reflected and amplified the fears already within her. Here, she was an outsider intruding into a domain of terror: an atmosphere of zealous, manic fear with its own agenda. It guarded that agenda with obsessive determination, insistent on subduing all wills to its own.

Diakrina sat up and looked at the opening. Again she reminded herself that she must not linger, for she had a journey ahead of her that must be completed before the sun rose. How she longed to see the sun! But she never would if she perished in this darkness.

Still, her hand held tightly to the torch. Surely it would be foolish to give up this precious source of light. Had it not illuminated this rock ledge, allowing her to escape the beasts at her heels? She couldn't have made it this far without the torch.

Her eyes fell once again on the words at the foot of the opening:

*"For You are the fountain of life; in Your Light we see light."*
And . . .
*". . . do not depend on your own understanding."*

Just then a slight breeze wafted across the Altar and caused the torch flame to flutter. In that moment, her eyes caught something scratched into the edge of the slab. It was not an artistically etched inscription like the others, but more of a scratching, like someone had fastidiously scraped the stone with a pocketknife. The letters—carved along the right, top edge of the slab—were not deep, and were only just legible. As she knelt down to decipher them, she noticed a rough arrow scratched into the top surface of the Altar, pointing from the words to the cross-shaped opening. Soon, the style of the hand began to make sense to her and she read slowly:

*"Die . . . before . . . you die. There . . . is . . . no . . . chance . . . after."*

Then she read it all together: "Die before you die. There is no chance after." A few more scratches, lighter still and barely visible followed. Obviously, less care had been used in adding them, and they appeared to be an afterthought: a hurried signature, perhaps? Diakrina could not quite make out the name, but it began with two initials: a "C" and an "S." The rest was not legible.

Though she never learned the name of the pilgrim who had obviously preceded her and had left his own testimony of struggle and heroic decision, she was forever grateful for his advice. To avoid the death she feared, she must die to the life she was clinging to. Only by choosing to give up her own life—if that is what it cost to trust the Living One—could she hope to find the Life He offered her. Only by dying to her own rights and desires to see and save herself by her own hand, could she be saved by His. This was the point of decision.

She straightened up from crouching over the engravings and repositioned herself at the foot of the cross. Then, raising herself up on both knees, she stretched out her left hand holding the torch—handle down as Strateia had instructed—out over the middle of the opening.

The night lay still and quiet. Once she dropped the torch, she would be at the mercy of the dim glow of her sword illuminating only the step in front of her at best. Even with her newfound resolve, the finality of letting go made her pause.

Then, in the stillness, the most beautiful, quiet, yet firm voice she had ever heard came gently from every corner of space around and above her: "Do not fear, I will be with you."

A flood of peace and tears washed over Diakrina and suddenly she knew she *would* trust Him. Her heart would not let her do anything else. She looked up, still kneeling over the cross-shaped opening, and whispered, "Thank You!"

Then she let go.

The torch did not drop immediately into the opening as she had expected. Instead, it hovered for a moment and then began a slow descent into the heart of the Altar. Diakrina leaned over the opening and watched as it descended down, down, down, continually fading into the dark depths until, after about three minutes, it finally disappeared altogether.

Diakrina stared for a few more moments, pondering the strange descent and wondering at the depths of the opening. Then she stood up and looked blindly into a night as black as the pitch puddle that had nearly swallowed her foot. Though a faint crimson glow emanated from her sword hanging from her right hand, everything else was utterly dark. Instinctively, she waved her left hand in front of her face and noted that she could not even detect its presence unless she was looking down directly at her sword.

She stood there for several moments—two or three minutes, perhaps—hoping her eyes would adjust to the dark, but they did not. Finally recognizing that her sword was indeed the *only* light in this place, she began pointing it in various directions around her feet until she found the edge of the stone slab and carefully stepped down onto the face of the Altar, determined to begin her journey through Nekus.

The moment she stepped off the slab onto the Altar, the stone beneath her shook with incredible violence and knocked Diakrina off her feet. A low rumble erupted from deep beneath the Altar and rushed up toward her. Frantically, she stumbled to her feet, only to be thrown onto her back once again by the convulsing rock. Suddenly, a blast of brilliant light burst from within the heart of the Altar through the opening in the slab and pierced the night sky like a powerful cross-shaped laser.

Diakrina stopped struggling to get up and stared with stunned amazement at the beautiful golden cross above her. Then another shudder ripped through the Altar with an ear-splitting roar. White light—whiter than any white she had ever imagined—burst through the surface of the entire Altar until the stone beneath her became completely transparent and shone like a white sun. The radiance from beneath her was so brilliant and so palpable that Diakrina felt like she was in a mighty rushing waterfall of light flowing upward from the Altar into the sky. And there, on the sky, she saw her own silhouette against a backdrop of otherworldly light.

CHAPTER FOURTEEN

# NEKUS CANYON

Diakrina couldn't be sure how long she lay there on the Altar—she lost all sense of time. However, when she came to herself, she realized the small crest of a moon had actually moved little since she had left Strateia.

Yet, she sensed an urgency to get started into the canyon. So, rising, she stood in the radiance of the white light flooding from the Altar's top, and looked out into the pitch-blackness of the Canyon of Nekus. Then gripping her sword tightly, she began the descent of the seven steps of the Altar down onto the ledge, which was the last thing illuminated by the light.

Beyond, all was black.

With every sense at full alert for the slightest indication of the beasts she had previously encountered—or any new horror that might be lurking just beyond her sight—she took a deep breath and leaped down from the ledge into the inky stillness. Before taking a single step, she lowered her sword in front of her feet and moved its tip slowly from side to side searching for the promised footprints.

At first she saw only the bare earth of a path that was interrupted, here and there, by clumps of green grass and intruding rocks. Then, just beyond a rock that reached into the path from the left, she saw a faint, crimson glow in the shape of a human's left footprint. She moved toward it and immediately, a stride beyond it, she saw a matching footprint of a right foot. With this second footprint she wasn't sure if the light of her sword had manifested what was already there, or if it had actually been laid down, from heel to toe, as the light reached that spot. She resolved to watch more closely on the next footprint as she stepped forward again. Yet, once again, the effect was as if the actual laying down of the footprint was just beyond her sight by milliseconds, or that the effect of the sword's light advancing over the footprints from heel to toe, made it appear as if it were only now being imprinted. She could not be sure which.

Cautiously, and still searching the darkness with her eyes, ears and even, as it seemed, with the very sensitivity of the surface of her skin at heightened awareness to the slightest change in breeze or temperature, Diakrina followed each crimson footprint as it manifested. The footprints followed a winding path for about 50 yards until the path emptied onto what appeared to be the main canyon floor. Here there was no path but only piled boulders to her left, right and ahead. Diakrina wondered if this was the condition of the rest of the canyon floor, as she could see only about a yard ahead and to the sides.

At this point Diakrina became conscious of how loud the sound of flowing water to her left had become. It was the river from which Strateia had taken the fish. She stood still for a moment to try to decode the sounds around her so as to get some sense of the canyon. The river seemed, from the sound of the water reflecting off the canyon walls, still to be about 100 yards away. Diakrina presumed that this must be the place where the river, coming from the southwest, entered the south end of Nekus Canyon, which ran north from this point as far as she had been able to determine before sunset. The river appeared much louder here, she reasoned, because it narrowed, deepened and quickened as it made a bend into the mouth of the canyon. The nature of the sound suggested that the far side of the river ran against the canyon wall.

But it was other sounds far ahead and below her that made her aware that Nekus Canyon was not only narrowing, but in the darkness ahead was also descending to a great depth. As Diakrina's ears analyzed these deep, distant sounds, she determined she was not hearing them directly but as echoes high off the canyon walls ahead of her and to her right. She deduced from this, since the floor of the canyon just in front of her was blocking the sound from reaching her directly, that she was still some distance from where the canyon made its steep descent. She was in a kind of sound-shadow caused by the ground ahead. But by way of the reflections and echoes coming from above and around her, she realized the air outside the bubble of this sound-shadow must be vibrating with a continuous thunder.

From the unremitting nature of these echoing roars, Diakrina suspected she was hearing a huge, thundering waterfall plunging to the lower floors of the canyon. Just then, a small swirl of air, damp with tiny water droplets, blew across her face reinforcing her theory of a nearby waterfall.

Diakrina looked back at the ground and could see a faintly glowing footprint on the boulder immediately before her. She pointed her sword toward it and moved ahead. Immediately another footprint became visible farther up the rock and she pointed her sword toward it and continued.

The footprints led her in a kind of winding manner over and through large boulders. With each step she took the deep roars she had discerned grew louder, richer and more distinct as they became increasingly interlaced with higher pitched sounds—the subtle spraying sound of falling water hitting rocks and the higher tones of the swishing and swirling of water rushing past river-embedded boulders.

Then, in one step, she was simultaneously blasted in the face with a strong, cold, mist-drenched wind and an ear-shattering rumble; both of which rose to meet her like a stampeding herd of horses. The crashing of the river into the floor of Nekus deep below was so violent, and the canyon so resonant, that its sound could have been compared to an unending avalanche of boulders.

Diakrina froze instantly and tried to adjust her senses to this ocean of reverberation echoing from every surface and pressing forcefully on her from all directions. Two people standing and screaming into each other's ears could not have made their voices heard in this place. For quite some time, Diakrina feared to move.

As she stood there, drenched in sound and mist, she had the sense that in the inky blackness before her lay a vast space, like a long roofless cathedral, larger than had ever been conceived by any race of men. But it was no holy place. It was a not a *place* at all, but a space—a space haunted with a stern and desperate pride; its sternness calculated to hide its desperateness.

The roaring water screamed the space's unrelenting defiance against the whole of creation. It was a space filled with a terrifying, cruel spite that raged against all it had not yet consumed; a space inhabited by a maddening discontentment—enraged, unquenchable thirst; gnawing inextinguishable hunger—desiring to fill its bottomless emptiness with every thing and person it could devour. It recognized no beauty and respected no authority. It hated all equally because it had no virtue by which it could value any differently.

Diakrina felt fear more intense than she had ever imagined could exist. Yet, the very wet and thunder of the place activated her baser instincts of survival and suppressed the rising fear-fraught thoughts.

When finally she had braced herself against the onslaught, she stretched her sword forward to look for the next footprint, but found only the edge of a great abyss in front of her. Turning the sword to her left, however, she spotted a crimson footprint alongside the edge, parallel to the great drop and moving in the direction of the river and the thundering fall. She followed the footprints along the great edge for about two hundred yards. All the while, the roar of the great fall came closer and closer and the rising mist soaked her skin and hair. Soon she noticed—at first subtly but then with increasing vibrato—the rock slabs under her feet pulsating with the roar of the water.

As the thunderous reverberations increased in the inky black, she began to lose her nerve. She didn't realize she had stopped. Suddenly coming to her senses, she stood staring at the next footprint in front of her, but was unable to move. Her feet defied her will to take another step.

Total sensory confusion had gripped her. The bones in her legs quivered with the shuddering of the rock beneath her, sending waves of tremors up into her guts. The physical trembling mixed with her fear made her stomach churn. She felt weak and nauseous.

The unrelenting, intense darkness had strained her visual senses to a point of exhaustion, while all her other senses were pummeled by extreme overload. This unnatural imbalance, mixed with the certainty of the vile and haunted nature of her surroundings, led to a rising panic about her blindness. She frantically wanted to see. For a few moments she gave vent to an insane urge, swatting and scratching wildly at the space in front of her eyes trying to somehow remove the suffocating blanket of sightlessness.

The thought of the word *suffocating* made her realize that the darkness had been increasingly pressing in on her since she left the stone Altar. Camouflaged among the other overwhelming sensations, it had coiled its way around her like a constrictor snake around a sleeping victim. Now with its victim fully awake and helplessly in its coils, the darkness seemed to be squeezing the life out of her. The hideous blackness suddenly felt like much more than merely an absence of light. It was a conscious and malevolent predator and she was its defenseless prey. It conformed itself to every contour of her body and slowly crushed her breath away.

Desperate to escape, she turned around as if to retreat, but the blackness behind her offered no comfort, no hope, no hint of an escape route. Her eyes craved something on which to focus like a starving man craves food. But there was nothing; not even a faint footprint to indicate the path she had taken.

Diakrina broke. A moment of sheer madness caved in on her. She began screaming and swinging her sword as she spun around and around in mindless circles. Then, suddenly, she ran. She ran blindly and wildly, retreating from the sounds of the great waterfall. But her frenzied retreat was cut abruptly short after just a few strides when she stumbled over a large stone and fell violently forward toward the rocky slab beneath her.

After spinning frantically in circles, her sense of direction had been tricked by the canyon echoes, and she had inadvertently rushed headlong toward the edge of the cliff. This mistake nearly killed her, and it also saved her. For had she fallen so violently in any other direction, her head would have savagely pounded the rock slab. As it was, she landed with the upper part of her body out over the precipice. Instead of hitting a rock slab, her head hit open air and a gust of cold vapor that rushed up from the fall below.

The blast of wet cold air on her face and the swelling roar startled her instantly out of her madness. After a few seconds she collected her wits and quickly assessed her predicament.

Mercifully, her left heel had caught under the ledge of a rock as she fell. Otherwise, she would surely have tumbled helplessly over the edge. The good news seemed to end there, however. Her entire upper body, from just below her waist, dangled precariously out over the precipice. One wrong move and she would plummet to certain death in the darkness below her.

At such moments, one needs to be calm and calculating. Diakrina, however, had depleted all such reserves. Hanging by a tenuous foothold over an abyss and too weak to pull herself back toward safety, Diakrina trembled and sobbed in self-pity and despair.

Suddenly, despair gave way to sheer terror. Something, or someone, grasped hold of her free right ankle and began to pull. Diakrina screamed, lifted herself and swung her sword thoughtlessly and violently back to her right toward the edge of the cliff. In so doing, she dislodged her left foot from its hold under the rock's edge and the left side of her body slid off the ledge. The only thing holding her from falling now was the hand grasping tightly to her right ankle.

Diakrina was in a state of total terror. She continued to slash frantically, as best she could, at whoever or whatever held her fast. Like a fear-crazed animal, she screamed and swung her sword with no thought of the consequences of succeeding in getting the hand to turn her loose.

But all her flailing availed nothing. The hand not only held her firmly, it lifted her into the air and pulled her back over the edge of the great drop and deposited her, still swinging and thrashing onto her back and turned her loose.

Now free from the grip of the unseen appendage, Diakrina leaped to her feet brandishing her sword in a crimson figure 8 in front of her, determined to slash whatever was there. But nothing was there.

After about five seconds of this mad slashing, Diakrina stopped and crouched in the darkness with her sword swaying in front of her as she circled slowly. She was certain the attack would come, but from where? For over a minute she circled and swayed waiting for whatever horror might pounce. But nothing did.

The roar of the water drowned all other sounds, even her own heavy panting. This unrelenting thunderclap coupled with the impenetrable darkness rendered her functionally both deaf and blind.

Slowly she lowered her sword. As she did, her starved eyes spotted a morsel of vision on the ground just beyond the tip of her sword. Two bare feet—not footprints, but feet!—faced her. Before she could raise her sword to see the person they belonged to, the feet turned and stepped into the darkness in the direction of the waterfall, leaving glowing, crimson footprints on the rock.

Diakrina surprised herself by crying after the figure, "Please don't go. Come back!" as she hurried after him. She could not hear her own voice over the roar of the waters, so she knew the fellow traveler could not hear her. But then, somehow, over the deafening thunder of the fall, a kind and firm whisper reached her ears and touched her heart. "Come, Diakrina, follow me."

In that instant, a wonderful and precious realization flooded Diakrina's spirit. These footprints she was following through the night were not just remnants of some long ago traveler. They were fresh and new with every step. They were signs of a very real and very present companion who knew her name. She was not alone. She had never been alone in the dark of this night. And if she followed the footprints, wherever they may lead, she would not be alone. This unseen friend, this guide, had saved her from plummeting over the precipice in her madness. These footprints were more than a sign, they were a source of hope and comfort in a hopeless and distressing place.

Diakrina hesitated for a brief moment. These footprints of hope—the one glowing thing in this black night—led straight toward her worst fears: the thundering waterfall. Something in her wanted to turn and run from the terror of the awful cataract. But a deeper resolve quickly exerted itself, for she longed more than anything else to be near the one whose feet she had glimpsed in the dark. Yes, she would follow, no matter what. She was done listening to her screaming, disoriented senses and fears.

With newfound determination, she lowered her sword and stepped after the faint footprints toward the thunderous fall. As she descended toward the fall, the rock beneath her grew increasingly treacherous. The path, now soaked by the spray, was slick and the rocks shuddered with the rolling reverberation of rushing water. She felt that she was trying to walk on ice in an earthquake. Yet, the crimson footprints glistened even more brightly on the shimmering rocks, and Diakrina resolved to keep following.

The footprints led to the edge of the river and then turned right toward the top of the waterfall. Diakrina paused briefly and stretched her sword out over the water. Its glow extended about three feet from the shore, revealing a violent, rolling torrent rushing past, just inches from her feet. She lowered her sword once again to the path ahead and resolutely continued her cautious trek in the tracks of her barefoot guide.

By now the sounds of rushing, cascading water had swelled beyond the limits of her hearing. A kind of silence swept over her as the sound waves turned her entire body into a vibrating membrane. The roar drowned all other sounds and yet was, itself, too loud to hear. The noise immersed her until she became part of it. Her ears seemed to give up and shut down, leaving her in a deafening blast of pulsating silence.

Still heading in the general direction of the waterfall, the footprints veered slightly away from the river's edge until coming against a solid stone wall, about six-feet tall, running parallel to the river. Diakrina's crimson-marked path now led between the river on her left and the stone structure on her right.

The stone had strange inscriptions of what appeared to be many different languages, with writing that seemed to flow vertically, instead of horizontally. As Diakrina walked she shifted her sword into her left hand and lifted it just enough to cast a gentle glow on the rock, and examined the inscriptions with her right hand which was nearest the stone. After about 20 paces, the footprints brought her to what appeared to be a stone base with rough-cut steps, and she realized that the inscribed "wall" that she had been walking alongside was actually a large pillar lying on the ground where it had fallen.

The stone base stood at the head of the precipice where the great fall plunged over the edge into the black abyss. Diakrina's sword illuminated only the first stone step and part of the second, each seeming to spread about three feet deep. The entire structure appeared ancient, and Diakrina felt as though she had stepped into a scene from lost antiquity. From the little she could see, she determined that the scale must be enormous.

The massive pillar had fallen from a large pedestal to the right of the steps. Approaching the left of the steps, Diakrina discovered another pedestal, this one supporting a colossal, rough-hewn stone pillar— apparently identical to the first—that had not fallen.

She lifted her sword to see as far as she could up the pillar, but it continued into the darkness above the reach of the light. She surmised that it would be approximately the same dimensions—about 20 paces high—as its fallen twin. Each pillar stretched about six feet wide and again that deep, making it roughly square at its base. Based on what she had seen of the fallen pillar, they maintained these proportions all the way to the top, with little or no tapering.

Like its fallen counterpart, the upright pillar had inscriptions of various languages etched into its face. About five feet up from the ground, Diakrina spotted English letters and running the tip of her sword along the text she read, *Entrance to the realm of Thanatos.*

She stepped around to the right of the pillar, expecting the message to continue. Instead, the inscription merely repeated, *Entrance to the realm of Thanatos.* When she surveyed the back of the pillar and found the same words, she concluded that the final side would say the same and opted not to look, for it would have meant navigating a very narrow, quivering ledge—little more than a foothold wide—between the base of the pillar and edge of the great waterfall.

Feeling that the inscription seemed somehow incomplete, Diakrina walked over to the fallen pillar and located its English inscription, again about five feet from what would have been its base. Turning her head and reading from top to bottom, she mouthed the words into the deafening roar of the night, . . . *from which there is no return.*

These words completed the inscription with a ring of somber finality that sent a cold fear through Diakrina. *Entrance to the realm of Thanatos from which there is no return.* Surely all human experience proved that entering the realm of the dead is a one-way journey. Mortals do not return from this place.

At that moment, a question penetrated her mind. She was never quite sure if she thought it herself or if it was somehow imposed on her. "Why is the second pillar fallen and why in that direction?" The question seemed odd and even a bit irrelevant, and yet it demanded an answer.

On closer inspection, the base of the fallen pillar appeared to be broken cleanly, as if snapped by a powerful hand—not crumbled, as she had assumed, by the natural vibrations of this awful place. Neither had it fallen, as one would expect, into the precipice, but outward as though pushed by a force from inside the realm of Thanatos.

And—the thought wrapped around her like a warm blanket on a cold night—the pillar with the ominous declaration of *no return* was the one that had fallen! Diakrina suddenly knew that it was true that *someone* entered the realm of the dead and came back, knocking this damnable pillar down as he returned.

Returning to the task at hand, Diakrina reminded herself that her night's mission was to find and recover the Fruit of Immortality, and that meant ascending the stone stairs into the realm of Thanatos. She feared and detested this place. It felt unnatural and somehow *wrong* that she should enter. But as she approached the first step slowly, the glow of her sword illuminated a single crimson footprint; its toes pointing up the stairs.

The image of two bare feet came to her memory: the ones she had spotted briefly on the path. They had looked entirely human, she thought. And yet they tread this dark place with confidence and purpose. Yes, she would follow.

Putting a foot on the first step, she pushed upward as to mount the stairs. Instantly, she felt something like a soft, wet, invisible wall. She retreated quickly back onto the rocky ground and began probing the air above the step with her sword. It met no resistance, and she could see nothing unusual. As she leaned forward and her sword hand crossed the threshold above the first step, she felt that same cold, soft, watery wall again. At the same instant, she saw a subtle ripple in the air in front of her as though she had pushed her hand through the surface of a pond. It looked and felt like a pool of crystal clear, icy water suspended vertically in front of her, hanging like a curtain at the threshold of the first step.

She pushed her arm into the curtain up to her elbow and felt her hand come out the other side, as though the wall of water were only about a foot thick. Then she again put her foot onto the step and pushed her body against the invisible substance and began pressing her way through it. It felt like walking, fully submerged, through bitter cold water and it reminded her of the sensation of passing through the Door of the Rose as it was closing around her. Only the Door was not cold. The Door, in fact, though she had not thought of it until now, had been deliciously warm. This icy wall reminded her of the cold darkness that snapped at her heels as she ran toward the Door of the Rose and leaped through it.

When she had finally pushed her way through onto the first step, she paused and took a deep breath. It seemed strange that she was not wet nor covered with any residue at all. The air here, however, was noticeably colder.

She turned to press her hand back through the invisible wall to examine it once more, but discovered that it now felt as hard and impenetrable as marble. She pushed harder and leaned against the wall, but it did not budge. Oddly, however, her sword sliced through the barrier without any hint of resistance. The transparent wall seemed to interact with Diakrina's body, but had no effect on the sword.

Pushing down a rising sense of panic, Diakrina turned toward the next step and lifted her sword in front of her. There, glistening on the second step, a crimson footprint beckoned her onward.

She reached forward to find another watery curtain between her and the footprint. Something in her drew back. She did not want to cut herself off further from any possible retreat, and she now knew that this doorway only opened in one direction.

An idea borne of desperation came to her. Turning sideways she pressed her left hand against the solid wall on one side and reached her right hand, gripping her sword, just inches into the soft wet wall on the other. Then, with this tactile connection with both surfaces at once, she walked slowly to the left end of the step, searching—futilely, as she would discover—for a break in either wall. Reaching the end, she turned around and repeated the same, all the way to the right end of the step. With this notion shattered, she made her way back to approximately the center of the stairs where the crimson footprint had ascended, and she sighed deeply. She felt like she was in a long, narrow coffin.

This second step seemed soberingly final. The pillar, though fallen, warned of a plight now confirmed by the invisible wall of stone behind her: this path was one of no return. The next step would double the certainty.

Again, the image of two bare feet and the remembrance of those firm and kind words, "Come, Diakrina, follow me" asserted themselves onto her mind.

"Yes," she whispered, "I will." With that, she pushed her way up and through the bitter cold curtain and onto the second step. Here the air was colder still, and Diakrina felt chilled to the bones. Turning, she pushed against the wall through which she had just passed and discovered, as she had expected, that it, too, had hardened like steel behind her.

This time she wasted no time. Spotting the crimson footprint on the step above her, she pushed through the icy wall onto the next step. Again and again she repeated this, determined to get to the top as fast as possible. Each step found her on an even colder landing.

At one point, her curiosity took over and she paused to experiment. Halfway through a transition to the next step, she halted and tried to back out. The parts of her body that were fully immersed in the substance refused to budge backwards, while the parts still entering the wall were free to back away. Somewhere in the middle appeared to be a point of no return. Though she found this phenomenon fascinating, the unbearable cold trumped her curiosity and she quickly pushed through to the next step.

She counted nine steps before she reached the top onto a ledge just above the fall. Here the report of the water crashing below sent blasts of air pressure up the throat of the abyss and hammered her body like relentless and rapidly pounding ocean waves. She could hardly keep her balance against the impact of the sound waves.

She followed the footprints, which turned to the right away from the waterfall and continued about 30 feet until they came to a large boulder. Here, several feet from the edge of the ledge, she found some relief from the pounding pressure waves, though she could still feel their pounding through the rock beneath her feet. The footprints stopped some four feet from the boulder.

Diakrina had stood there for about a minute in the sound-canceling roar, wondering what to do next, when a sudden flash of lightning pierced the night from a narrow strip of sky visible between the towering canyon walls. After hours of total darkness, Diakrina's eyes suffered an instant and total whiteout. She winced in pain and covered her eyes with her left hand, but by then, darkness ruled the night again. But not for long. Just as she dropped her hand from her face, another flash of lightning streaked the sky, sending Diakrina's eyes into another total whiteout.

It was maddening. The lightning pummeled her light starved eyes with a brilliance as blinding as the darkness had been. A third flash lit up the night for a full three seconds, and Diakrina once again covered her face. She noticed with the third flash that no thunder could be heard. The roar of the fall deadened even this great voice of nature.

Diakrina lowered her eyes and braced herself for the next volley of lightning. Instead of lightning, however, another flash pierced the night. This light looked different, and it was at ground level and appeared to be coming from a few hundred yards away. Diakrina partially covered her eyes, not knowing what to expect next, and watched as the light flared up and began to move toward her.

Like the lightning, the intensity of this light blinded her, and its deliberate and steady motion in her direction alarmed her. Someone or something had detected her and she had nowhere to hide. Backing away from the light and shielding her eyes from the blinding glare, Diakrina stumbled over a rock and landed on her back, holding her sword up in front of her. The light blinded her as completely as the night had. She could see nothing else, not even her own sword in front of her.

As her pupils mercifully constricted, she began to ascertain a form and, after several minutes, her eyes adjusted to the outlines of a . . . a *thing*. A growing conviction settled within her that this *thing* was more of a *what* than a *who*. She later described it as "oppressively unnatural."

This glowing, flaming creature was immense. Taller than Strateia by at least four feet, Diakrina estimated it to be about 12 feet tall. It was human-like, yet very different. His dark grey tunic reached almost to the ground, and his large breastplate—cast of a shiny black metal—nearly covered the top of a wide belt that appeared to be made of the same black metal. A sheath and sword, larger than any Diakrina had imagined, hung from his belt. Judging by the length of the sheath, the sword must have been about six feet long with an immense handle, too big for Diakrina to grip with both hands.

He stood looking down at her with a flaming head of black hair that seemed to wave like fire fluttering in the breeze rising from the abyss. His complexion was of a color Diakrina had never seen before and could never find anything in the world around her to which to compare it.

"His flesh had no flesh-tone. He was almost white—not white as we mean when we call a person white, but actually white—but it was a dirty white with a kind of greenish, grey hue to it," she once said in an attempt to explain. "His flesh looked lifeless as if in a state of decay just under the surface." And in fact, even with the wind and mist rising from the waterfall, she detected the settling of an acrid, rotting odor saturating the space around her and the creature.

Now, on further inspection, she realized that the light of this creature was not white at all, but a kind of pale, greenish color like its skin. The handle of his sword radiated the same sickening, nauseating green, only more concentrated.

As her eyes became more accustomed to the light, she began taking in her surroundings. She was in a very large stone paved courtyard which got broader as it receded from her. All of it was dimly glowing with the greenish light. About 300 yards beyond and behind this towering creature, on the far side of the courtyard, stood the edifice of a Gothic-style stone temple, from which the creature had likely come. It was carved into the face of a wide arching wall where the canyon turned and circled in toward the east and formed this wide ledge on which the courtyard and temple stood. The canyon wall then came at Diakrina on her right at an angle toward the fall, which resulted in the ledge becoming very narrow just as it approached the stairs.

In the face of the temple, high up between large angry columns at the top of massive steps, was something like a throne, which dominated the front of the edifice. This temple glowed with pale, greenish light and cast its dim glow over the area. The whole place looked haunted and vile.

In the center of the courtyard, about halfway between the stone temple and Diakrina, a large obelisk stood defiantly. Its square foundation stone measured about 10 feet high. From each of its four corners the carved head of an ibex (wild goat) protruded outward and upward. From the center of the foundation the obelisk rose about 60 feet. The greenish light from the stone temple caused the obelisk to cast a long, dagger-like shadow toward Diakrina.

Diakrina was cold and shivering and still lay helplessly on the stone pavement in front of the creature. Studying the creature's countenance—if you could call that death-like expression a *countenance*—Diakrina's sense of danger escalated. This truly was a creature to be feared. He looked wicked, prideful, vile and cruel.

She could not pass back down the stairs (it was nine-times locked against her), and she could not retreat to her left toward the waterfall as the ledge ended there. She could not run to her right as the rock wall of the canyon was there; and in front of her was this greenish, 12-foot creature with a six-foot sword and the stench of death radiating from him.

Diakrina looked up at the creature and he glared down on her. She saw his lips move to speak. But sound did not come from him, for when the creature spoke, the roar of the waterfall itself formed the words. He haunted and possessed even the noise of the cascading waters and reverberating rocks!

"I AM THANATOS! WHO IS THIS ENTERING MY DOMAIN? PRESENT YOURSELF!" came the question and command. Words, riding on such a medium, were devastating to any courage Diakrina had tried to retain. The *voice*—this speaking thunder—pounded her with every syllable.

The voice was inhuman, self-absorbed, merciless, angry—wicked. In the most emphatic way in which it could be true, she had been shouted at as a thing, an object, a non-person; she had been addressed as an annoyance to be resolved. The pronoun, *who*, had been used out of mere accurate recognition of a *fact* for which the speaker had contempt. In his regard she was being consciously demoted in the order of existing entities; she was being reduced and dissolved: disintegrated.

All the life seemed to go out of her. She wanted to scream but had no strength even to attempt it. Besides, she had no voice in this place. The loudest scream she could produce would be nothing more than a silent yawn within this ocean of thunder. What is more, how could she answer when she could not make herself heard?

But evidently, she was not expected to answer. The question and the demand had both been merely rhetorical, as she would learn. Without any regard for her response, the voice of the waterfall of Nekus spoke again.

"I SEE YOU POSSESS THE CRIMSON SWORD. DO YOU ACTUALLY THINK IT IS OF ANY USE TO YOU HERE?" snarled the creature. And with that, he threw back his great head and the most maddening, piercing howl roared through the canyon from the waterfall. It was so shattering that the very canyon walls seemed as if they would crumble, and the rock ledge beneath Diakrina shook back and forth as if in a violent earthquake.

Instantly, Diakrina sensed madness—insanity—in this howl; a veiled rage which seemed to shriek out some deep and incurable pain. The intensity of this howling rage made Diakrina feel as if her teeth would shatter, as all the strength in her jaw could not keep them from crashing violently together. All she could do was hold tightly to her sword as she continued to curl up in a heap on the ledge.

When finally the long howl ended, the creature looked down on her and spoke again. "YOU HAVE BUT TWO CHOICES. EACH CHOICE DEPENDS ON WHAT YOU DECIDE CONCERNING THE SWORD. IF YOU RELINQUISH THE SWORD BY THROWING IT OVER THE EDGE INTO THE FALL, I WILL ALLOW YOU TO PASS THROUGH MY DOMAIN BY TRAVELING THE DOWNWARD PATH. IF YOU WILL NOT RELINQUISH IT, BOTH YOU AND THE SWORD WILL BE CAST OVER THE EDGE INTO THE FALL. THE CHOICE IS YOURS. THERE ARE NO OTHERS."

Diakrina felt a cold terror almost literally take her by the throat. The thought of being cast over the edge into the thundering blackness to certain annihilation swept over her like a tidal wave of irresistible fear. But give up the sword? The sword was her only tie to hope. What is more it continually reminded her of Strateia who had given it to her. How she longed in this dark, stench-filled place to see his face again. Suddenly it rose up within her and she shouted with all her might, "NO!" It was the shout of a silent movie. She had no voice at all in this terrible place.

The creature, Thanatos, took no notice of her attempt to be heard. He simply stepped aside and took his large sword from its sheath. He walked toward the rock wall to Diakrina's right and, with both hands, swung the sword over his head and down against the rock. Diakrina felt a shudder but heard no sound other than the waterfall; the action was once again that of a silent movie. The sword ripped through the rock and a fissure in the rock crumbled producing an opening about ten feet high that began as a mere crack at the top and widened to around two feet at the bottom.

This done, the creature turned back to Diakrina. Once again, the bloodless voice of the waterfall addressed her.

"I HAVE THE AUTHORITY AND POWER TO THROW YOU AND THAT SWORD OVER THE EDGE AND NONE WILL STOP ME: IT IS MY RIGHT IN THIS DOMAIN. HOWEVER, HERE IS AN OPENING TO THE DOWNWARD PATH." He pointed to the breach in the rock. "WHO KNOWS TO

WHERE IT MAY LEAD. BY IT, YOU MAY PERHAPS SAVE YOURSELF AND LEAVE MY DOMAIN, THE CANYON OF NEKUS. THOUGH NO MERE HUMAN EVER HAS, WHO CAN KNOW THAT YOU WILL NOT BE THE FIRST? IT IS A VERY, VERY LONG PATH AND THE POSSIBILITIES ARE SURELY MANY. THROW THE SWORD OVER THE EDGE AND I WILL ALLOW YOU THIS OPTION. IT IS MY *ONLY* OFFER. REFUSE, AND I WILL THROW BOTH YOU AND THAT SWORD INTO THE BLACK, ENDLESS DEPTHS OF NEKUS FALLS."

The pounding syllables of each word drove the cold verdict home. Deep inside she knew these were her only choices. And the determined, matter-of-fact manner of the ultimatum made it quite clear she was already being pushed toward one or the other of these two dreadful destinies. There would be no delay. She would choose. And she would have to choose now.

Diakrina knew her voice could not be heard, yet still she could not keep herself from crying out at the top of her voice, "Living One, please, help me!" Her voice made no dent in the prison of black thunder, and she heard only her own screaming heart within.

Diakrina looked at the sword in her right hand and pulled it close to her. She had vowed never to give it up. This downward path seemed to offer a terrible option, but an option all the same. At that moment, it seemed that Diakrina's life had been reduced to a single nightmare, offered to her as the only hope of escaping the terror and destruction of Nekus Fall. But, then, what terrors waited on this downward path? Did it leave Nekus Canyon or go ever deeper into it? Was it only a longer path to the same destination?

These frantic thoughts were forcefully interrupted by the demanding voice of Thanatos. "THE MOMENT OF DECISION IS NOW. WHAT IS YOUR CHOICE?" Diakrina struggled to her feet shaking like a leaf in a thunderstorm.

As she stood, the sword seemed too heavy to lift and she let the point fall to the rock beneath her feet. Then, as she looked down at its glowing blade, she suddenly came to herself and realized she was looking at a crimson footprint at the very tip of the blade. It was pointed toward the edge, toward Nekus Fall. She lifted the blade tip forward and saw another footprint even closer to the edge. She took a step and pointed the tip out even further. There was a third footprint and it was on the very edge of the ledge where the liquid sound of Nekus pulverized all sensibilities. She stared hard at the footprint as if trying to remember what they were all about. The meaning of the footprints was foggy, as if shrouded in some long lost memory.

Then she heard two voices, one after the other. The first was soft and sweet, a mere whisper that drowned out the thunder of Nekus Fall.

"Follow me, Diakrina, follow me."

The second was the voice of the creature, Thanatos. He had mistaken her slow movement toward the fall as an indication she was preparing to cast the sword over the edge, "THAT'S RIGHT, THROW IT OVER!" came the command.

Instantly, Diakrina came to her senses. Strength came into her and resolve flooded her heart. She would not relinquish her sword—her source of hope and connection to the Living One. No matter what the cost she would cling to it with her last breath.

She turned and looked up into the greenish, dead face of Thanatos and smiled. Then she took two steps toward the edge, and holding the sword in front of her with both her hands and focusing her mind on nothing but its crimson promise, she jumped.

CHAPTER FIFTEEN

# The FALL

As Diakrina dove from the ledge, she heard the voice of Thanatos, the cataracts of Nekus, thunder a deep, long, insane howl of maddened, incurable pain. But her only thought was to hold tightly to the sword and peer deep into its crimson glow.

And glow it did, brighter than she had ever seen it glow before. As Diakrina fell further and further down, the mist from Nekus Fall became so thick that it was like falling in a very wet fog where little could be seen except the blaze of the sword as it created a crimson halo around itself in the water droplets rushing by with ever-increasing speed.

The glow of the sword increased until Diakrina, herself, was engulfed in a crimson circle of light as she fell headfirst with the sword held out in front of her. The effect, as the light reflected off the millions of passing water droplets, was to make everything inside this bubble of crimson light visible and in motion. The edge of the bubble was opaque, due not only to the darkness beyond it, but equally to the reflection of the light from off the mist. And so, outside this capsule of light, nothing seemed to be in motion.

The reverberation of water hitting numerous protrusions from the rock wall created thunderous pressure waves that smashed into Diakrina like bursting bombs, and the much quicker pulse of the impact of cascades ending their descent somewhere far below pummeled her as she fell. She could tell the sound was becoming greater, not because she could hear any increase—the sound was already too large to be heard—but because the pressure waves caused by the sound were escalating to the point it was becoming physically punishing.

Of course, there were the great questions as to what was about to happen. Would she survive? Would there be a miraculous rescue? Would she merely be pulverized into nothing by the massive hammering of the water as she fell closer and closer to the termination point? Or would it be the collision with the bottom of the canyon that would finish her?

And what of her quest for the Immortal Fruit? Had she failed?

While these questions raced through her mind, she kept reminding herself she had followed the footprints as she had been instructed: she had been led to jump. Whatever happened, it was now out of her hands.

Diakrina tried to keep her mind focused on holding tightly to the sword with all her strength. The vibrations coming through the sword blade and handle were so violent and quick her hands and fingers and even her arms were beginning to go numb from the assault.

Just when she was truly afraid she could hold on to the handle no more, she noticed the frequency of the pulses began slowing—not the intensity, just the frequency. In the darkness, Diakrina had lost all sensation of falling except for the endless stream of crimson-illuminated mist flying through her capsule of light and the increasing frequency and intensity of the pressure waves. They had been an indication of her speed. Now, as they decreased, she had a sensation of the speed of her fall diminishing.

Suddenly, without any warning, she was flipped upright, then onto her back and then spun around several times. Some kind of air-pressure was pushing up on her. This, added to the sound pressure waves, seemed to be lifting against her fall. The mist, instead of racing upwards past her as it had, now pulsed as if caught in a giant circle of vibrating air and water. Her tiny light-capsule continued to spin and tumble.

Suddenly, she believed she understood the strange physics at work around her. The force of water hitting the narrow canyon floor was displacing the air and driving it upwards along the canyon walls. Since she had not jumped into the center of the waterfall, but in the air along its side, the combination of sound waves and displaced air were holding her aloft on an acoustic and pneumatic cushion.

Then a great and long flash of lightning came from overhead, high above the canyon walls, illuminating the whole canyon for several seconds like someone had turned on a light switch. Because it had only been seconds since her eyes had left the greenish blaze of Thanatos, and because of the continual blaze of her sword as she fell, this time Diakrina could see. *What* she saw made her eyes go wide in astonishment and terror.

She was indeed suspended, high above a torturous, swirling, pitching pool of water about the size of a football field into which the torrent of Nekus Fall fell like the volume of the mighty Amazon. Waves rolled out from the point of impact like monsters far too large for a pool this size. Like mighty, rising and falling mountains they reached up to claim her, then fell with a shattering, crushing, demolishing force that caused the entire pool to surge fiercely outward in all directions away from the fall and hit the canyon walls with a shudder.

In those few seconds, when these watery mountains collapsed and the pool rushed outward, the whole surface of the pool sunk into a bowl-like shape. Diakrina could see that the waterfall had blasted out this bowl deep into the bedrock. The water, which rushed away from the fall toward the downward descent of the canyon, was washed out of this bowl-like, concaved area with such force that it rose over the rim and became a huge tsunami crashing down the canyon some 100 feet to the river below. The whole effect was not a steady flow, but a pulsating series of violent, mammoth waves washing over the rim of the basin and plunging into the canyon beyond.

Diakrina was being suspended and tumbled by the violent forces at work here pushing the air upward like a powerful hurricane. Also, she could not but believe the sound waves were interacting with her body and lifting her as they passed upward and through her. Somehow, she was being lofted about 75 feet above this violent scene.

She saw all this in a series of continuous lightning strikes that made it like daylight in the canyon for several seconds. Just before it went dark, out of the corner of her eye she saw something else just beyond a descending wave. She could not make it out, but it was some kind of large circular pattern in the water over next to the far canyon wall.

Just then the lightning lit up the canyon again, but at the same moment the rising hurricane tumbled and swirled her until she could not fix her eyes on anything. She did realize, however, that she was being tumbled across the canyon toward the far wall. At times, the pressure beneath her would seem to fail and she would be dropped violently for about ten feet before being caught and tossed back upward and over.

When finally she was able to turn onto her belly and stay there long enough to focus on what lay beneath her, she saw the circular pattern clearly, for she was almost over it. It was a huge torrent moving in a swirling circle—a massive whirlpool. At its center a deep depression in the water's surface swallowed thousands of gallons of water every moment. She realized that the tsunami waves splashing over the edge were only a fraction of the water descending from the fall above. This hungry, circling mouth was greedily devouring as much of the river as it could consume, leaving only the renegade waves to pour over the edge. To her horror, the hungry mouth was not only swallowing the river water, but its sucking vortex extended up into the mist above it and was beginning to pull Diakrina into its circling motion.

She attempted to air-swim away from the monstrous gaping mouth, but of course, it was no use. Pushing down her rising panic, she told herself that all her efforts now should focus on holding tightly to her sword, no matter what. She pulled the handle of the sword close to her waist with the blade in front and several inches from her face, and held on with both hands gripped as tightly as she could. Then she watched helplessly as the lightning lit up the canyon for long seconds and she slowly circled the great mouth of water, sliding closer toward its center with every turn.

As she was nearly over it, a great flash of lightning illuminated everything and the yawning mouth, which had been dark, was lit so she could see down into it. Down, down, down, like a long tunnel it descended. She could not see its end as it turned outward, under the rim of the cup and toward the canyon and the river below.

Diakrina quickly turned her head, looked out over the rim and spotted a stream of water, some 20 feet in diameter, spewing out over the river from the direction of the vortex beneath her. The stream hit the water not more than 60 feet from the far wall of the canyon. She instantly realized that this was the water from the gaping whirlpool into which she was being pulled.

Her eyes were fixed out over the rim when the next flash of lightning lit up the canyon. What she saw struck her with a new level of helpless fear and drained any remnant of courage out of her in an instant. For the first time, she looked downriver and saw that yet another fall, just beyond this one, sucked the river into another great abyss, and that abyss swallowed the river underground!

Swallowed underground in Nekus Canyon—the thought filled Diakrina with total despair, and nothing now could save her from the fate. She was a helpless victim on the current of an unstoppable force. Turning her gaze back toward the throat of the great vortex immediately below her, she saw that she was making her last circle around it before being sucked down into its gullet.

As she stared helplessly into its swirling throat, a moment of total bewilderment struck her as she saw that on its swirling, circling surface were crimson footprints that led down into its belly. She was still wide-eyed and trying to sort her thoughts when all went dark, and she felt herself sucked downward with a great force.

Diakrina pulled the sword handle close and braced herself. Fortunately for her, the force of the whirlpool pushed the water, which was much heavier than the air she was riding on, outward to form a great moving tunnel. The air, along with Diakrina, was forced and sucked to the middle of the vortex.

The air spun violently and twirled her like a top. Down, down the vortex pulled her to where the tunnel began to turn to go under the rim of the great cup. Here, as it turned, the walls of water closed in on Diakrina and the air and water churned into a kind of froth and foam. As the tunnel tightened around her, her speed accelerated, as did her spinning. She held her breath and clutched her sword.

For a few moments the water completely engulfed her. Then, without warning, she was shot out into the thunder of Nekus Fall about 30 feet above the river just as the lightning flashed. Somehow, her velocity catapulted her beyond the shooting stream of water on a trajectory that appeared to be dropping her only about 25 feet from the far canyon wall. In those few milliseconds, Diakrina caught sight of a ledge jutting out from the canyon wall some 15 feet deep and about 2 feet above the water level where a person might pull themselves out of the river if they could reach it before being swept down into the underground belly of Nekus Canyon.

She tried to orient herself to know which way to swim once she hit the water. About halfway through her diving arc, all went black, except for the sword, and she braced herself for the plunge by gripping it with every ounce of strength she could find.

Her impact with the water took her down far below the surface. The water was deep and cold. As soon as she could, she tucked the sword backwards in her right hand so the blade pointed back and away from her, and began swimming with all her might toward what she hoped was the river's bank and the ledge. The current of the river was incredibly strong and she knew she would likely get only one chance to reach the bank. By keeping the current oriented to her left side she could keep some sense of direction. When she came to the surface, already swimming hard, huge waves hit her like a stampeding herd of elephants. The more she thought of being pulled down into that terrible abyss, the harder she swam across the current, hoping the whole time she was indeed going the right direction.

Lightning flashed over the canyon again, and Diakrina raised her head trying to see the canyon wall and bank. She was only a little off target, pointed almost back up stream and slightly away from the canyon wall. It was not more than 10 feet away but it seemed like hundreds.

When she turned herself directly toward the canyon wall, the current began to drag her more swiftly downstream. She knew she would have only seconds before the pull of the current would become too strong for her to swim across—she had to reach something quickly she could hold on to.

At last, she felt a rock, and she grabbed for it. But it was smooth and slick and she was pulled past it as the strengthening current took control of her. She lunged with strong strokes toward the wall and in the darkness actually smashed her face into a large rock. She grabbed with all her might and managed to get the slightest hold on the up-current side of the rock with her left hand. But her hold was slipping and the current was relentless.

Slowly she was being pulled back into the stream. Just before she lost her hold all together, in a frantic, desperate move, she stretched her right arm out to her side as far as possible, and holding the sword like a very long dagger, she thrust its blade downward onto the back of the rock.

With an explosive burst of light the sword melted itself nearly down to the hilt into the boulder. Diakrina grasped the sword handle with both hands and then pulled herself toward the rock. She then reached out to find that there was another rock closer to the canyon wall and she wedged herself between it and the first boulder. This put her somewhat behind the first boulder and the current turned her loose. She leaned back against the second rock and pushed against the sword handle to keep herself from moving back toward the river.

Another flash of lightning several seconds long revealed that she was only a few feet from the ledge. Diakrina gathered herself and pulled hard on the sword. It came free from the stone and she pushed herself back toward the bank.

When she reached the bank, she put her right hand with the sword on top of the ledge and began to climb onto its upper side. When at last she was able to stand, she dropped the sword tip down on the ground in exhaustion.

There as she looked down at its now soft, crimson glow, she saw a faint footprint just at its tip.

## CHAPTER SIXTEEN

# REVELATION

On seeing the footprint, Diakrina collapsed in a pile of exhausted relief. Strangely, she found, as she pulled herself up to lean against a nearby boulder, that as the footprint still glowed in response to the crimson sword, she began to feel a kind of levity: a kind of lighthearted cheerfulness.

She had survived. She was alive—well, at least so far. She had jumped from a height greater than the world's tallest skyscrapers without a parachute and was alive with nothing more than a few scratches and bruises to show for it. Who at home could she ever tell all this and they would believe it?

She had done the unthinkable and accomplished the improbable. Once again she had an inner awakening. Some part of her had come to life. She had faced death—literally—and had chosen it instead of distrusting her invisible guide. In facing death, she had found a new and deeper means of being alive.

Once again, she looked at the glowing footprint and realized she actually owed everything to him—or was it *Him*? Could the one leading her actually be the Living One, Himself? Would the ultimate King and

Lord of Life be willing to get so involved in the dangerous, dirty, infamous issues of her predicaments? Would One so great stoop so low? And if so, why?

As she thought along this line, her understanding of greatness began to change. In fact, she began to see, one of the very characteristics of greatness was its willingness and ability to stoop. The great can descend. The low cannot ascend. The low can pull down, but the great can lift up. Wasn't it always the small of character, the weak of will, the bankrupt of virtue that were criticizing, judging, slandering and mocking others, pulling down in a vain attempt to make themselves appear up?

Was it not equally the giants of character, the sturdy of will, the fruitful of virtue that were always lifting up the unfortunate, encouraging the discouraged and timid, correcting injustices and finding pleasure in caring for the least important? Diakrina determined that from this day forward she would *lift* more.

When finally she stood, another flash of lightning lit up the canyon for about five seconds. She turned toward the downstream abyss and could now see from the ledge that the river disappeared into its gaping mouth. She could not know, for she could not see how far it dropped, but she sensed it was almost bottomless.

What added to this conclusion was the fact that all the noise and thunder of the place were still coming from the first great fall. As close as she was to this second waterfall, which plunged into the abyss, she could sense none of the sound or vibration coming from out of its mouth. It was as if the great river fell into silence because it found no bottom and sent no thunderous report echoing back up the great shaft.

Diakrina remembered the small streams that had been torn by the great Chasm that had created what Strateia called the Severed Lands. Those streams fell away into silence.

Strateia had also informed her the great Chasm had no bottom a created being could reach. Could it be this abyss into which this fall descended was indeed the great Chasm? If so, this second fall into the canyon of death would have been irrevocable—there could be no path back out of its silent throat.

As terrible and life-numbing as the roar of the upper fall was on Diakrina, a deeper horror emanated from the silent abyss below her. A cold, self-perpetuating hopelessness seemed to exert absolute control beyond its rim. It telegraphed out from its devouring mouth a darkness so absolute that utter, irrevocable despair was its only light. When Diakrina realized how close she had come to actually going over the edge, she shuddered with gratitude. By a miracle of guidance, she had safely crossed the cold river of death just a few yards from the abyss of its devouring mouth.

The darkness returned, and the footprint remained. She took a deep breath and pointed her sword in the direction it indicated, which was, thankfully, away from the silent horror. But she was too weary to take a single step. The pounding she had taken from the report of the water, from which she now was somewhat protected by the shadow of the great rim above her, had taken its toll. She tried to move forward toward the footprint, which is all she could see in the darkness, but her eyes would not focus and the footprint seemed to be spinning. She sank onto her knees and lost consciousness.

When Diakrina awoke, her first conscious thought concerned a strange sense of weightlessness. She lifted herself up on her hands and found that the weariness and soreness that had previously overcome her were completely absent. What is more, somehow, though there was no source of light in Nekus, she could dimly see the features of the whole ledge on which she was lying, the canyon wall to her right and the tortured surface of the river to her left.

As she stood, unfamiliar sensations flooded her whole being—it was exhilarating. She peered toward the fall and found she could make out its general features. She began to wonder if some form of light were dawning on the canyon. But as she turned her head to look straight up where the sky should be high above the canyon walls, she found no indication of light coming from above.

Looking down, she saw her sword lying on the ground and instinctively knelt to pick it up. Just before her hand touched it, she caught a glimpse of the outline of a human hand curled around its handle.

At first, she was merely puzzled. The hand was not easy to see—it was somewhat translucent; the handle of the sword seemed to be visible through the hand—but the hand was clearly human, and female in shape. As she paused for only a second, a flash of lightning again crashed through the canyon. What Diakrina saw in that instant made her start, and she leaped backwards from the spot where she stood.

There in front of her lay the form of a young woman crumpled on the ledge with the sword clutched in her right hand. She wore a garment woven from grass in a very unique pattern. Around her waist was tied a scarlet cord and a belt which held a sword sheath.

Diakrina found her mind suddenly blank with astonishment. The garment, the cord . . . they both seemed so familiar, yet preternatural. Her mind raced to find a context to help make sense of it all. Yet, nothing would come.

The young woman was not moving. She lay with her face to the ground and her long hair covering her features. Diakrina tried to say something, but the absence of the sound of her voice reminded her of the communication blackout enforced by the roar of the fall. Even while she was trying to speak, not really knowing what it was she was trying to say—and never hearing what she actually uttered—the realization that someone else was holding her sword jolted her into a kind of panic.

She quickly stooped and in a single, integrated motion attempted to grasp the sword handle by pushing the girl's hand away. But the hand did not move; nor did it present much resistance to her push. Instead, her own hand seemed to pass through and into the girl's hand. As it did so, she felt the sword handle in her grip.

This froze Diakrina. She knelt there, over the girl's body, motionless. She stared wide-eyed at her own hand somehow within the hand of the unconscious girl. Slowly, she turned loose of the sword and rose to a standing position, looking hard at the girl lying there as if trying to recognize her.

Then she saw them. Just to one side, slightly under the body, lay two golden stones carved in the shape of a rosebud, attached to the ends of the scarlet cord tied around the girl's waist. Diakrina slowly knelt again and fingered one of the two stones.

Then, as if she had been hit by a jolt of electricity in the form of crystal clear memory, she dropped the stones and, jumping straight into the air, landed about two feet from the body. As she landed, she saw something move in the air like a silver whip just to the left of her head. Defensively she swatted at it.

Her hand struck some kind of strong cord, and as she did so something tugged stiffly on the back of her head. At the same moment, she caught sight of the rest of the cord whipping downward toward the girl's body. The wave rolled down the cord until it ended at the back of the girl's head.

Diakrina tried to turn toward the cord and grasp it. But where it was closest to her, it moved as she moved her head and she missed it. She reached at it again, and this time she caught it firmly in her left hand. As she pulled it toward her, she felt again a tug at the back of her own head.

The whip-like cord was silver in color. It was sinewy, yet flexible, and about as big around as a one-inch thick rope. Diakrina slowly took hold of it with her right hand. Then using her free left hand she followed the cord slowly around behind her until she found where it ended . . . attached to her own head!

The cord made no sense to her—yet it clearly connected her and the girl on the canyon floor. And what had made her jump in the first place was the recognition that the stones, carved like a rosebud, at the ends of the scarlet cord, were the ones Strateia had given her in the Garden.

The realization she was staring at her own body took Diakrina's breath away. She had no categories of experience to engage this realization. How could she be looking at herself, from outside herself?

"Am I dreaming?" she heard her mind ask. "Am I . . . dead?"

This last question obliterated any other questions that might have been on its heels. Diakrina's mind was suspended in a vacuum of *conceptionless* input. She stood there like a person who had been thrust into a world where everything she saw was unrecognizable. No object suggested any concept or name or category by which it could be identified.

"No, Diakrina, you are not dead," came a firm, yet gentle voice.

She heard the voice not with her ears, but inside her own head.

"The silver cord is not broken. Until it is broken there is no death, even though you are presently in the realms of Thanatos."

The voice, not being heard with her ears, offered not the slightest clue as to what direction she should look to engage the speaker. Diakrina was looking around her in all directions, when from above her came a soft radiance descending toward her. Yet as she looked up, it proved to be much higher and further away than it first appeared.

As Diakrina watched, the radiance continued to descend, becoming brighter and brighter causing her to shield her eyes. With it came a fierce yet comforting heat, dispelling the chilly, damp air of Nekus.

There, in front of her, stood a beautiful being whose essence seemed to be nothing more or less than moving flames of white, gold and blue fire. The flames composed the shape of a man unlike any she had ever seen or imagined. His whole body was comprised of these white, gold and blue flames in constant motion. Yet, somehow, this constant motion obeyed a very precise composition of features that consistently defined him with exceptional clarity.

In his right hand he held a torch. To Diakrina's amazement, it looked very much like the torch she had dropped into the altar at the mouth of Nekus.

Now that the being stood in front of her, he spoke to her mind again. This time, Diakrina took note that the voice and the medium of words used transcended language, as we understand it. The form of communication transmitted more than sound-symbols to be interpreted in the context of the *hearer's* own mind. Somehow she knew that what she was receiving was this being's own thoughts transmitted with the context in accompaniment—if you will, the being's own personal definitional and connotative dictionary, his own personal intent of meaning.

With such communication it was impossible for one to misunderstand or be misunderstood. It was almost like Diakrina and the being were sharing a common consciousness and thought process that formed a single perspective and meaning on the content being shared without blurring the personal distinctions of response or understanding to the message. For there was yet a clear distinction between her amazement and the being's . . . well, peace, understanding, graciousness and patience. The *speaker* and the *hearer* were never mingled or blurred.

Also, as he *spoke*, she could *feel* his emotions just as she could feel her own. But there was no confusion which were his, and which were hers. The comprehensiveness of this form of communicating made Diakrina feel as if she had never spoken anything in all her life more profound than baby cooing. Human language was a single note on a piano, while this, by comparison, was a 120 piece orchestra in majestic, ever-changing crescendo.

"Diakrina, I am the Guardian of the Altar." He then turned to look at the torch in his hand, and holding it out somewhat toward her he continued. "In an act of faith you gave me the sacred trust of this torch. This torch, which is your reliance on your own understanding and abilities, I have kept.

"By turning from reliance on your own perception to put your faith in the guidance promised you, you have escaped the ever-hungry mouth of the second Fall of Nekus. By choosing death instead of disobedience leading to independence—by choosing faith instead of fear—you have leapt into the arms of Life and turned the very thunder of death's voice into a means of conquest. The roar of Thanatos—the roar of death—has been made to serve you and bear you over to Life. By your trust you have traced the steps of Him who has forever subdued Thanatos' power. And the result is you have obtained your own share in His conquest. This is His gift to you.

"Yet, you still stand in the Canyon of Nekus, with only four hours left before dawn. By dawn you must have passed from this part of the Canyon to the western branch. And we both know why you are here."

"I am here to reclaim the Fruit of Immortality which was stolen and hidden here." Diakrina had attempted to speak as always but found that it was unnecessary after only two words into her response. She could speak here with her mind and be heard.

"To find the Fruit of Immortality," said the flaming man to her mind, "you must go back toward the thunder of the fall, back to the place where the waters below the fall spill over the bowl-shaped rim down to this level of the river. There you will find, behind the water that pours over its edge, an opening. It leads to a passage that will turn to the right and lead you west, up and out to a second arm of Nekus Canyon that runs away from the river.

"You must enter this passage and travel its length. At its end you will find a portal similar to the one you entered coming into the realms of Thanatos. It is the Portal of Zoe, by which you will be led back to the realms of men in the Severed Lands.

"Unlike most who come this way—and all do ultimately—it has been determined that before you walk the path that leads to the realms of Life unending, you will pass back to the land of the mortal. There you will be given the opportunity to complete your quest and return through the Door of the Rose back to the realm of your own time. The Portal of Zoe will take you back to mortality. Follow the footprints. He knows the way."

"What about the Fruit of Immortality?" asked Diakrina. "Where do I find it?"

"Before you reach the Portal of Zoe, about halfway up the cave-like passage, on the left, you will find a cleft in the wall: a vertical break about 30-feet tall. It will just be wide enough for you to push your way through at first. Yet, after several feet, it will widen out into a room. You will find the Fruit of Immortality on a ledge about 100 feet back inside this cleft. Take it and do with it as you have been instructed."

"Will it be guarded in some manner?" asked Diakrina.

"Yes, but not as you might imagine. You will not be physically hindered in taking the Fruit, but you will be solicited. The guardian of the Fruit will entice you to partake of the Fruit. You must overcome this temptation.

"If you succeed, once the Fruit is safe in your possession inside the crystal container, beware. The rest of your journey will be under fierce resistance. Once you escape with the Fruit, you must continue on through the passage and out through the Portal of Zoe. Even after you pass through the Portal, do not let down your guard, for the terrible guardians of the canyon at the exit to the western branch of Nekus will attempt to stop you."

The mention of these "terrible guardians" unnerved Diakrina. She wished she could avoid any more such encounters, but this seemed unlikely.

"Also, Diakrina, I must give you another warning. On the same ledge with the Fruit of Immortality lies a set of great keys. Do not, I repeat, *do not* for any reason touch them. They are indeed guarded in ways you cannot imagine. If you tried to take them you could not succeed. In fact you could not even lift them, let alone carry them. Any attempt to take the keys would only result in your destruction and the failure of your mission."

"These great keys, what do they lock or unlock?" asked Diakrina.

"They are, to your race, the keys of death, hell and the grave: the keys used by Anomos and Thanatos to chain you to death. For now, he has a legal right to them. Even the Living One will not allow them to be taken by force until Anomos' claim is nullified.

"Anomos gained the rights to them by his conquest of your first parents, and they can only be recovered by a human. However, there is no human, yet, in this time, who can nullify his claim. In your time, by having become a man, the Living One will have done so. He will have taken the keys back and set your race free from the fear of death. But He, and only He, will be able to do this, and here that time has not yet come."

Diakrina wanted to take this all in, but she was still disturbed by her bizarre condition of being attached to the motionless body on the rock floor of the cavern by a strange silver cord. She found it hard to keep her focus.

Finally she could take it no longer, and it did seem the flaming man had paused for a moment. "Can you explain this to me?" she said pointing to the form on the canyon floor.

"Do not be frightened, Diakrina. As I told you, this is not death. Because you are to pass back to the realms of men in the Severed Lands, your silver cord is not broken; your spirit is not separated from your body. It is the severing of this cord that is what you call *physical death*. Your time is not yet."

Diakrina looked down at the form on the slab of rock beneath them. She traced with her eyes the path of the silver cord from behind her to the motionless form. "Is that . . . who . . . is she . . .?" She couldn't get the question out.

The Guardian of the Altar interrupted her attempts, "Yes, Diakrina, that is you, your soma, your body."

"Yet, I'm not dead even though I am disembodied?" she quickly interjected.

"No, you are not dead, Diakrina. The silver cord is still connected. This is not death, though some have mistaken it for death.

"You can read of this in King Solomon's writings. His book called Ecclesiastes describes death and the silver cord is mentioned."

Then the Guardian quoted what Solomon had written concerning death. The sense of the Hebrew he quoted which Diakrina heard by the Guardians own understanding of it was this:

*"Remember the Living One—before the silver cord is*
*severed, or the golden bowl is broken; before the pitcher is*
*shattered at the spring, or the wheel broken at the well, and*
*the dust returns to the ground it came from, and the spirit*
*returns to the Living One who gave it."*

"Diakrina, Solomon was using a Hebraic manner of speaking. You must discern the poetic form of his words, for he wove together three symbolic word-pictures and two literal statements about death in this description.

"The first literal statement is, 'before the silver cord is severed,' followed by three symbolic word pictures which give added understanding to the consequences of the silver cord being severed. The three pictures are the golden bowl being broken, the pitcher being shattered and the wheel being broken at the well. The broken golden bowl points to something valuable being rendered dysfunctional by its breaking. The other two word pictures, the shattered pitcher and the broken wheel at the well, both point to the impossibility of water being drawn so that life can be sustained.

"Then the form calls for him to end with another literal statement about what he is describing—in this case death. This final statement is very literal, like the first about the silver cord: 'and the dust returns to the ground it came from, and the spirit returns to the Living One who gave it.'"

"So, death is a *severing* in both cases?" asked Diakrina.

"Yes. The broken bowl, the shattered pitcher and the broken wheel describe the resulting loss of life and function which come from that severing," answered the Guardian.

Diakrina looked back at herself lying on the stone slab. "You say I am not dead. So is this some kind of out-of-body state? I have heard of this, and of strange cults that seek to obtain this state."

"Yes, Diakrina, in your time it is called an out-of-body experience or O.B.E. Times before you have called it many different things. The Greeks in the mystery cults called it an out-of-mind experience. It is not something you should seek. In fact, the Living One forbids it. It is a state you can no longer manage since you fell from the Great Dance. It can become a great source of deception if you seek to use this function of your nature on your own. It is lost to you until the Restoration of all things. And even then, it will not take this form—this near separation. For the new body—as the former—will not be left behind in this mode of perception."

"Then why am I now experiencing this?" Diakrina asked with concern.

"This is the point at which most who pass through this canyon experience the temporary separation of spirit and body—what you call physical death," answered the Guardian. "This has been aborted in your case because it is determined that you are to pass back through the Portal of Zoe and the Door of the Rose.

"This is not your time to die, Diakrina. You conquered Thanatos by your trust in the Living One. Death had to be risked to bring you into this realm for the sake of the quest. But by faith, and your obedience that came by that faith, you have overcome him. Therefore death has been aborted for you for the sake of the quest. You are within death, yet you live by His power through your faith in Him."

"So, I am not dead as long as this silver cord is intact?" asked Diakrina again, seeking reassurance.

"Correct, Diakrina. The concept of death, at its most fundamental level, means *separation*. It does not mean to cease to exist."

This seized Diakrina's attention and she asked, "Can you explain to me what you mean?"

The Guardian turned somewhat and motioned toward the rock wall behind him. Suddenly flames from his body leapt onto the wall in a baseball size globe. Then the white, gold and blue flames spread outward like a ring. Inside the ring, light pulsated outward like ripples in a pond. And as the flaming man began to explain, Diakrina saw three-dimensional, holographic-like images that illustrated his explanations.

The first scene she could not explain. It had to do with a vision of the Living One and how all things have their existence—their being—and can only truly live as they were created to live by having an unhindered relationship to Him. That relationship is determined according to the kind of thing or being He has made it to be.

She saw thousands of living beings, most of which were beyond her power to recognize. And somehow she could discern their connection to the Living One by their place within the Great Dance.

The Guardian's explanation, as she watched all this unfold, can be paraphrased something like this: "As I said, death does not mean to cease to exist. Death is separation that gives rise to a progressive abnormality. Each new level of abnormality results in a new form of separation, or severing.

"It is true that in the progression of the various separations caused by death, some aspects of life are lost and cease to exist. *But that is a consequence of death, not death itself,*" said the Guardian with extra emphasis. "Death itself is a terrible severing from Him who alone is the Source of all Life and beauty.

"When a branch is severed from a tree"—here Diakrina watched a branch being torn from its source of life and then watched as it began to wither—"the loss of the relationship of life to the tree is the first separation and loss for the branch. But it is not the last. If not grafted back in, the branch will, in this state of being severed from the tree, begin to decay, disintegrate, and separate in itself. Thus death as severance leads to a process of death as disintegration. This is what your species was warned about by the Creator."

"Strateia spoke a little of this to me earlier," interjected Diakrina.

Then changing his voice and inflection so that it was clear he was quoting a text very sacred and solemn, and doing it in such a way that Diakrina heard very distinct sounds of words being articulated; בְּיוֹם אֲכָלְךָ֫ 'מִמֶּ֫נּוּ מוֹת תָּמוּת : וּמֵעֵ֫ץ הַדַּ֫עַת טוֹב וָרָע לֹא תֹאכַל מִמֶּ֫נּוּ כִּי

Though the language was unfamiliar to Diakrina, his communication revealed the Guardian's own understanding of the language. The translation is roughly this: *"And from the tree of the knowledge of good and evil, you shall not eat of it: for in the day that you eat of it, from it, you (by) dying shall die."*

"Notice, Diakrina, that while many of your translations of this command translate, מוֹת תָּמוּת, as "surely die," the phrase is actually "to-die you-shall-die." While in the Hebrew language the repetition of a word often accentuates its emphasis—and so it is in this case—it is also more than emphatic. This gives a technically precise expression of the curse that has come on your race. Through death as severance from your proper relationship to the Creator you have been brought into a process of death as disintegration by which you are constantly in the process of dying. From birth to death you fight an unending battle against the loss and degeneration that is working within you and among you."

"You said there are many forms that death takes. What do you mean?" asked Diakrina, as a desire to understand this dark enemy grew within her.

"For you and your race, many progressive forms of death telescopically unfold into your lives. Separation from relationship with the Creator, what some call spiritual death—the severance of your spirit from a relationship with His Spirit—is the primary death that generates all other forms. It is the *dying* by which you *shall die*.

"From this first death—separation from the Source of Life—comes another stage of decay. This second form comes from the first like maggots from a corpse."

Here Diakrina saw within the images the troubled faces of thousands of people, young and old. She could read their faces and know their minds. They were filled with self-doubt, fear, insecurity and ignorance. Many were angry and depressed as they found life inscrutable. The questions, "Who am I? Why am I here? What is the meaning of my existence? Is there some purpose for it all?" seemed to take a million forms.

"You can call it psychological death," continued the Guardian, "a separation from the knowledge of your own true identity. For if you do not know Him—of whom you were created a reflection—you cannot know yourself. You become an empty mirror separated from the Light that gives you identity. Your purpose and meaning for existing are lost to you and you try to invent both for yourselves.

"Your humanity is achieved by Divine reflection. Without Him you cease to be fully human just as a mirror without light ceases to reflect and thus be a mirror."

The Guardian paused for only a moment to let his words sink in. Then he continued.

"From this second form of separation comes a third. You may call it sociological death: the separation of man from man."

Diakrina watched as hundreds of families argued and fought. Children cried and begged their parents to stop, but the anger and rage continued. Then she saw bloody battlefields with men and children being butchered by the thousands. She saw murderers ambush their victims and merciless thieves rob the poor of their only means of survival. The pictures made Diakrina want to hide her face.

The Guardian continued his explanation while all these terrible scenes unfolded.

"Men, like light-deprived mirrors," said the Guardian, "all suffer from a loss of true identity, each trying to use the others to find some sense of worth and security. Without a proper relationship to the Creator, they are reduced to living in competitive comparison with each other. Relationships are turned into a search for significance rather than a celebration of each other's significance.

"The competitive comparisons by which significance is sought pollutes relationships with judgment, jealousy, anger, bitterness, hatred, rage and despair. Each is trying to put himself up by putting others down. Some try to feel good about themselves by equaling or excelling the performance of some person or standard they believe bestows worth and significance when achieved. Some use others as dispensable objects to be manipulated and consumed for their pleasure or power. Some try to get from others what others cannot give, and rage when they fail to get it from them."

"But," interjected Diakrina, "are we not to expect to receive from others by means of relationship?"

"Yes," answered the Guardian, "but what we receive from others must first be given them by the Creator. And what we are intended to receive directly from Him cannot be received from others. Do you understand, Diakrina?"

"Yes, I think so."

"True identity comes only in our relationship to Him who creates and sustains us. Darkened mirrors looking into each other will not find the light of significance. When each has found Light in the Creator, they can reflect it to each other, but not before. Do you understand, Diakrina?"

"Yes."

Then, as if pressed by time, the Guardian resumed his discourse with a sense of urgency. "A fourth form of death then flows like oozing decay out of the third. You can call it governmental death or circumstantial death. Mankind, having been separated from direct relationship to Life and from the knowledge of his true identity and purpose, and separated from each other through the isolation of impoverished relationships, is then dead to the ability to have proper dominion over the realms of responsibility and creativity.

"Besides losing relationship and knowledge of the Creator, of themselves and of others, mankind loses the healthy skill of synergistic accomplishment. They find their own physical and spiritual nature invaded and manipulated by alien forces they cannot control or resist. Rather than being the steward of circumstances, they become the prisoners of circumstances. Mankind becomes circumstantially controlled.

"And the circumstances that control them are shaped and used by Anomos and his minions. This is the death of man's governmental powers. By being dead to the Creator, men find themselves separated from adequate wisdom and power to create and preserve. By being in rebellion to the Creator, all nature, even their own, is taken captive to a sinister power that uses their own nature as a weapon against them.

"Everything man designs and builds has the seeds of its demise germinating within it from the moment he begins its construction. All gardens grow weeds, all buildings tumble into ruin, all civilizations fall. Every life tends to sink beneath that which it should rise above. One man destroys what another man built. And so the rubble of past hopes and dreams keeps piling higher and higher with time.

"This, Diakrina, is what gives your history on this planet such tragic pathos. So much is dreamed and accomplished only to be lost in the end. All beauty fades. All conquests are reversed. All treasures are scattered. And only the gift of hope keeps the story in process."

While the Guardian spoke of these things Diakrina traveled through a flowing relief of images in which she saw great civilizations rise and great works of architecture and art flourish, only to be burned, destroyed and scattered as another arose to take its place, only to suffer the same fate. Over and over, like great rising waves that always crashed upon the rocks of time, she watched the unfolding of human history.

"And finally, Diakrina," continued the Guardian, "we come to the fifth expression of death, the one which men most fear and which has become, for them, its primary connotation. Like the first thunderous Fall of Nekus, it roars terribly in the hearts of men. This expression of death is the separation of spirit from body, the dissolution of man's fully soulical expression as embodied, eternal spirit."

Then once again, the Guardian, changing his voice and inflection so that it was clear he was quoting a text very sacred and solemn,

said, "וַיִּיצֶר יְהֹוָה אֱלֹהִים אֶת־הָאָדָם עָפָר מִן־הָאֲדָמָה וַיִּפַּח
בְּאַפָּיו נִשְׁמַת חַיִּים וַיְהִי הָאָדָם לְנֶפֶשׁ חַיָּה:"

And as before, while the words were unknown to her, their meaning was not. The Guardian's own understanding of the language was simultaneously communicated to her, like a real-time translation that needed no second voice. What she heard translates something like this: *"And the Yahweh Elohim is forming the human from soil from the ground, and He is blowing into his nostrils the breath-spirit of life; and the human is becoming a living soul."*

Within the swirling light on the rock Diakrina saw a most amazing thing as the flaming man quoted the passage. "I can't put it into words," she later said. "But I saw man's body being formed, every organ and part from the microscopic to the complete man. I watched as the Living One imparted His breath to the formed man and gave him consciousness, self-consciousness, mind with will, reason, imagination and emotion. He stood up, a wonder to behold."

The Guardian directed Diakrina's attention to what she was seeing and said, "A human soul, Diakrina, is not some *part* of you, it *is* you: the whole of you. Body plus spirit equals a living soul. You were created to live fully in both the realms of the spirit and the realms of the material. For unblemished Man there was no division. And the union causes synergistic characteristics and functions to emerge that are not merely spiritual or material.

"Your separation from the Creator, who is Spirit, has made you dead to direct perception of the spiritual realm. Thus, you cannot even know God in your present form except indirectly. Even your own spiritual dimension is darkened to you and can only be known indirectly by observation of its effect and its interface with your material essence. And, therefore, you can only know others indirectly through the medium of the material realm. You have become imprisoned in your five physical senses, separated from direct perception of more than half the reality you live within."

Here Diakrina saw on the rock wall men and women moving through life conscious of only material things and physically visible manifestations while a whole world of spiritual beings, both good and evil, acted and interacted around them. They seemed to be oblivious to the real flow of events and the real causes and effects. Yet they often concocted elaborate theories, many of which were very foolish, by which they attempted to explain everything merely from the things they could observe.

"The Creator," continued the Guardian, "by many merciful means, causes the material creation to reflect into mankind's senses, and through the senses to his mind, knowledge of Himself and of the spiritual sphere. He has also spoken light into your darkness by many words through chosen spokesmen and by one all-inclusive Word, through the Living One, Himself. You were never intended to know the separation of spirit from body; it is an abnormality to human existence. Disembodied human spirits are less than fully human."

This was a point of great correction for Diakrina. She had often accepted, without even thinking it through, that man's soul or spirit escaping into a kind of bodiless existence was the ideal. Clearly this was wrong.

"This," said the Guardian, "is why physical death, which causes the body to return to the dust from which it was taken, and leaves only the human spirit to return to God, is one of your great enemies. Its greatest power is that it, like the first Fall of Nekus, leads to the greater unending fall beyond it, a fall with no bottom and no remedy. And the second fall's silence is the great stealth by which it forever astonishes its victims.

"This is the sixth and final form of death, called in the Great Book, *the second death*. By some it is rightly called eternal death, for it is eternal separation from Him who is Life and from all that He creates to be enjoyed.

"And by all I have told you," he continued, moving somewhat closer to Diakrina so as to have her full attention, "you should understand that all these forms of death—psychological, sociological, governmental, physical and ultimately eternal—flow out of the first: the separation of the creature from a Life-giving relationship with the Creator.

"But it is that sixth form of death—sometimes called the *second death* because it follows physical death—that plunges the soul into the most terrible abyss. It is the death of hope, as the whole person, spiritual and physical, passes forever beyond the reach of Life. It is the eternal separation of the human spirit from Him who alone can heal it, and the eternal separation from the beauties of the material creation that will sustain His obedient creatures in joy forever. For those who refuse His help, there is no cure for the bottomless, silent Fall of Nekus by which the soul eternally retreats from the realms of light and Life and joy."

Here Diakrina saw unfolding within the light on the wall a fearful scene of doomed evil spirits and doomed human souls being sucked into a terrible darkness, which cannot be described. No light ever pierces it. No soul can touch or know another within it. All are forever locked inside their own self-consciousness without hope of knowing or experiencing any other thing or person. The scene so traumatized Diakrina that she reached the verge of screaming uncontrollably. However, the Guardian knew this and the scene vanished from the wall as the flames returned to him.

"This is why, Diakrina," said the Guardian with a countenance that made the flames that formed his face blaze with fierce passion, "the Creator has made the first Fall of Nekus so thunderous and fearsome. By its terrible voice He communicates to men the real incurable horror that lies silently beyond. He wants them to take the first fall very seriously, for what follows is irrevocable. Men are deaf to the greater thunder of the second Fall of Nekus. It is too great a sound for any creature to hear. Only the Creator can perceive it."

"Then," interjected Diakrina, "no man has ever returned from beyond the second Fall of Nekus?"

"Yes, and no," answered the Guardian. "No *mere* man has or ever could. For any creature it has no bottom that can be found. It is a constant crashing through endless bottoms of despair into ever-increasing blackness and isolation. This second Fall of Nekus has bottoms that are not an end. Each is the beginning of greater despair, for hope has vanished forever.

"But when, before your time, the Living One became one of your race, while remaining who He eternally is, He willingly came here, and to our utter astonishment, He surrendered Himself to the current of the river and allowed it to sweep Him over the silent fall. The lands of the living held their breath that day."

"Could He . . . did He . . . return?" Diakrina impatiently pleaded.

"Yes, Diakrina, He drowned its creaturely-endless-depths with His Aseity—His self-generating, eternal, infinite Life. And by His victory He has defeated its power and claims over any who place their trust in His conquest by deeding their lives into His care.

"To them He gives His uncreated Life by giving them His Spirit to live within them. Over them this second death has no power. His victory becomes theirs."

The Guardian paused and Diakrina stood with him in a very pregnant silence.

"Now, Diakrina," he said, breaking the silence, "it is time for your journey to continue. But first, I have a question for you.

"When you first placed this torch—the torch of trusting your own perception—into my care, you did so with great fear and trembling. As you have passed through the trial of the Canyon of Nekus, there have been many times you have earnestly wished to have this torch in your hand. It is trust, resulting in obedience, that has brought you this far and saved you from the great silent fall. This is something this torch could not have given you the power to do as it would be weakened by its dependence on your own perception.

"But I now give you a choice. Will you continue by trust? Do you wish me to be your Guardian still? Or do you wish to take the torch?" And with that, he held the torch out toward her.

While Diakrina longed for the comfort of the torch in the darkness ahead, she knew deep inside that she could not depend on it. If she had taken it into the Canyon, she would now be descending in the eternal fall. Her Guide, His footprints, alone had led her to safety. She would not cease to trust her Guide now.

"I reaffirm the trust I have given you," answered Diakrina. "I will follow the footprints in trust."

"Then I will leave you and you must take the passage I have told you about."

Then pointing toward the base of the first great Fall of Nekus, he said, "In the direction of the entrance, you will find your Guide's footprints."

Then the Guardian paused and looked deeply into Diakrina's eyes as if to arrest her full attention to what he was about to say. Diakrina looked back into his eyes, which were flames of utter beauty that communicated a profound and overwhelming personality.

"Diakrina, remember what I say next; do not forget it." Then he paused and moved slightly closer to her.

"The next time you experience a state like this one—when your spirit is separated from your body, yet still attached by the silver cord—beware! Anomos can use this state to weave a great illusion. He can misuse not only material beauty, but also spiritual beauty, to deceive."

The Guardian paused again to let his thoughts sink deep into her mind. Then he continued.

"There is a vast spiritual creation full of beauties you cannot yet conceive. Some of it—like the material realms of earth—is under Anomos' control. He can spin very convincing lies by exposing people to the beauties of this spiritual world.

"As beauty is often used to bait the cruelest hooks of evil in the material world, so it can be in the spiritual world. Not everything that is spiritual and beautiful is holy or true. Remember my words and be warned. For evil's greatest power is to hide its ugly face behind glorious and harmless beauty. The poisonous serpent hidden in the bouquet of beautiful, fragrant flowers—an expression I believe you are familiar with—is the right word picture. When the fragrance of the flowers is fully embraced and enjoyed, the serpent strikes."

Again the Guardian paused. Then he said, pulling a little back from her, "I have told you. Be diligent to not forget my warning."

And with that, the flaming man began to rise. "Sir," cried Diakrina, "you have not told me your name; only that you are the Guardian of the Altar."

The flaming man smiled as he continued to rise and then spoke with a voice that seemed to echo from the canyon walls, "I am a Seraph. My name is Revelation!"

And suddenly, Diakrina felt the cold stone lying beneath her and the warmth of the sword in her right hand. She turned over and looked up into the sky where Revelation had ascended. There was nothing above her but darkness. And the soreness and weight of her body seemed to press heavily upon her as she attempted to stand.

CHAPTER SEVENTEEN

# The IMMORTAL FRUIT

Dreadful darkness once again reigned over the canyon. Only the slight pulsing glow of Diakrina's crimson sword gave her eyes anything on which to focus. The roar of the upper fall was once again deafening to her ears.

She checked to make sure she had not lost the clear, crystal water container which she had placed over her head and shoulder as she entered Nekus. It was still there.

She stretched and rubbed her aching limbs, then slowly began picking her way through the boulders which lay between her and the rim of the great bowl below Nekus Fall. It is hard to imagine the effect of the violent cataract on her each time the lightning lit up her surroundings for a few seconds. The water pouring over the rim of the bowl at the base of the fall was itself a waterfall of immense proportions. Its rim was over 100 feet above her and stretched across the great river from side to side in a sweeping, outward arc away from the even greater fall above. This immense 100-foot drop of water was like a giant Niagara.

But imagine standing at the base of Niagara in the darkness, and every time the lightning turned the canyon around you to daylight for a few moments, you looked up to see this great Niagara just in front of you dwarfed by a hundred times larger waterfall above it! (Diakrina estimated that Nekus above this bowl dropped at least 10,000 feet.)

As the lightning flashed, she considered the large stream of water shooting in a great arc from a hole in a rock face that jutted out below the rim of the bowl. This, she realized, was the stream of water that came through the sinkhole and had spit her out near this side of the canyon.

She momentarily became absorbed in the need to find the passageway Revelation had spoken about. She looked for the edge of this great cataract in order to find some way to get behind the falling water. The intermittent flashes of lightning made it difficult to stay on course and she soon found herself up against a falling wall of water she could not pass.

After several attempts, she remembered she should not be trying to set her own course, but she should be looking for the footprints to guide her. Amazingly, when she finally remembered this fact and began searching for the footprints with her sword, they immediately appeared before her.

The footprints did not lead toward the edge of the fall, but to the left. But eventually, they turned to the right, and she was led into the fall at a point where the water was broken by some obstruction high above so that it formed a narrow passage through the 40-foot deep wall of falling water.

Once beyond the wall of water, the footprints led to a very narrow opening in a solid rock wall. Diakrina turned sideways and pushed herself slowly through the tight crevice in the wall.

Eventually, it opened up into a wider passage and then finally, into a very large cavern, the course of what had been an underground river. It then turned to the right and led her away from the great fall.

For about 45 minutes she climbed a very steep path upward. And every minute she traveled, the roar of the fall lessened, until it finally faded altogether. As she climbed, she constantly searched the cavern wall to her left for any sign of the cleft Revelation had described.

When she finally spotted it, the opening appeared quite unimpressive. It would have meant nothing to her if she had not been told to look for it. The footprints, however, turned in the direction of the opening, confirming she had found the right place.

It was indeed a tight squeeze to consider entering. The opening was very tall, but terribly narrow. Putting the sword in her right hand, she extended it into the opening ahead of her and then, stepping sideways, began sliding into it herself. It was a little unnerving being pressed into such a tight spot in the darkness. But she comforted herself by occasionally glancing down over her right shoulder to see the footprints still leading the way.

After about 10 feet, the rock walls she was wedging between began to expand outward from one another and she was able to turn and walk normally. She kept the sword in front of her and continued to check for the footprints.

Presently, the space widened into what felt like a large room. From the echoes of water drops here and there, she surmised it to be about 50 feet across and 100 feet deep, with a ceiling at least 100 feet high.

And it felt very haunted. Though there was no sound of any other animate thing, Diakrina could not convince herself she was in any way alone. It was more than the sense of some *presence*, but of *presences*.

At the back of this space, very high—Diakrina judged about 60 feet in the air—glowed a soft, golden light. She walked toward it cautiously.

As she approached the back wall, Diakrina lost direct sight of the glowing object, though she could still see its glow indirectly, because it seemed to be atop some great structure. The structure clearly rose from the floor up toward the high ledge from where the soft glow emanated.

As she came closer to the structure, she raised her sword in order to cast more light. The mouth of a circular staircase opened before her, to the right of the large structure. The stairs wound upward to the left and ascended toward the soft radiating glow. The glow, Diakrina reasoned, must be coming from the Fruit of Immortality.

She walked cautiously up to the stairs and then moved around them to the right in order to look behind. The stairs were about 20 feet from the back wall. By lifting her sword she could see the staircase did not attach to the back wall except at the top where a landing appeared to transverse the 20-foot span. It was then that Diakrina realized that the glow of her sword seemed stronger in this place, allowing her to see a bit farther into the darkness than she had experienced earlier on the path to the fall.

She saw no one but constantly had a sense of the presence of some *things*. Everything in Diakrina was at full attention. She had been told there was a guard, of sorts. And in this haunted space none could doubt it.

Seeing no other way to get to the upper ledge but by the circular stairs, Diakrina approached the wide mouth of the staircase and put her foot on the first step. Instantly the whole structure erupted in a blaze of greenish-white light. For a moment Diakrina was blinded by the intensity of the explosion. When finally her eyes adjusted she could see and feel faint flames of the same greenish-white color coming off every surface of the stairs. The heat was not unbearable and was actually somewhat welcomed by Diakrina, as the realms of Thanatos, in Nekus Canyon, were always bitter cold. Nothing else happened and the light did make it possible to see the whole of the cavern around her.

It was the faces that immediately caught her attention. Starting at about 10 feet above the floor, the walls were carved with a mass of large hideous faces that appeared to be fighting to peer past each other in order to look down upon her. In the eerie light that the greenish-white flames cast on the walls in a flickering manner, she found it very disconcerting that the carved faces seemed at times to be moving or changing expressions. She tried to tell herself it was only the effect of the flames. Yet the more she looked, the more she questioned whether this was true.

As you can imagine, this made the sense of the place being haunted very strong indeed. The carvings were of evil faces, distorted faces, each twisted with inexplicable hatred. The sheer mass of the faces pushed in on Diakrina with a smothering pressure.

But nothing or no one spoke. All was dead silent.

Diakrina turned upon the first step and began slowly ascending the staircase with measured movements. The steps circled its center three time on the way to the landing and Diakrina was somewhat forced to view the space and its carved faces from every angle.

The higher she ascended the more the light from the stairs seemed to animate the faces. But one could never be sure the stone countenances actually moved or just flickered in the shifting light. By the time Diakrina reached the landing, the sense of haunting was overwhelming.

The effect on her now was not that the carved faces themselves were changing, but that behind each face, or perhaps overlaying it—she could never decide which—a living face seemed to be using the carving as a portal out of which to peer at her. In some faint and ephemeral sense the greenish-white light interacted with thousands of ghostly expressions. Still, no sound could be heard except the subtle dripping of water drops somewhere in the space.

Diakrina stepped onto the landing and turned toward the back wall. She immediately felt a bit precarious as there were no railings on this landing and it was only about 4 feet wide and stretched 20 feet out in front of her toward the wall.

And there, on a ledge a little more than waist high, perched a glowing, Golden Fruit about the size of a small melon. Carved into the rock behind the Fruit protruded a large face about three feet tall and two feet wide. Unlike the others, this face did not appear evil or hateful looking. Its eyes were closed and the face had no distinct expression etched into it.

Diakrina moved very slowly toward the glowing Fruit and the carved face. Being 60 feet in the air made the 4-foot wide landing feel like she was walking a narrow plank. The audience of malevolent carved faces all around seemed to taunt her, wishing her to fall.

Finally, she stood in front of the ledge. On it lay a single golden piece of Fruit, glowing with an unearthly radiance. And to the right of the Fruit, about three feet away, was a six-inch round ring of iron a little more than one inch thick, joining three oversized, intricately ornate keys. They looked to be made of some very dense material and, as the Guardian had warned her, were no doubt too heavy to be lifted by any mortal hand.

Diakrina turned her attention back to the Fruit. She had always heard that the Fruit of Immortality, like the fruit of the other tree, would likely be an apple. However, she considered this to be mere myth. But in the moment she approached it, she knew that both what she had heard and what she had concluded about what she heard, were wrong.

This Fruit indeed looked very much like an apple in shape. But that is where the similarities ended. It was much larger, very gold and shiny on its surface, with a radiance coming from its skin. However, somehow, you could see inside it, beyond its surface, where a swirling sphere of light flashed every color of the rainbow, plus some colors Diakrina had never seen.

The Fruit was entrancing! And its real power to cast a spell of desire soon hit Diakrina in the face, for it gave off a fragrance that was immediately and overwhelmingly intoxicating.

Diakrina had never experienced anything so captivating in her whole life. It created an intense inner urge to possess it and become one with it. What the other fruits from the Garden had done to Diakrina upon tasting, this Fruit did to her with a single touch of its fragrance. Something inside Diakrina rose up in ecstatic anticipation of lifting the Fruit to her lips. So powerful was this urge, Diakrina had to literally take hold of her sword with both hands to keep herself from reaching for the Fruit with the wrong intention: an intention, that once unleashed, she knew she would not be able to stop.

Diakrina backed away from the ledge a single step to put the Fruit just beyond reach while she collected herself to carry out her task. She placed her sword in its sheath and lifted the strap of the clear crystal container over her head and shoulder.

She took a deep breath to steady her resolve. And with a prayer for strength to do the right thing, she was about to step back toward the ledge when, without warning, the eyes of the carved face behind the Fruit suddenly opened and came alive with a questioning expression.

"Seeking immortality, my lady?"

The voice startled Diakrina. It had indeed come from the large carved face in front of her. Diakrina ripped her sword from its sheath again and lifted it up between her and the now animated stone countenance. The crimson light of the sword blazed up and mixed with the greenish-white light that glowed all around her.

Diakrina wasn't sure if she *should* engage this *creature* or not. She stood there for several moments looking into the unblinking eyes of the stone face as they searched her countenance. The question she had been asked continued to hang in the air.

Then the face spoke again. "You must be very special to have made it this far. Certainly immortality would be the proper reward for such an achievement."

Diakrina still wasn't sure how to proceed, but decided to address this stone creature. "I have my own reasons for being here. And I am not sure they concern you."

"Not concern ME!" shot back the stone face with an air of indignation. "This great treasure is my charge and I am determined to see someone worthy of it receive its gift—the gift of immortality. Perhaps," and here it paused for effect and lowered its voice in a stressed and descending way on each syllable of the words that followed, *"you are that person."*

Diakrina knew this was the beginning of the temptation: the attempt to get her to succumb and eat the Fruit. She was in no mood to even consider it.

"What you call your charge, I call your scheme. This Fruit is to my kind, now, forbidden fruit. Nothing good can come of eating it. So please do not waste your breath on trying to convince me to do so."

"Far be it from me to try to convince you to do anything," shot back the stone face. "The facts can do that all by themselves. Look at the Fruit and tell me what you see."

In spite of herself, Diakrina looked intently at the glorious Fruit. And once again it cast its spell over her.

"Just to look on it is to desire it," began the face again. "That is clearly how it is created to affect your kind. So, of course, it must be *right* to partake of it or it would not have been designed to have this kind of power over you. Just one bite and you will see, and know so clearly, that this is so.

"A great door lies before you," it continued. "It would be such a shame to pass it by and never look within when such beautiful possibilities certainly lie just beyond it."

Diakrina felt as if she were falling under a spell as the face continued to speak. Then the face behind the Fruit took a deep breath and gave a slow, prolonged exhale over the top of the glowing and living sphere. The fragrance from the Fruit hit Diakrina in the face like a splash of utter joy. It filled her with pleasures and wonders. This was what she had been born desiring!

Just the fragrance of the Fruit was so full of strength and power that it caused Diakrina's body to surge with a kind of vitality she had never felt before. Her very soul seemed to expand and rouse out of a slumber she did not know it was in. Sensations and senses she never dreamed she possessed were unleashed from some prison deep within her. A strength, clearly supernatural, began rushing through every part of her body until she felt as if she could easily leap 100 feet into the air.

The passion and hunger to devour the Fruit was terrible beyond description. Everything in her mind was screaming, "Step back! Step back!" But her body was trying to step forward. The result was a kind of twisting battle as Diakrina strained to control her limbs. She could see her left hand drop the crystal container filled with water and begin reaching toward the Fruit. Fortunately, the Fruit was slightly out of reach because of her having stepped backward from the stone face earlier. But the battle to keep her feet in place, to keep the fatal, forward step from actualizing, began to cause beads of sweat to pop out on Diakrina's forehead. In just a matter of seconds her whole face was dripping with perspiration.

Slowly, hideously, she was being pulled inch by inch toward the Fruit. She was about to take the deadly step. And somehow she knew if she did, she would be doomed to the forbidden act.

She wanted to cry for help, but her voice would not come. And still the pulling continued.

Strangely, the strength she had received from the fragrance of the Fruit was not only being used by her body to struggle toward the Fruit, but it was also being used by some deeper part of Diakrina to resist. She felt like her body was going to be torn into two halves by this tug of war. In utter desperation Diakrina gathered herself trying to find her voice. For she sensed that in the next moment, if no help came, she was lost.

With an effort of terrible proportions, she gasped in a deep breath and forced her vocal cords to obey her. All that came out of her was a loud, desperate cry: "Living OOOOOnnnneeee!"

The sword she still held in her right hand exploded with crimson light and everything around her turned blood red. The pull toward the Fruit stopped so suddenly that Diakrina was thrown backwards onto the landing with such force that she tumbled onto her back and somersaulted over onto her stomach as her body began spinning around and around along and across the landing toward its left edge. She would have launched helplessly over the edge if she had not had the presence of mind—and some of the strength from the vitality of the fragrance of the Fruit still working in her limbs—to quickly drive the point of her sword into the landing and cling to it with both her hands.

The sword sank deep into the stone and she held onto it with superhuman strength. She came to an abrupt and jarring halt with all but her head and shoulders hanging precariously over the edge.

Diakrina hung there for a full fifteen seconds panting in wide-eyed shock. Slowly she came to herself and began pulling her body up and onto the landing. She rolled over onto her back and continued to gasp for air. As she did, she began calming herself down and trying to regain her focus.

After about a minute, she stood up and looked back toward the stone face and the Fruit. On the floor in front of the ledge was the crystal container lying on its side. She pulled her sword, with great effort, out of the stone of the landing, and walking back up to the ledge, and bending over, picked up the container. As she did, she heard the voice of the stone face speak again.

"Now, where were we?" it said in a voice that chilled Diakrina to her bones.

The sword in her hand surged with crimson power again and Diakrina felt a wave of strength go up her arm and fill her body with a resolve that was clearly a gift. With the container in her left hand, and the sword in her right, she jumped instantly to her feet and thrust the sword into the forehead of the stone face.

The sword sank in up to the hilt. The face contorted and a great roar surged from its mouth with such force that Diakrina lost her grip on her sword and fell backward to the surface of the landing. Then a hideous howl began, high, long and descending. It made shivers crawl up and down Diakrina's spine.

But, then, it was over. The countenance of the face went ridged and it became nothing but carved stone again. Diakrina stood up, took the handle of the sword, pulling hard until it came lose and pulled free of the stone.

She then looked down on the Fruit and, feeling the same sense of desire beginning to come over her again, realized she needed to work quickly. She determined she could not trust herself to touch the Fruit: it was far too risky.

She sheathed her sword and then removed the cap from the container. She quickly drank long and hard from it until all the water was gone. This, in fact, helped her look away from the Fruit and focus, if only for a moment, on something else.

Then turning the crystal container upside down, she approached the ledge and placed the container's mouth onto the top of the Fruit. The light from the Fruit filled the container and made it easy for her to see the letters carved on its inner surface. She turned her head sideways so she could read the inscription. Then gathering all her resolve she spoke firmly and loudly the word, "*Pepoithos!*"

The Fruit began to glow ever so slightly brighter for several moments. Then, as Diakrina watched, it gradually lifted from the ledge and passed into the crystal container. The mouth of the container was not large enough for the Fruit of Immortality to pass through it naturally, as it was only a small opening made for drinking. But somehow, defying any natural laws of physics, the Fruit slowly rose and passed through the container itself until it was inside.

Diakrina turned the crystal container upright and the fragrance of the Fruit coming from the opening hit her once again. She shook her head to try to clear it and quickly placed the cap back over the opening. She lifted the strap over her left shoulder and head and allowed the container to swing around somewhat behind her for carrying.

When Diakrina turned around, the walls of the room erupted into greenish-white flames as the faces sprang to life. Diakrina instinctually pulled her sword out again not having any idea what might happen next. It was then she heard hissing, whispering voices by the thousands begin chanting:

"The scheme has come to pain,
The temptation has been slain,
Crush! Crush! Or all is vain."

As this chanting continued the whole cavern shook and rumbled with deep grating sounds. The two sidewalls of the haunted space were moving, shudder by shudder, rumble by rumble, toward each other. Diakrina stared in disbelief trying to put what was happening into context.

Then it hit her: the cavern was closing in on her to prevent her escape. It was going to crush her before she could get down the spiral stairs and exit at the far end where she had entered.

Diakrina burst into action and ran across the landing toward the circular stairs, then down them as fast as her legs would carry her. With every circle of the stairs she could see the walls moving ever closer and the faces of the walls glaring down on her like coliseum spectators jeering at a victim about to be devoured by lions.

And all the while, the mantra continued and grew louder. However the chant had been shortened to its last line intoned over and over:

"Crush! Crush! Or all is vain.
Crush! Crush! Or all is vain.
Crush! Crush! Or all is vain."

When Diakrina finally reached the bottom of the stairs she rushed out onto the cavern floor in an all-out sprint. What concerned her most was that the opening through which she had come was not perfectly center of the cavern. It was slightly closer to the right-hand wall, and that wall was quickly moving toward the exit. If she didn't make it in time she would be trapped between the crushing walls.

By the time she was still about 30 feet from the exit, the cavern had been pinched into a 20-foot wide corridor. Judging her speed and the pace of the advancing walls, she kept telling herself, "It will be close! It will be close!" but she thought she could make it.

That is, until two fierce looking four-legged beasts materialized out of the advancing walls between her and the exit. They were about the size of African elephants and looked like a cross between a very large saber toothed tiger and a wolf. They roared, revealing gaping jaws full of savage teeth fronted by huge saber-like fangs.

Diakrina's natural reaction would have been to pull up short at the sight of these monsters and run in utter terror away from them, which would have meant never reaching the exit in time. But as the beasts were materializing from the walls, Diakrina heard a *whisper* surround her and enclose her so that the chanting was drowned out. The voice was melodic, calm and reassuring:

*"Don't stop, Diakrina! Keep running toward the exit. Run straight toward the beast on your right, the one which is directly between you and the opening. When its jaws are nearly on you, thrust your sword straight into the roof of it mouth as it leaps."*

In a flash, in her mind's eye, she saw a detailed, move-by-move, frame-by-frame sequence of pictures of her doing exactly what she had been told to do. Diakrina later said it was the strangest thing to experience in a split-second something like a slow-motion, step-by-step demonstration of what to do with wild beasts nearly on top of her.

So, without even a pause, she kept sprinting and pulled the bunt of the sword handle up close to her stomach with the crimson blade pointed forward and slightly up. She had just obtained this position while still in an all-out charge herself, when the fierce creature leapt through the air toward her with an ear-splitting roar blasting from its bared teeth.

Diakrina searched with her eyes for the roof of its mouth and then, instinctually adjusting for both her speed and the creatures, she gave a loud cry and thrust the sword upward as she too leapt into the air to meet its attack.

Both the sword point and the mouth of the beast arrived at the same point in space at the same time. The sword cut through the beast's head like a hot knife through butter. At the same moment, as she had been shown, Diakrina twisted the sword clockwise with her hand and arm and then straightened her arm in such a fashion that she could use the weight of the great creature to spin herself off to the right of its charging mass by using the handle as a point of leverage.

Still, the right side of the creature slammed into Diakrina's back and sent her catapulting toward the right-hand wall. And since she held tightly to her sword handle—as she had been shown to do—even though her arm was pulled out and up behind her by the spinning movement, the force of the sword was now turned toward the wall as she pulled it in a striking motion over her head.

This resulted in completely severing the top of the beast's head from its body. And as her sword came striking down in front of her, while she was flying through the air toward the advancing barrier, the eyes and upper head of the beast were propelled ahead of her and splattered with a thud against the cavern wall.

This move had, at the same time, put the airborne body of this monster between her and the other creature which had been on Diakrina's left. Diakrina hit the wall hard and fell to the cavern floor. She quickly scrambled to her feet and began running along the wall toward what remained of the exit. She could hear the other beast's claws digging into the cavern floor as it was reversing its course to pursue her. But the body of the decapitated beast slammed into it and sent it sprawling onto its back.

The beast was up in a flash trying to scramble over the carcass between them in order to catch her in time. But Diakrina was no longer focused on this creature. If she did not make it through the very thin opening just in front of her before it closed, it would hardly matter whether the beast killed her or the walls crushed her: either way she was doomed.

She was still 15 feet away from the opening and running hard, but it had already narrowed to that point that she feared not being able to fit through it. Three long strides later she leaped toward what was left of the exit, turned her body sideways in midair with her right hand and sword stretched out in front and her left hand flung straight behind, and hit the opening dead center. The moving wall on her right slid like course sandpaper down the back of her calves as she fell into the narrow passage that led back out to the main cavern.

While still lying on the passage floor, she turned and looked behind her to see the jaws of the second creature gaping through a one-foot-wide opening as it gave one last horrifying roar and pulled its nose back just before the opening could crush it.

Diakrina had too much adrenaline in her system to be still. She got up, moved as quickly as she could through the narrowing passage, and squeezed out through the tiny crevice into the larger cavern that she had traveled from below the rim of Nekus Fall.

Instead of turning right, back toward the fall, she—without stopping—made a sharp left and began running up the inclining cave with her sword stretched out in front of her so she could see. For at least twenty minutes she ran as fast as the sword's illumination would allow her to go. Up and down, and around large piles of boulders and deep depressions she ran, scampering like a mountain goat; and always gaining altitude.

Finally, out of breath, she slowed down and then came to a stop. Turning around she listened intently behind her to see if she could detect any sounds of pursuit. She heard nothing as she stood there panting for several minutes. Her body literally quivered all over from the surge of adrenaline.

Noticing a nearby rock about three feet high, she sat down to rest for a few moments and tried to calm herself. As her body began to relax, she noticed a soft glow behind her. It startled her and she turned around, but no one was there and the glow turned with her and stayed behind her. It was, of course, the Golden Fruit of Immortality softly shining through the crystal container.

Lifting the strap, she pulled the container around in front of her. There in the cavern this Fruit of unearthly beauty cast a welcome glow to add to the sword's illumination. Even though no fragrance escaped the sealed container, just the sight of the Fruit was overpowering.

Diakrina found herself looking longingly at it, turning the container from side to side so as to examine every contour. She became lost for several minutes just staring at its swirling color. Mesmerized, she could not take her eyes off the beautiful object.

She lifted it up close to her face as if hoping to catch just a small hint of its fragrance. It was then her sword flashed a bright crimson burst, which startled Diakrina out of her trance.

She looked down at the blade still pulsing very brightly. Then looking up toward the surface, which she knew was up above her somewhere, she said out loud with a sense of gratitude, "Thank you!" and pulled on the strap until the container was once again behind her and out of her sight.

## CHAPTER EIGHTEEN

# The BEASTS of PARANOIA

Rising from her resting place, Diakrina continued climbing upward toward what she hoped would be the surface, until at last she came to a level place. She had not gone far on this plateau when she abruptly collided with a clear, crystal wall. It seemed, on inspection, to be like the ones she had passed through as she ascended up the stairs into the inner realms of Thanatos on the far side of the canyon.

Diakrina pushed against the wall, but it refused to give way. Searching for a way around it, she found none, and so she continued pushing against it in various places with all her strength, becoming increasingly frustrated at the seemingly impossible obstacle. She had nearly lost her temper when once again she remembered the footprints. "How easily," she thought, "I resort to my own attempts to find a way through instead of remembering to look for guidance."

She placed her sword out in front of her and at once a glowing footprint appeared. She followed it, and then the next and the next as they led her far to the right along the clear wall. When she came up against the rock wall of the cavern, a small light began to glow in front of her. As the glow gradually increased, Diakrina traced it to its source, and there, in a small crevice in the cavern wall about waist high next to the clear barrier, lay a glowing open book.

As she approached the book to look at it, a glowing page tore loose and fluttered toward her. It floated in the air in front of her until she slowly reached out her hand to take hold of it. Pulling it toward her and looking at the page glowing warmly in her hand, she suddenly saw her life pass before her eyes. Some of it was her past. But some of it was adventures and days she had not yet experienced. But it passed so quickly she could learn little from it other than the fact that it was about her.

But the most overwhelming sensation that came over her was an awareness that the page was only a single passage from a greater and more profound story. Her story did not make any sense by itself. It was like finding a single passage from some great masterpiece but being denied the rest of the great adventure.

The desire to know the rest of the story—before and after her part of it—became strong. For the first time in her life it was not her own story that mattered most. Somehow she knew—and knew emphatically—that her own story derived its value from its context within the whole of a greater story. Apart from the greater story, her story had no lasting meaning.

As she held the page, looking into its drama, she heard the distinct and unmistakable voice of Revelation: "Fold this page and place it in your garment. You will need it at the end of your quest." Then the voice added, "Then, holding your sword in both hands, approach the barrier and speak the word, 'ZOE.' Then press the sword into the wall and follow it through."

Diakrina looked thoughtfully at the page for a moment, folded it neatly and placed it inside her grass tunic in the folds above where her belt and cord passed tightly around her waist. Then, holding her sword in both hands, she pointed it toward the transparent barrier and said loudly, "ZOE!" As she pressed the tip of the sword against the clear wall, it passed through, but the real test would come, she knew, when her body contacted the wall.

As her hands touched the wall, a warmth of energy from the sword passed into her fingers and her hands slowly began to pass through the barrier as though it were liquid. As she pushed forward, her whole body began to pulse with energy so that she easily pressed into the now-supple barrier.

As before, the wall felt icy cold and chilled her to her bones. She pushed through for several seconds until she was fully encased in the chilly substance. The wall was thicker than she remembered from the stone steps into the realm of Thanatos, and it took her more than 10 seconds to push through to the other side.

When at last she stood beyond the ice-cold barrier, she blinked several times as light filled her eyes. The light, though not bright, was still temporarily painful as she had been so long in the dark. After nearly a minute, as her pupils adjusted, Diakrina discovered that she was standing in a shallow cave mouth, and just beyond it the light from a sunrise was splashing over a canyon that stretched out in front of her.

She stepped from the shallow cavern and took several paces onto the canyon floor. About 35 feet from the opening, the warmth of morning sunlight hit her back as the sunrise peeked over the canyon wall behind her and cast long, soft, westward shadows down the narrow length of the canyon in front of her. The canyon was framed on each side by nearly vertical walls of rock that ascended, as far as Diakrina could estimate, over two thousand feet into the air.

Diakrina was very tired. She found a rock not far from the cavern mouth and sat down for a few moments to watch the growing light of the blessed dawn. As the light increased, a kind of giddiness—a relieved, dancing joy—rose up inside her.

The giddy, dancing joy was not superficial, however. It ascended upward into a sacred delight as her whole body and soul drank in the glory of the light. Never had a sunrise seemed so beautiful. She turned her head around toward the east and found that the place where she had exited came out of a small outcropping about 20-feet high, not at the edge as she had suspected, but in the middle of the canyon floor.

Beyond this outcropping, the canyon stretched eastward toward the sun. The light of the dawning day seemed to roll at Diakrina like waves of life washing away the suffocating darkness of the preceding hours. She stood and stretched out her arms toward it and began to drink in the sunrise. With the sunshine came something greater and more important than mere physical light, and it filled her soul with a fresh breeze that allowed her to breathe once again with hope.

"Hope, yes, hope! Hope!" she found herself saying to no one in particular. That is what came flooding over her with the dawn. Where she had been, save for the hope given her by the promise of the sword, hope was totally missing.

It quickly occurred to her that she had always taken for granted—and therefore, it had gone unnoticed—the hope that flooded life in the realms of the living. It was an atmosphere one breathed and never gave a second thought.

But she had been, like an astronaut, where this atmosphere of hope was missing and could not be freely inhaled. She now realized the sword, and the footprints it revealed, had been her oxygen supply. Without it she would have suffocated in the realms of death, never to escape.

She stood with her face toward the rising sun for nearly an hour as it rose higher into the sky. She could not get enough of its physical warmth or breathe in too much of the atmosphere of hope that pressed, now palpably, upon her. She could feel strength and health returning to her whole body.

She would probably have continued for several more hours simply drinking in the warmth of the morning if she had not suddenly heard what sounded like a stampede of large animals behind her. Diakrina spun quickly around toward the west as the crescendo of the thunderous sound sweeping toward her shattered the morning calm.

Two huge, donut-shaped rings, like enormous black smoke rings, yet heavier and more solid, raced toward her across the canyon floor, expanding as they came. She just had time to hit the ground as they passed over her, missing her by only inches.

As they rolled over her, Diakrina felt an ice-cold wave of air pass across her back. She jumped to her feet and looked down the canyon in the direction from which the two black rings had come. Not far down the canyon, now made visible by the increase of sunlight, stood two huge cobra-like serpents. They stood over 50 feet high each and were glaring at Diakrina.

While the two hooded heads swayed 50 feet in the air, only about 10 feet of the length of their lower bodies was visible. The rest of their bodies were enveloped in a black mist. From the part Diakrina could see, she estimated that the serpents' bodies must be about 10 feet in diameter.

They appeared parallel with each other, with a little over a 130 feet between them, and were both looking directly at Diakrina as if they had just become aware of her presence with the growing light. Evidently realizing she had escaped the two dark circles, they made a spitting motion toward Diakrina and two more black, rolling rings formed in the air and began to expand toward her.

These circles of darkness, like rings of smoke, seemed to dissolve light as they expanded outward toward Diakrina. And their approach—she now thought—sounded like an oncoming locomotive in all its fury.

Not knowing what else to do, she took her sword in both hands and crouched in a bracing stance waiting for the force of the rings to hit her. And hit her they did.

Like the force of a bomb blast, the first ring swept over and around her, knocking her from her feet and up against a rock about 10 feet behind her. Immediately Diakrina could feel the all-too-familiar-cold of the darkness as the ring swept around her.

Then the second ring hit and the bitter cold blackness swept her up and threw her forcefully against some rocks a little farther back. As it rolled over her, she not only felt its bitter cold sucking away the warmth of the morning sunlight, she also felt a thick, sticky black substance splash over her and soak her from head to foot. With it came an instant feeling of cold panic soaking into her. It seemed to be seeping deep into her very being, and her head began to spin with a maddened, irrational terror.

Whatever this substance was that came with this second rolling ring of blackness, it quickly changed Diakrina. All she wanted to do now was run, but she couldn't.

At the same time the terror began to course through her veins, she felt a strong, almost irresistible force pulling her toward the two serpents. She was turned around in her tracks and the eyes of the serpents were powerfully drawing her towards them.

She turned away from the beasts and forced herself to run in the opposite direction. To do so, she had to fight constantly the mesmerizing pull toward the serpents and the terrible panic that was taking possession of her. She heard the shattering roar of what had to be two more dark rings erupting from the mouths of the serpents behind her. Diakrina let out a scream of manic determination against the panic-filled force that was drawing her toward the serpents, and ran toward the sun as fast as her legs could carry her.

But she had gone no more than 40 yards when the first ring of blackness rolled so close to her that it blasted her to the ground onto her face. The next black ring rolled over her, and once again she was splashed with the sticky black spray that filled her soul with panic.

Diakrina's eyes were now wild with fear, and she picked herself up and ran toward the sun as fast as she could go. She heard another set of rings coming and she quickened her pace in crazed paranoia. After about 100 yards, she came to a very large rock to her right that rose high into the air from the canyon floor. She ran past it and then, darting to the right, ran behind it as she felt the cold sweep of the first black ring rush past her.

The shelter of the rock kept the ring from impacting her, and she pressed her back up against the rock's backside and watched as a second black ring rolled past splashing the tarry goo on everything before it. Diakrina stared in wide-eyed terror as it rolled on down the canyon toward the sun and toward the main part of Nekus canyon.

With a moment's reprieve she took note that she was covered in the sticky spray. It soaked her hair and skin. She tried to pull it off, but it was like trying to wipe off a thick covering of sticky honey. She was frantic to get the cursed tar off, but there was nothing she could do to remove it. She could feel it soaking into her bones. And as it did, she felt a near irresistible terror starting to fill her stomach and bowels with a trembling weakness.

She was sick all over. Nausea turned her stomach upside down, and she began dry heaving with nearly every breath. When finally her convulsing stomach subsided, she curled up in a fetal position, swaying back and forth like a frightened child behind the great rock.

She sat, continuing to hold herself for several minutes as she tried to get a grip on herself and figure out what had happened to her and to the beautiful morning. The sun still shone with delicious warmth, but she could find no joy or assurance in it. The panic that was soaking into her distorted everything around her until the morning no longer seemed to offer any promise of hope or life.

Nothing was different with the morning, but everything was different with Diakrina. This sticky black bile from the beasts had changed everything.

As Diakrina rocked back and forth, she increasingly fought to keep control of her perception and will. She blanked-out for a few seconds—like a person driving a car and fighting a severe need to sleep—and then came forcefully awake to discover with horror that she had risen to her feet and was starting to take a few steps from behind the rock and toward the serpents.

Coming to, she clawed her way back behind the boulder and forced herself to retreat farther behind the rock than before. But once again she lost consciousness long enough to wake up again, a few steps back toward the edge of the great boulder. She retreated again and forced her back up against the rock trying to fight the blurring of reality that continued to seek to master her.

When this happened the third time, she shook herself awake, and retreating, quickly took her sword from its sheath. She knelt down and rammed the point of her sword deep into the rocky floor of the canyon, just inches from the rock she'd been hiding behind. The blade flashed bright red and seemed to melt its way into the canyon floor until only about a foot of it protruded up from the ground. Sitting down with her back to the rock and her side tight up against the sword handle, she quickly unfastened her belt, wrapped it around the sword just below the hilt, secured it firmly around her waist and buckled it tightly. When she had no sooner done so, she lost consciousness again.

She started back to awareness, likely only a few seconds later, to find herself twisted and contorted in a struggling attempt to stand up, but her makeshift tether had held. She righted her position and checked to make sure the belt was firmly in place just before her eyes rolled back in their sockets and she lost consciousness again.

Once more, she awoke to find herself straining at the belt. And once again, she squared herself against the rock and made sure of her restraint. This happened over and over again until Diakrina lost count.

But then, awakening, she saw him. He came walking toward her and he still shone as bright as the blazing sun in the daylight around her. "Revelation!" she shouted and tried to jump to her feet only to realize she could not move.

The man of moving flames of white, gold and blue fire smiled and opened his arms toward Diakrina. "Come!" he said with a voice that shook the canyon. And like a frightened child, she quickly unbuckled herself and ran into his arms.

As she did, she did not find the man she expected. Instead, she was engulfed in white, gold and blue flames that licked at her whole body. Instantly, she could feel the panic being pulled out of her as the foul black substance was burned from her skin and soul without the slightest sense of pain.

Diakrina turned in circles within the blazing fire that surrounded her and wondered where Revelation had gone. But then, she heard his voice and realized he was all around her.

"I see you have encountered the Serpents of Paranoia," said Revelation in a very matter-of-fact way.

"Is that what you call them?" asked Diakrina.

"It is a proper name for them," answered Revelation.

Then, suddenly, the flames that surrounded her vanished and Revelation, himself, stood before her. "You are going the wrong way, Diakrina," he said looking deep into her eyes. "The spring where Strateia waits for you is beyond the beasts and the western mouth of this canyon. The serpents are driving you back toward Nekus."

Diakrina did not know how to answer. The panic that had filled her only a few moments before was gone. But even the memory of it made her shudder still.

"It seemed I could not help myself. The rolling blackness from those serpents covered me, inside and out, with terror." Then recovering herself enough to once again become inquisitive, Diakrina asked, "What kind of beasts are these Serpents of Paranoia?"

"They are, as their name implies, beasts of fear and terror. They are always associated with death for those of your race," answered Revelation.

"But why now?" countered Diakrina. "I have come out of the heart of Nekus Canyon and the realms of Thanatos. Shouldn't I meet such creatures of fear going in, not coming out?"

"But you did meet them, Diakrina," said Revelation as he raised one flaming eyebrow at her with an expression which said, *"Don't you remember?"* "They came on you the moment Strateia left you at the mouth of Nekus. You found safety from them by running to the shelter of the Altar of Trust."

Diakrina's eyes widened with the remembering. "You mean that these towering serpents were what was chasing me and leaping from the rocks like giant tigers as I ran toward the Altar?"

"Yes, but they were not towering serpents then. They were more like what you would call saber toothed tigers the size of African elephants," interjected Revelation.

The expression on Diakrina's face was a wordless question: "How?"

Revelation continued: "The Serpents of Paranoia have a thousand and more forms. They morph to the circumstances and to their intended victim. They feed on fear and so, like an animal that feeds on blood, they slash at their victim's soul with their lying threats, in order to cause their victim to bleed fear for them to feed on.

"Your sword and the refuge of the Altar saved you at the first meeting. They would have dissolved you to pure terror in the darkness of Nekus if you had not run to the Altar of Trust. If you had left the Altar without committing the torch to me, they would have used the flame of your self-reliance to manifest themselves to you in such terrible forms that the life in you would have been dissolved into manic terror, and you would have entered the realms of Thanatos like a dried-up corpse. Those who come to Thanatos sucked dry of life by the terrors of the Serpents of Paranoia are cast into his river and carried over the second, nearly endless, Fall of Nekus.

"You mean these are the beasts of Nekus that Strateia told me were too fearful for me to look upon and survive?"

"Yes," answered Revelation. "There are times when trust is the only means of sight that can save you. And if the Living One calls you to trust Him because He has put you into darkness, He is teaching you how to use the eyes of your heart.

"It was not just your physical eyes that saw the crimson footprints that led you through Nekus. It took more. Physical eyes do not understand. It is the eyes of your heart that believed and trusted His leadership.

"Your vow of faith at the Altar, and your act of faith in committing the torch, gave you eyes of trust by which to see Him and trust Him. By means of that trust He could lead you through the beasts without harm and bring you out of the realms of Thanatos."

Revelation paused and then asked Diakrina, "Do you not remember the instructions of the prophet on the wall at the Altar of Trust?"

"Yes, I do. They are seared into my mind's eye," answered Diakrina. And with that she began to quote:

*"Who among you fears the Lord and obeys the word of His servant?*
*Let him who walks in the dark, who has no light,*
*trust in the Name of the Lord and rely on his God.*
*But now, all you who light fires and provide yourselves with flaming torches,*
*go, walk in the light of the fires and of the torches you have set ablaze.*
*This is what you shall receive from My hand:*
*You will lie down in torment."*

"You remember well, Diakrina," said Revelation with approval. "And now your adventure of trust has opened the eyes of your heart wider so that you now *see* the words of the prophet with greater discernment and understanding."

Diakrina turned back toward the beasts that were beyond the great rock. "I am no longer in darkness, Revelation. The Living One has led me to sunlight again. I now see these great serpents, and I seem to be powerless against them. Their black, rolling rings of darkness soak my soul with terror so that I cannot fight them. What am I to do?"

"You are to have the eyes of your heart made wider, still," answered Revelation with a knowing smile. "Do you not realize, Diakrina, that you passed through these terrible beasts without harm even though they were constantly with you in the darkness of Nekus?"

"Yes, I know that now," said Diakrina even as the thought of it made a wave of horror run down her spine. "But they are *very visible* at present and I have no ignorance of them to keep their terror from overtaking me. How will I fight them in the light of day?"

"You will fight them by faith and knowledge—truth, if you please—Diakrina. You must come to understand in the light what you have come to know in your heart because you have walked in trust with the Living One in the darkness." Then pausing for only a moment as he allowed Diakrina to digest mentally all he had just said, Revelation added, "Let me ask you some questions, and I think all will be plain.

"Why do you believe the beasts could not dissolve you to terror to devour you while you were in Nekus?"

"Well, I now know that it was the Living One, Himself, who was with me," answered Diakrina.

"That is true, *and it is true still*," confirmed Revelation with strong stress on the last phrase. "And because you trusted Him instead of your own perception and wisdom, these beasts could not effectively generate a great and consuming fear in you because the power of their lies, through their threatening forms, was obscured. You felt their presence and, therefore, felt fear in the darkness of Nekus. Do you remember the feeling of being caught in the coils of a great serpent as the darkness seemed to tighten around you?"

"Yes! And I was out of my mind with terror!"

"But this fear was small compared to what they could have generated in you. If they had had the door of your own perception—your self-reliance—to capture your mind and soul with their many threatening forms, you would have been lost; all would have been lost."

Revelation paused for a moment to allow his words to sink in. Then he continued.

"Diakrina, when they roar and bare their fangs here, you hear and see their threats and you believe them. But, what is the truth? Do they really have any power over you that does not come from your fear of them?"

Diakrina's eyes widened as this question hit home. Indeed, she found these questions were beginning to frame in her a new attitude toward the serpents. She began to understand things in a totally new light. Revelation continued, giving answers to his questions.

"The Living One conquered these serpents. And all who have placed their trust in His victory have His victory and power over these serpents given to them. If you hold to this truth and refuse to believe their threats, they lose every foothold within you.

"But this truth will do you no good if you do not believe it to be true. If they can make you endorse their lying threats by a response of fear, they will feed on you and gain a foothold to suck life from your soul.

"The proof that what I am telling you is true is that they could not destroy you when you could not see and believe their threats. Now, knowing this truth, they cannot destroy you even if you see their threats, if you know—and therefore, trust—that their threats are a lie. As long as you confess your faith in the Living One's victory over them, and believe that He has given that victory to you if you trust in Him, they have no power over you. His conquest is your victory. And it is revealed and confirmed to you both by my words and by your passage of trust through Nekus."

And then, looking very serious indeed, Revelation began to glow with a brilliance that made Diakrina have to shield her eyes as he said in a voice that shook the canyon floor:

"I AM REVELATION. I HAVE COME TO GIVE YOU HIS WORD OF TRUTH. HE IS THE WORD, AND AS THE WORD HE IS THE WAY, HE IS THE TRUTH, HE IS THE LIFE! BY TRUSTING HIM, YOU SHALL NEVER BE PUT TO SHAME AND SHALL NEVER KNOW DEFEAT THAT HE CANNOT TURN INTO VICTORY. HIS VICTORY IS ALL THERE IS. THERE WILL SOON BE NOTHING OTHER!"

Diakrina's eyes widened even as she had to cover them from the surging brilliance of Revelation. The power and meaning of his words hit deep in the very core of her being: they changed her.

Revelation then reached inside some kind of fold in his flaming garments of light and pulled from it a burning torch: the very torch Diakrina had entrusted to him at the Altar on the other side of Nekus.

"Diakrina, I will now give back to you what you entrusted to me. For what you lose by trusting Him, you keep forever in a new transcendent form."

Diakrina was about to ask why she should need a torch in this sunlit canyon, when the torch in Revelation's hand began to burn very brightly as two descending arcs of light formed downward toward the base of the torch from the flame at the top. As Diakrina watched, the arcs came together at the bottom of the torch. Then the circle of flames which resulted began to grow outward until it was a flaming disk about three feet in diameter.

Then the flames began filling in the circle until Revelation was holding a burning shield, which blazed with blue, gold and white flames like those that composed the features of Revelation, himself. And just like the living, burning flames compose Revelation, the flames seemed to compose the very structure of the shield.

On the shield's face two symbols formed in crimson red. They were A and Ω, side by side; the first and last letters of the Greek alphabet. Diakrina would learn later that these two symbols formed one of the names of the Living One, which declared His victory over evil and all death: the realms of Thanatos. This name declares that He is the first and the last and, therefore, Master over everything in between.

Revelation moved toward her, took hold of the top of the shield and turned it around to reveal a retainer strap for her left arm to pass through and, on its right side, a wooden handle for her left hand to grasp as she held the shield. It was clear that the wood of the torch had become the handle by which the shield was to be held.

"Your trust—your faith—has become your shield. For in trusting you have come to illumination and understanding that can penetrate beyond what is merely seen by your physical eyes. By it you can extinguish all the fiery lies of the evil one who uses the Serpents of Paranoia against you. This shield is your trust in the Living One and your faith in the words of truth that I, Revelation, have brought to you, as His messenger. Your faith in Him overcomes the kingdom of the Severed Lands.

"Its weapons against you are lies and fears. His shield, delivered into your hand, is faith and understanding, which have been activated by your choices of trust. For it is He who works in you, Diakrina, both to will—to choose—and to act on the choice, when it is according to His purposes for you, which will become your future pleasures."

Diakrina took the flaming shield by putting her left arm through the strap and then grasping the wooden handle with her left hand. There was no sense of heat coming from the shield. The flames of light blazed on its outer side but no heat came toward her.

Once she had the shield on her arm, the brilliance of Revelation began to grow again until Diakrina could no longer look directly at him.

"The cool spring in the valley awaits you, Diakrina," came the voice of Revelation from the blazing light that had grown to a blinding oval of blue, gold and white flames that shone like the sun.

"Take the shield and your sword and face the fears that lie between you and your destiny," came a clear command. "For the curse you carry in the Fruit of Immortality is an immortal one. You must dissolve this curse for mankind with His aid. Do not give in to fear!"

And with a flash of blinding light, Revelation was gone.

CHAPTER NINETEEN

# The PATH BETWEEN FEARS

Diakrina stood in her place for about a minute trying to take in the fact that Revelation had left and she was alone again with the awful serpents towering 50 feet over her path forward. She knew she could not stay where she was, for she had to get to the spring where Strateia waited for her.

And, of course, this meant she had to venture from the protection of the rock into the protection of the truth that had been given to her by Revelation. The memory came forcefully over her of the panic that had soaked her to the core of her soul and had made her nauseous with terror and irrational fears.

She hesitated and backed up to the rock. But it was clear she could not stay here. She gave herself a stiff talking to as she rehearsed the truths Revelation had taught her only moments before.

Finally, she checked to see that the crystal container with the Immortal Fruit was secured on the strap over her shoulder so that it was protected as it rested in the middle of her back, and that the page torn from the glowing book still nested safely in her tunic, secured by the cord around her waist and her sheath belt. Then, with a clear and determined resolve to trust what she knew deep within to be true, she pulled her sword from the canyon floor and stepped slowly out from behind the great rock.

Immediately the two serpents spit rings of rolling darkness that came expanding toward her with such thunder they made the ground quake. She raised her new piece of armor, and the shield glowed ever and ever brighter as the rings of blackness bore down on her.

Without warning, just before the rings of blackness hit her, a blazing wall of white, gold and blue light burst out from the shield. The light shot up to the sky, down to the ground and out to her right and left as far as her eyes could see.

The expanding rings of blackness hit the wall of light and Diakrina felt the impact of the cold blast quenched by the light and power coming from the shield. The fact that the rings had not soaked her with the black pitch-like substance that had before drenched her in panic and terror gave Diakrina a firm grip on her newfound boldness.

Even though the light-wall from the shield disappeared immediately, she continued to walk forward with the shield before her and her sword held tightly in her hand. The serpents turned fully toward her and spit out two larger rings of blackness that echoed terribly in the canyon like a hundred locomotives.

Again, the expanding, rolling circles of blackness came racing toward Diakrina. She braced herself with the shield held out in front of her; and once again the force of the cold blackness hitting her was met and repelled by an exploding wall of blinding light. A deep bone-jarring impact struck Diakrina, but the wall of cold darkness shattered into a spray of grey steam.

Recovering from the slamming concussion, Diakrina ever so slowly continued toward the serpents. They did not spit, now, but watched her every movement as she came closer and closer. Their unblinking eyes shown with a sickening, greenish light.

As she came within about 50 yards of the serpents, their features became most distinct. They were like overgrown cobras. The cold, pale green light shining from their small, fierce eyes gave them a demonic quality that was quite unnerving.

Diakrina was puzzled as to why they did not charge at her as they were quite intent on her every movement and clearly wished to stop her. But for some reason they remained in their places, side by side, a little over 130 feet apart. Both faced her and seemed to be waiting for her to come closer.

Diakrina felt very small and vulnerable as she came nearer and nearer to the towering beasts. She could feel fear, like a liquid atmosphere, surrounding these creatures. It pressed against her shield as she pushed ever closer. She still could not see the lower 40 feet of the serpents as the black mist swirled around them.

She was soon within almost striking distance of the serpents and wondered why they did not move to strike. Surely it would take only the slightest maneuvering on their part to come within reach of her. And of course, she was still terrified at the prospect of their dark rolling rings hitting her at blunt-force range. It might be more than she could withstand, even with her fiery shield.

But though the serpents swayed back and forth, they never moved toward her. It was almost as if they couldn't move—as if they were fixed in place. But if so, how and why?

Not being able to see through the black mist that surrounded them made it impossible for her to answer this question. But her mind tried to form all kinds of reasons for this strange and inexplicable behavior.

Diakrina held the shield and sword in front of her and stood studying the two creatures for a long time. They continued to be obsessed with her, swaying rhythmically and never taking their eyes off her, but they never moved forward.

At last, Diakrina realized she needed to do something. She could not stand here staring at them all day. She was afraid to proceed, but nothing but death lay behind her. She had no choice: *she had to move forward.* Her path led straight between them! But how?

Standing there behind the new shield and gripping her sword, while her mind searched for some possible solution, she remembered how, outside the cave, her sword had freed her when the Mist had tried to drag her in. She also remembered how her sword, and the sword of Strateia, had slain the Mist in the cave.

Diakrina looked down at the crimson blade as it pulsed slowly.

"If only I could get close enough to use the sword on that black mist, perhaps I could find out why these beasts are not moving toward me," she finally said out loud to no one but herself.

As if responding to her words, her sword suddenly glowed brighter and pulsed very rapidly. Diakrina stared at the sword wondering what this response could mean. Again she spoke aloud, "Should I attack the black mist with the sword?"

The sword flashed a brilliant crimson and the pulsing increased into a steady blaze. Diakrina felt sure this was a confirmation. She needed to attack the mist.

But how? Attacking the mist would mean moving even closer to the serpents. So close, in fact, she'd likely be easily within their reach. But then, she thought, was she not already in their reach? Their primary weapon seemed to be the rolling black rings which they could, presumably, spit at her at any moment.

Yet, looking up at the towering serpents once again, she tried to talk herself out of doing such a risky thing as moving any nearer to them. Then again, she really had no choice but to move forward, though the path ahead was covered with the black mist.

It was then she thought of something. The distance between the two serpents had not changed all the time she had been observing them. There was, as best she could determine, a space between them slightly greater than the height of the two serpents combined: about 130 feet. They never moved closer to each other. Could it be that they couldn't? And if so, why?

She tried to imagine what could be hidden in the mist that would keep these two serpents fixed in place. Something was keeping them from charging her—though they clearly seemed to want to do so. It appeared they could not move toward each other but were restrained a fixed distance apart.

Then a thought struck her and she spoke out loud again before she realized what she had done, "Are they *indeed* restrained somehow?"

The shield suddenly blazed up in white, gold and blue flames as if to join the sword in giving a positive response to her question. And instantly, she knew what she had to do.

Bracing herself to this possible insight, and realizing there was really no option, Diakrina began walking, ever so slowly, toward the very middle of the space between the serpents where the black mist swirled on the canyon floor. The two serpents turned inward toward her and began stretching out their hooded heads. But they still did not move forward with their whole bodies.

As she got closer to the wall of black mist, the serpents both quickly spit at her and two black, swirling rings raced toward her, now coming from both sides at once. Diakrina lifted the shield on her left and the sword on her right in a defensive motion. White, blue and gold light exploded on her left and crimson light exploded on her right, and the two rings simply vaporized with a sizzle.

For a moment, Diakrina wanted to retreat. But just then her eyes fell on a faint crimson footprint just ahead of her, pointing directly into the black mist between the two serpents. This was all the confirmation she needed, and Diakrina—with shield in left hand and sword in right—ran as fast as she could in the trail of glowing footprints.

The mist retreated before the blazing lights she carried and cleared a path nearly 20 feet wide ahead of her. As she ran, she could see a clearing beyond the mist some 100 yards ahead, and a new burst of optimism raced through her.

Suddenly, the massive head of a serpent crashed through the dark mist from the right of the path, and Diakrina jumped left to avoid the swiping slash of two fierce fangs, which sprayed poison on the ground around her. No longer in the center of the path, she now caught movement to her left out of the corner of her eye, instinctively leaped to her right and raised her shield to her left just in time to escape the bared fangs of the other serpent. The shield flashed white, blue and golden as poison sprayed up against its blazing wall. Swinging her sword wildly, she miraculously clipped the end of a poisonous fang and broke off its tip a split second before it would have pierced her arm.

Diakrina took several steps back away from the serpent, but remembered just in time that she was moving into reach of the serpent on the other side; the one which had first struck at her. Both serpents once again retreated into the black mist, but she knew their heads could come striking at any moment through the black walls.

Unexpectedly, a breeze came blowing from ahead of her. In it was the most beautiful calm whisper. Diakrina stopped. She stood perfectly still with her sword blade suspended over her right shoulder in an aborted swing.

*"Be still, Diakrina,"* whisper the golden voice. *"In quietness and in confidence you will find strength and safety."*

Frozen by the beauty and comfort of the voice, Diakrina found she was standing in the very middle of the path that led through the black mist. She now realized, standing here, that the serpents could not reach her. If she quit reacting in fear to either one of them, they could not put her in reach of the other. And here, she had only to use her shield and sword to defend against the black rings and spewing poison.

She stood there for about ten seconds while the beautiful breeze kissed her face and hair. She relaxed and took several deep breaths. Then with her sword raised toward her right and her shield toward her left, she steadied herself for the attacks she was certain would come.

Then, in a horrifying flash, the serpent on her left struck through the black mist. It took all the will power and control she could bring to focus to stand still and not react. The terrible head came within about five feet of her as it struck and then retreated back into the vapor. And once again the shield blazed up enough to protect her from the splash of poison that shot from its fangs.

Then the one to the right did the same and also failed to reach her. A crimson flame from the sword vaporized the poison it ejected while it was still in midair.

This happened several times and each time she steadied herself and stood firm. Then with the shield and sword still held in place, she began to walk slowly forward until she was beyond the black mist. After a few steps she turned around to face where she believed the serpents were in the mist behind her. She continued to walk slowly backward, not stopping until she was beyond the mist by about 50 yards.

When she finally stopped, the breeze which was now to her back began to blow with such great force that she had to lean backwards into it to steady herself. In a matter of moments the air cleared allowing her to see plainly what had been hidden in the black mist of lies.

On the canyon floor stretched the two serpents, still towering into the sky, but now with their whole great lengths lying visible. Each serpent was fettered by a great chain of steel over six inches thick, with links about two feet in diameter. The one chain held its serpent to the south canyon wall, while the other chain bound its serpent to the canyon wall opposite. Studying the chains and their length, Diakrina could now see that they were just long enough for the two serpents to come nearly together in the middle of the canyon if they stretched out their full length and strained at the chains.

As Diakrina sized up the two serpents and their restraints, she realized that the words of Revelation and the crimson footprints had led her through a narrow safe zone where neither of the two serpents could strike. The two great Serpents of Paranoia, as seen from this side, were deadly and fearful to see, but clearly bound and helpless except for their black rings of rolling fear.

Their sole strategy was to frighten their prey into carelessly stumbling into striking distance of one another. If she had fallen to their ploys, these creatures would have dissolved and shriveled her soul. Surely her greatest danger had been her own fear, and her only safety had been in refusing to react to her fears and follow the path of truth.

For some reason the two serpents seemed to lose all interest in Diakrina now that she had managed to pass the corridor they guarded. And in like manner, now that she was past them, she too had no more desire to look at or even think about them. So turning again toward the west, she moved on.

She had reached the western end of the Canyon of Nekus and looked with pleasure over a green valley that stretched out below her. She suddenly felt exhilarated. She had not become a corpse in Nekus, and now she felt truly alive as she detected subtle, pleasing smells of the forest ahead, coming to her on the soft breeze blowing from the west over the trees.

A well-defined path descended down into the green valley and wound its way into the forest below. The thought that Strateia was waiting for her somewhere down this path near some cool and inviting spring put Nekus out of her mind. She strode light-footed down the path toward the green, living landscape that stretched out before her.

The path soon led her into the shade of the trees; old-growth timber with large oaks, elms and old-world poplar trees that reached high into the sky with massive twisting and forking limbs spreading in all directions. The morning sun was just getting high enough that the warmth of it made the shade under the arms of these great titans feel welcoming.

As she passed under their green canopy, the songs of cardinals, mockingbirds and finches presented a morning concert that drenched Diakrina in what felt like a long-forgotten symphony of life. The spirited chatter of these living creatures so absorbed in the action of living formed intricate melodies that seemed to celebrate the pleasures of being alive. Diakrina took a seat on a large rock along the path and drank in this concerto of life. She could do nothing but relish the amazing contrast of this music of life to the roar and thunder of the dark canyon of stark, barren death from which she had just escaped.

And as the sunlight streamed through the canopy and created patterns of golden light on the soft shade of the path that lay ahead of her, Diakrina felt very grateful, indeed, to be alive.

## CHAPTER TWENTY

# The APPOINTMENT

When finally Diakrina resumed her journey, it proved to be a pleasant and uneventful walk. The farther she traveled into the great woods, the more at peace she felt. The impression of *hauntedness* that had accompanied her all through the realm of Thanatos was slowly fading and the icy grip of Nekus was letting loose as she journeyed back into life.

The fragrance of flowers along the path soon filled her head with delight as the breeze, passing over their bright velvet petals, picked up their delicate scents. Diakrina paused now and then to take deep, slow breaths and sort the wonderful bouquet that subtly rearranged itself at every step.

About half an hour into her walk, the path up ahead turned gently to the left—south—as the forest climbed a steep hill to her right. Just as she reached the turn in the path she heard the sound of running water straight ahead. She noted with delight this sound was not the roar of Nekus Fall, but the babble of a laughing, yet quiet place somewhere down to the right of the path where the water sounded as if it ran deep and calm.

She then noticed a break in the foliage to her right and in the break a simple square wooden frame of old lumber, about 10 feet high, with a small, unpainted and weathered gate. The gate entered onto a narrow trail that led from the main path down toward the gurgling water at the base of the hill.

A rope attached to the inside of the gate stretched to a stake in the ground at the edge of the narrow trail beyond the gate. Tied to the rope, about halfway between the gate and the stake hung a rock, about eight inches square, pulling the rope down into a shallow V shape and creating just enough tension to hold the gate closed. Yet as Diakrina pulled, the rock gave only the slightest resistance; the gate opened with the pleasant creaking sound of weathered, outdoor hinges.

She walked through the gate, and when she turned it loose it swung shut with a small clapping sound that reminded Diakrina of the wooden screen doors on her grandfather's farmhouse. When they were children they ran in and out all day long in the summertime and she had heard that homey sound hundreds of times. The sound took her back to very happy times.

The path beyond the gate wound slightly downward through the trees toward the base of a forest-covered hill, which had grey, rocky bluffs protruding out from it. Beneath these bluffs was a large, deep and clear spring rolling from the hill. It turned left and flowed peacefully toward the south.

The stream, which was not more than 50 or 60 feet wide—but did seem to run quite deep—had a small, upward-arching, wooden bridge that crossed from one bank to the other. And there on the other side under a large spreading oak tree, sitting on a boulder that protruded—like a table—out of a beautiful circle of green grass with brightly colored flowers gently waving in the breeze, all encircled by the forest rising up the hillside across from Diakrina, was Strateia.

As Diakrina came through the trees, he stood to receive her, his face beaming with joy. She couldn't help herself and ran like a delighted child up and over the bridge to greet him.

The stately warrior clasped both her hands and welcomed her. He peered deeply into her eyes and then exclaimed, "Welcome back, little one."

Strateia turned and pointed to the top of the rock where he had been seated and Diakrina saw he had once again spread out a banquet of Garden fruits on its surface.

"This is a place for you to renew your strength, Diakrina. Bathe in the cool waters of the spring and wash away the scent of Nekus and the black pitch of fear from your face and hands. The waters will refresh you and renew you. Eat and rest here under the great tree. Today is a day of rest, a Sabbath from your quest. For it is right for us to celebrate."

As Diakrina did not have access to a mirror, she was unaware that small amounts of pitch from the serpents' black, rolling rings of darkness had splattered on her face and matted through her hair as she passed between them in her last battle. And the *scent* of Nekus, as Strateia had so politely called it, was the acrid, rotting odor that clung to her from having been in proximity to Thanatos and his realm. It was the smell of a corpse.

His kind words made her aware of both her likely appearance and unpleasant odor. Strateia smiled at her and excused himself to give Diakrina leisure to bathe in the spring.

She did not bother to take off the grass dress which Strateia had so skillfully woven for her after the Great Dance. She removed her sword, the crystal container with the Immortal Fruit inside, the folded page from the glowing book, and turning over her shield like a large bowl in which to hold them, laid them all on a nearby rock.

As she set the shield down on the surface of the rock, sunlight from between the branches overhead flashed on the Immortal Fruit within the crystal container. The beauty of the Fruit, and the memory of its irresistible fragrance, poured instantly over Diakrina like a great thirst. She found herself motionless and staring longingly at its surface. It seemed to call to her with a silent voice that canceled all the sounds around her. It created a kind of solitude around her and itself. Slowly, like steel cables being steadily wound up, she was being drawn into a kind of obsession with its every feature.

Time stood still and for a moment everything else faded away. Then she felt a firm hand on her shoulder and heard what seemed like a distant voice. Slowly the voice became audible, and she realized it was Strateia standing right next to her.

"Turn away, little one. This is a moment to flee not fight. Turn away."

Diakrina came to herself with a start. The sounds of the spring and the singing of the birds flooded her senses again. And with a conscious effort she turned to look up into Strateia's strong countenance.

His eyes were full of concern but also understanding. Diakrina took a deep breath and then whispered, "Thank you."

Then, turning, she dove into the spring, dress and all. The cool water was startlingly refreshing, as the morning was already growing warm with the sun. The water was so clear it was like bathing in liquid crystal. Her senses flooded again with the beauty of her surroundings.

She bathed and splashed around for nearly an hour, and it felt like she was soaking in life itself. She became saturated with joy. Diakrina began to wonder if this water was only water as it felt like it was doing amazing things to her body: it seemed to inundate her with health and strength. She drank deeply from the spring, and it soaked her very insides with a sense of utter satisfaction and tingling power.

Presently Strateia returned. Diakrina exited the water and began drying her long hair in the warm sunshine as she sampled and delighted in the Garden fruit. She felt really alive! Strateia watched her enjoyment with an expression of vicarious pleasure, and his unguarded expressions of delight at her delight only deepened Diakrina's own enjoyment of the exquisite meal.

The birds continued to sing contentedly all around the spring, and the quiet babbling of the deep water as it entered the large brook and flowed off through the forest drenched Diakrina in a calm, yet eager sense of health and wholeness. All, as never before, seemed right with the world.

As if intending to introduce the information in a way that would dovetail into the serene context of Diakrina's oasis retreat, Strateia, as he leaned back against the large rock in the center of the green turf, softly and subtly mentioned the fact that she had an appointment that morning. At first Diakrina hardly responded as she was dreamily gazing at the blue sky with its harmless white clouds floating by above the green canopy of the forest.

But slowly, like a person realizing someone has been calling your name for several moments, she came to herself and sat up with a questioning look on her face. "Appointment?" she blurted out. "What do you mean, Strateia?"

"I mean just that, an appointment," responded the warrior while never changing his demeanor, as he too seemed to be taken in by the restful and healing atmosphere of their surroundings. "I have been informed that in a short time you will be summoned."

"Summoned?" repeated Diakrina suddenly sitting up on her hands and looking back at Strateia. "Summoned before whom?" she pressed with a sense of earnestness that cut through the restfulness of her surroundings.

"Before the King," said Strateia with an air of obviousness. "Who else? It is the King that summons us."

"But what is the purpose, Strateia? What is the reason I am being summoned?"

"That is not something I have been told, little one. The King speaks to each of us about our own chapters within His Unending Story. It is a matter between Him and you."

"But what must I say and do to be ready for this summons?" gasped Diakrina as she jumped to her feet with a new sense of alarm and concern.

"There is nothing you can do to be ready for it," said Strateia. "He already knows all. Any preparations you would make as a kind of façade for presenting yourself would be futile—meaningless. The very actuality of His all-knowing presence melts all such facades like snow cast into the mouth of a volcano. It would be best if you come transparently and humbly, aware that He already knows you better than you know yourself."

At just that moment, a shaft of blinding white light shot down from the sky and surrounded both her and Strateia in a dense and steel-like blaze about 12 feet in diameter. Strateia stood slowly to his feet and then gave a forward bow with both his arms outstretched while he backed out of the circle of glory. Diakrina instantly knew this was her private and personal audience with the King.

The first words she heard were, "DIAKRINA, YOU HAVE TREAD YOUR FATHER'S FALL INTO THANATOS BACKWARDS BY MEANS OF TRUSTING ME. YOU HAVE WALKED IN CONQUEST. YOUR FAITH HAS SAVED YOU."

Diakrina fell to her knees and looked upward into a blaze of glory. At this point, in trying to relate to us what followed, she always became overwhelmed with both emotion and frustration in searching for the right words. In the end, she simply asserted the fact that most of what she experienced in that moment will never surrender to speech and will forever remain a necessary secret between her and the King.

The first thing she tried to relate is how she was instantly aware of being in a different place. "In fact," she added, "the word *place* is very inadequate. It was not merely like finding that you had been instantly transported somewhere else—somewhere . . . higher. It was not just a different place. It was also a different state of being, of . . . existence.

"Being in His presence was utter love and perfection. I believe a very religious Jew or devout Christian would have called it fierce goodness and passionate holiness. I was delightfully drowning in this consuming, yet preserving fire. And while it was beyond question that He was so . . .well, so . . . *Other*, that He infinitely transcended every concept that could ever be formed of Him, yet the attitude of His whole Being was a firm resolve to bridge this vast chasm between Himself and you: to give Himself to you.

"He not only came to me . . . He . . . completed me in inexplicable ways. He loaned me the use of His vast gifts by creating in me new powers to receive and use them. He did this so that I could understand more, receive more; so He could give me more of Himself than I could, on my own, receive.

"I found myself," said Diakrina, "so recreated in His presence that I transcended my previous self in every way yet remained, still, Diakrina. Yet, not the Diakrina I had ever been before. In one sense, I felt like a goddess: I was filled with strength, wisdom, beauty and joy. Oh! How unspeakable the joy! But at the same moment I was drenched—steeped—with sanity and humility. It filled me with adoration and love for Him that quenched, absolutely, any possible spark of pride.

"And, yes, I was in a different *Place!* But who could describe it! This *Place* was not created to surrender to description, but only to experience.

And that experience came with the gift of hyper-intensified, trans-sensory powers of perception.

"I am sure I was somewhere in the Great City. But it was more like being in a garden. It was both wild as a vast wilderness filled with free, untamed creatures and vegetation, while also being as cultivated, nurtured and designed as a greenhouse.

"Nothing was tame, but nothing was lawless. Nothing was safe in the sense of *predictable*. Yet nothing was unsafe in the sense of threatening or dangerous. All were free, yet all willingly expressed their freedom for the sake of things and persons outside themselves. It was a freedom that bowed to a higher purpose. It bowed with great strength and joy."

Diakrina kept mentioning over and over how enormous and vast was the *space*—if it could be called that. Yet nothing was remote. Its remoteness was removed in the most marvelous way: a way that did not remove the adventure of discovery.

For example, one might discern something as simple as the beauty of a brilliant flower filled with dancing light all through its petals. That flower could be, by earthly standards, thousands of miles away and would take the expenditure of great energy just to transverse the perfect wilderness between you and it. But here, where there was no pain or weariness or hurried schedules, but only strength and perfect health bristling with unbounded energy and delight, one might undertake such a quest and conquer every challenge just for the delight of gazing at the beauty of this flower face to face for a single moment.

She said, "The *vastness,* the *immensity,* the *enormity* of this intimate *Place*—these *are* the only words I can think to use—would make the whole universe, contemplated with its billions and billions of galaxies expanding in unbounded space, seem, by comparison, like being locked in a cramped coat closet.

"And who could communicate the colors, the fragrances, the constant delight in the explosive creativity of the *paint brush* of perfect Life in unfettered expression all around? Yes, I was in a very different *Place!*" she exclaimed.

Then Diakrina's eyes narrowed. "And in that *Place* He filled me with knowledge. It was like living water being poured on a thirst so deep within; I did not know it existed or troubled me until it was quenched."

At this point she would search for words with a look of hopelessness on her face and then suddenly exclaim, "It's all too big, too comprehensive . . . yet, too intricate for words! There is no series of sound-symbols that I can conceive of that could contain what the King communicated to me. He used words, like a skeleton on which the living flesh of His meaning was built. But this *living meaning* was not just the words themselves, they were His very thoughts being implanted in my understanding."

She was once asked if it were anything like what she had experienced when Revelation communicated with her in Nekus after she came out of the river, for she had said that his very thoughts and intentions about what he was sharing accompanied the *words* he used. Reproduced below is the record of that moment as it was recorded earlier.

Now that the being stood in front of her, he spoke to her mind again. This time, Diakrina took note that the voice and the medium of words used transcended language, as we understand it. The form of communication transmitted more than sound-symbols to be interpreted in the context of the *hearer's* own mind. Somehow she knew that what she was receiving was this being's own thoughts transmitted with the context in accompaniment—if you will, the being's own personal definitional and connotative dictionary, his own personal intent of meaning.

With such communication it was impossible for one to misunderstand or be misunderstood. It was almost like Diakrina and the being were sharing a common consciousness and thought process that formed a single perspective and meaning on the content being shared without blurring the personal distinctions of response or understanding to the message. Fortherewasyetacleardistinctionbetweenheramazementandthe being's . . . well, peace, understanding, graciousness and patience. The *speaker* and the *hearer* were never mingled or blurred.

Her response to this communication being the same was, "Yes . . . and, No."

Then she admitted, "In one sense it was the same *manner* of communication. However, *what* was communicated was so much greater that it never occurred to me to correlate them until now. The content overwhelmed any thoughts of the medium being the same. But now that you mention it, I would have to say they were like a common language. Both were ancient and elegant."

Diakrina said she experienced so much while in the circle of glory that it would take a lifetime to distill it all and explain it. However, she did try to relate one very particularly overwhelming interaction between her and the King.

"I heard Him say, 'Come with Me.' Instantly, I was drawn into a place where there were billowing clouds that filled everything. There was nothing else, no land, no sea, no plants; only billowing clouds.

"These clouds were beautiful for they were filled with white, gold and blue light that danced all through them and between them. Yet, even in the beauty of the place in which I was suspended, the very atmosphere was one of serious creativity, as if something very important was about to take place.

"Suddenly the clouds parted and I saw I was suspended over a massive book. It was open and lying at a slight angle as if sitting on an ancient angled writing desk. It was so large its open pages lay like a great landscape below me.

"There were no words on the pages. They were completely clean and blank.

"Then I saw the most perfect Hand; the King's Hand, and in it a writing quill. It was dipped into an inkwell which would have been the size of a pond in our world.

"I watched as He wrote a single word on the first page. What he wrote in shining crimson letters was, αγαπη. I knew instantly this was the Greek writing of the word, *agape*—Divine-Love.

"Then from this single word came a profound understanding of all created time and history. As I read the word, and continued to read the word, layer after layer of meaning and stories came riding, as it were, on great horses out of that single expression.

"I learned that all that exists, except the King, had been created: had a beginning. I learned that all that He created He created out of pure love and for the sake of love.

"No creature is necessary. None are needed. The King and His Father and Their Spirit are a unity of perfect relationship where life, love, joy, unending adventure, fulfillment and perfect contentment and peace exist—all ever and continuously new. Nothing needed to be added. Nothing could be added. They possessed all that could be desired. They *were* all that could be desired!

"Yet He was so infinitely full of life and love He overflowed with delight to create beings and things other than Himself. Not to supply some need in Himself. He had no need. Rather, He created out of perfect love so He could delight in causing and giving."

Then Diakrina related that under that single word, αγαπη, the page exploded open like a massive window onto a scene of creation. Millions of angelic beings of great beauty and splendor—breathtaking creatures of characteristics, beauties, intelligences and strengths so multidimensional that their essence transcended normal (as we know it now) human perception—came bursting from the page.

Each one was like a god, and each was so filled with the perfect knowledge and wisdom of the Living One who created them that they joyously danced and bowed in worship to honor Him. He in turn lifted them up and filled them with ever greater joy, knowledge and love.

A new circle of life had begun: life that had been caused; life with a beginning. And it had been caused by He Who Has No Beginning. And out of love He gave Himself to His creatures to fill them with all the power and beauty—glory—they could contain. For there was no end to what He had to give. He possessed all, and all He possessed He possessed infinitely.

There could never be a threat or a fear that He could be equaled. So, He gave. He was pure αγαπη.

Then the window on the page closed. And again the perfect Hand of the King picked up the quill and dipped it into the ink. On the second page across from the first He wrote two words that seemed joined by a hyphen. What His Hand wrote across the top of the second page was this: ελευθερος–κινδυνος.

Again Diakrina knew instantly what these Greek words meant. The first was, *eleutheros*, which is the word for *freedom*. The second was the word, *kinduros*, which is the word for *risk* or *danger*.

Then Diakrina heard the King speak.

"I AM LOVE. I CREATE BECAUSE OF LOVE. I CREATE ALL OUT OF LOVE. I CREATE FOR LOVE. I CREATE TO ENABLE LOVE. IT IS LOVE THAT CREATES. I AM LOVE."

After a short pause, the King continued.

"LOVE CAN ONLY EXIST BY FREEDOM. IT IS A CONTRADICTION TO COERCE OR DECREE THAT LOVE MUST BE. THERE CAN BE NO IRRESISTIBLE LOVE. THAT WHICH IS IRRESISTIBLE IS NOT CHOSEN. BY ITS NATURE—MY NATURE—LOVE MUST BE FREELY CHOSEN."

There was another short pause and then the King spoke again.

"I GIVE THE FREEDOM NECESSARY FOR LOVE TO BE CHOSEN. MY LOVE FOR MY CREATURES TO KNOW LOVE BECOMES MY WILL TO GRANT THEM THE NECESSARY FREEDOM TO LOVE OR NOT TO LOVE. THIS IS MY SOVEREIGN WILL AND I WORK ALL THINGS ACCORDING TO MY WILL."

Again there was a short pause. And again the King continued.

"I EMBRACE THE NECESSARY RISK OF FREEDOM. THERE IS NO FREEDOM WITHOUT RISK. THE FREEDOM WHICH MAKES LOVE POSSIBLE, BY NECESSITY MAKES A THOUSAND OPPOSITES POSSIBLE. YET, THOUGH IT IS MY CREATURES THAT ARE AT RISK, IT IS THE RISK THAT ENABLES AND SUSTAINS THEM IN LOVE.

"STILL, THEY CAN CHOOSE AGAINST IT. IF THEY CHOOSE AGAINST LOVE THE LOSS OF

LOVE WILL BEGIN TO DISINTEGRATE THEM. YET FOR THE SAKE OF LOVE, WHICH ALONE CAN GIVE THEM MEANING AND PURPOSE, IDENTITY AND SIGNIFICANCE, THIS RISK OF FREEDOM MUST STAND. IT IS A RISK NOT TO MYSELF, BUT TO THEM. HOWEVER, MY LOVE EMBRACES THEIR RISK TO MAKE IT MY OWN; FOR LOVE WILL NOT STAND APART."

Then the King declared in a voice that echoed through the whole of creation:

"I CHANGE NOT. I ALREADY POSSESS ALL IN ABSOLUTE PERFECTION. MY CREATURES CHANGE CONSTANTLY. I AM. THEY BECOME. IF THEY CHOOSE AGAINST LOVE BY FAILING TO GIVE THE TRUST THAT LOVE DEMANDS, THEY WILL CHANGE BY UNCREATION. IT WILL BE CALLED SIN."

There was a short pause and then the Living One said,

"LOVE IS THE SUPREME LAW. LOVE IS THE PRIME DIRECTIVE BY WHICH I WILL BE SOVEREIGN. I AM LOVE. ALL WILL ULTIMATELY BOW TO IT. BUT THE CONQUEST WILL BE BY LOVE. YET ALL MY CREATURES MUST KNOW AND REMEMBER THAT MY LOVE IS NOT, AND NEVER COULD BE, WITHOUT JUSTICE, RIGHTEOUSNESS, HOLINESS AND BEAUTY. THEREFORE, I WILL JUDGE ALL VIOLATIONS OF LOVE IN MY JUSTICE, RIGHTEOUSNESS, HOLINESS AND BEAUTY. AT THE END OF THIS AGE, AND THE BEGINNING OF THE UNENDING AGE, ALL WILL BE QUESTIONED ABOUT LOVE."

Then the second page burst open like a window and Diakrina saw the Great Dance. Love, joy, beauty, strength, adventure, peace, pleasure, and satisfaction flooded the creation. All loved. All became increasingly the beings and persons the Living One continually poured into them. Eons upon eons were filled with ever-increasing goodness and beauty.

Then the second page closed. The King's Hand reached out and turned the page.

When the next page turned into view all was dark and chaotic. Its surface was swirling and formless. The King took the quill and dipped it in the ink. Diakrina watched as he wrote over the dark swirling surface three words: κακος, Διαβολος, εγκαλεω.

The first word, *kakos*, means *evil*. The second word, *Diabolos*, was capitalized as a name. It means *Accuser*. The third word, *egkaleo*, means *accusation*.

This time from each different word exploded a different scene. From the word, *kakos*, Diakrina saw a beautiful and powerful angel, more beautiful than any she could have ever imaged. He ruled a third of the Living One's creation. A third of the glorious ones obeyed him. He danced in the Great Dance more beautifully than any of the other creatures.

But as she watched, this beautiful and powerful angel turned from the Great Dance. He replaced it with himself. He turned the freedom of Love wrong-side-out and, instead of giving and sharing with others, he became obsessed with his own person and existence. He became a taker.

This turning inward with obsessive passion severed him from the Great Dance. He could no longer properly hear the Speaking Music. He attempted to make music of his own, separate from the Speaking Music.

However, he had no power to do so. So, he began repeating the Speaking Music's former themes. But he sang them out of time, out of step and willfully contrary to the beauty of the Speaking Music. He tried to make all hear *his music* by drowning out the Speaking Music.

The result was discord and ugliness.

What followed was thousands of years of chaos as angels fell and took hideous demonic forms. Because war and uncreation infected those parts of the cosmos this mighty angel ruled, he was cast out and his access to the upper realms of power were denied to him. He was brought before the King and judged. He was found guilty and condemned.

He had sinned against Love and therefore against his own wellbeing and the wellbeing of all who followed him and were under his care. And his rebellion endangered the whole order of the Living One's creation.

In loving justice, righteousness, holiness and beauty the Living One condemned this great angel's injustice, unrighteousness, unholiness and ugliness in order to protect the creation and the creatures He loved. He sentenced the great angel to be banished from the creation into an outer darkness where he and his followers could have no access to create chaos and death.

Then the scenes related to the first word faded. And the second word on the page exploded into narrative pictures.

Διαβολος (Diabolos) had been given great powers and great knowledge. He had much skill. Yet now, all his power and skill had become enslaved to cunning.

He rose to accuse the King. He claimed his condemnation was unjust. At this point Diakrina realized the great angel was none other than Anomos himself.

Anomos asserted that the King's power to cast him out of Heaven was an injustice. He claimed his attempt to create a new kind of reality—which was subservient to the *self*—had not been proven undesirable. He even suggested his act of independence was a reflection of the Creator.

"Isn't the Creator at the center of all He has created?" he asked. "Is not my attempt to make my self the center of all things I relate to a reflection of this?"

Diakrina in passionate rebuttal said, "Anomos, by sleight of hand, had tried to make his mad, *inward* obsession—his *taking* and *consuming* what the Creator has already caused to be—seem like a reflection of the Creator's outward focus of *giving* and *sustaining*. The Creator is at the center because He causes all that is to exist. The Creator is at the center to serve out of Love. Anomos puts himself at the center to dominate and devour. He is hunger not food. He is thirst not water."

Her eyes danced with a kind of defiance, which made it clear she had become personally invested in the defeat of Anomos' lie. In fact, a kind of otherworldly passion filled her as she continued.

"The Creator is the only Source—there is no other. He must, by the very nature of things be at the center of all that is. But He creates a center from which everything flows outward. He is the Original and Ultimate Giver. Anomos creates a center around himself into which everything flows inward and is consumed, like a black hole. And by this distortion and inversion he tries to imagine himself to be great like the Creator.

"But he is nothing more than a parasite on the face of the creation. He tries to subdue all the Creator gives. He tries to make it subservient to his own identity: making himself the ultimate taker." Then she added, "I consider the right word for it is, *thief!*

"In his insanity he imagines that to enslave someone or something to his will is the same as creating it. Rather it is anti-creation—distortion leading to death.

"Anomos and the Creator are nothing alike. The Creator pours into His creation His constant gift of Life. Anomos is the opposite. He gives nothing; he severs all he masters from the Creator's Life. He consumes and takes; he corrupts and destroys."

Then with fire in her eyes she added, "Anomos is a leech sucking the lifeblood out of everything. He is constant consumption. Yet his consumption cannot endanger the Living One's infinite supply. Thankfully Anomos' consumption is limited. Though he was created as a mighty being, he is a limited creature all the same."

Then with a passionate sense of injustice and contempt Diakrina added, "Anomos even had the outrageous gall to blame the King for all the devastation taking place to the creation in his sector of the cosmos. He *claimed* the devastation was the result of the King's making war against him. Instead, he should have acknowledged he had created a destructive cancer which called for radical action in order to spare the rest of the creation from the infectious devastation of evil he had unleashed.

"In like manner, he also claimed the cancer-like moral rebellion and stupor which came over all that he controlled, which clearly was not a result of the war, was—if you can believe such silliness—*'a necessary creative-process that would lead to a new evolution of existence never known before.'* These were his words. He insisted this *evolution of existence* could not be obtained except through a process he called *the self-centering of all reality.*

"This self-centering of reality is what he claimed *he* had originated. Oh, how he longed to claim to be an originator! And indeed he had originated this! He had originated decay and death. *And it is not evolution but a devolution!"* said Diakrina almost in a shout. "It is not creation but uncreation! Any moron can tear down!"

Diakrina's eyes narrowed as she paused for a moment as if gathering her thoughts. She then began in a very serious tone to describe a key part of Anomos' contention with the Living One.

"The one thing which I learned that began pulling everything together for me was the fact of Anomos' challenge," she said. "His challenge was that the King could not prove Himself just and right by using power. Strateia had spoken of this when he told me the ancient story at the Tree Bridge. But now I learned more.

"Anomos claimed the King's power to cast him out of Heaven was not proof the King was in the right. He intimated the King could not be trusted because—as he insinuated—*'He fears His creatures' potential.'*

"It wasn't true, of course. But the accusation had been made. In truth the King can fear nothing or no one. Yet it was a creative lie designed to infect with doubt those who heard it. And it would have to be answered. For if not answered it could infect with a doubt that would always be unresolved."

Diakrina paused and seemed to be remembering something very important. Then she continued softly.

"It is on this that Anomos made his cunning play. He dared the King to answer his accusations without using His power. He claimed that only an answer demonstrated through weakness by the King could prove the King was indeed acting justly."

Diakrina once again paused for a moment. She seemed far away in thought again. Then she slowly came back to the moment and continued.

"This challenge seemed to be unanswerable. Yet the King, in His prefect passion to justly cleanse all accusations from the minds of His creatures, accepted the challenge.

"The King's answer to Anomos was, 'I INDEED GAVE YOU GREAT GIFTS. AND I SEE HOW YOU TWIST TRUTH BY THE PERVERSION OF THOSE GIFTS. YOU USE THEM TO SPREAD YOUR INFECTION. YOU RAISE AN UNFOUNDED DOUBT. YOU TRY TO INFECT THE REST MY CREATION, THOSE WHO HAVE NOT COME UNDER YOUR DELUSION, WITH YOUR DOUBTS. FOR

WHERE THERE IS DOUBT, THERE IS DISTRUST. AND WHERE TRUST DIES, LOVE CANNOT LIVE. AND YOUR HOPE IS TO DESTROY LOVE IN ORDER TO REIGN.

"'SO, I ACCEPT YOUR CHALLENGE FOR THE SAKE OF LOVE. I WILL NOT ALLOW YOU TO DESTROY BY MEANS OF A LIE THE FOUNDATION OF TRUST BY WHICH LOVE EXISTS IN THOSE I HAVE MADE. AND I WILL DEFEAT YOU, ANOMOS. YOUR LIE WILL DIE BY MEANS OF MY WEAKNESS NOT MY POWER. FOR LIES ARE SELF-DEFEATED. AND THE VERY LOVE YOU SEEK TO KILL WILL CRUSH YOUR HEAD.

"'HOWEVER, UNTIL THIS ACCUSATION IS ANSWERED, YOU WILL HAVE LIMITED FREEDOM WITHIN YOUR OWN DOMAIN. THIS IS SO YOU CANNOT ACCUSE ME OF LIMITING YOUR APPEAL BY REMOVING ALL YOUR FREEDOM. AND WHEN YOUR ACCUSATION HAS BEEN ANSWERED, WHICH IT WILL BE, THE SENTENCE ALREADY PASSED ON YOU WILL BE CONFIRMED WITHOUT POSSIBLE APPEAL.'"

Diakrina said she then watched as Anomos and the angels that had followed him were cast out of the Living One's immediate presence; severed from loving relationship with Him. (Though, of course, none can be out of His ultimate presence for He is everywhere present.)

Then those scenes disappeared and from the third word, εγκαλεω (egkaleo) Diakrina saw an amazing event. To answer the *accusation*, the Living One took a planet which had been devastated by the war between His angels and the demons of Anomos. This planet was located in the domain of Anomos. (Yet, the Living One maintains ultimate authority over all realms of His creation, even those under Anomos' trust.)

The Living One began completely remaking this planet and the solar system in which it existed. He created a new and beautiful world within a few days right in the center of Anomos' realm. He named it Earth. In six days He completely renewed it and filled it with life.

After He filled it with life of every imaginable kind, the King knelt down in the dust of this new planet and took some of the earth and began forming an amazing being. The being was material, of the earth from which he was taken. Yet, the Living One made him so fearfully and wonderfully designed that his material essence could perfectly interface with a spirit.

Then the Living One breathed an eternal spirit into the body He had fashioned and the enfleshed spirit became a soul: a living being existing consciously in both the realm of material senses and the spiritual realm of intellectual truth, knowledge, freedom, responsibility and love.

This Adam, as He called him, was alive to the spiritual world and could interact consciously with it, and he was alive to the material world and interacted consciously with it. By means of his relationship with the King, he had power to resist the infectious corruption of evil and hold at bay the power of Anomos' principality, Thanatos.

This earth became an oasis of Life in a desert of evil and death. And man, Adam, was a walking mystery. Anomos knew that the Living One had placed him there in his domain as a beachhead to answer the accusation. Man was somehow to be a weapon in the King's Hand: intended to be used in crushing Anomos' appeal.

"And here an amazing insight was given to me," said Diakrina. "Mankind was the King's means of answering Anomos' challenge without using His power! We were to be the weapon of weakness by which the King would crush Anomos' head; that head from which poisonous lies pour through fangs of fear to inject itself into all of the King's creation.

"What is more, He created us in the sector of the creation ruled by Anomos. He exposed us to the power of both good and evil. And as strange as it seems, it would be in and through mankind that this great trial of Anomos' appeal would proceed."

Diakrina stopped and took a deep breath. Then she said, "Love, with its necessary freedom and risk would still be the prime directive even for men. Men were created love-capable. Therefore, they were to be moral. This of course meant they also had the ability to become immoral. Evil was not necessary—it need not be actualized—but the *possibility* of evil was necessary in order for love to be a choice.

"This is why the King placed two options in the Garden of man's home: a tree that made him immortal and kept Thanatos at bay, the Tree of Life; and a tree by which he recognized his need to trust, and therefore love, the King.

"This second tree, *The Tree of the Knowledge of Good and Evil*, was the boundary that a trusting creature willingly recognized between his

Creator and himself. This boundary was an undeniable fact: the Living One alone knew the true face of good and evil. But mankind must choose to live in the truth of this fact by trust. This trust was the only soil in which love could grow and thrive."

Diakrina learned that if man violated this trust, if he crossed that boundary and tried to be what he could never actually be—one capable of judging the boundaries of good and evil for himself—he would be cut off from his direct relationship with the King. He would be severed—die— to his spiritual source of Life. He would have to receive from the King by indirect relationship and receive his life by secondary medians through the material realm.

If he came under the power of Anomos and evil—if he were infected with his lie—then he would have to be isolated from the Tree of Life so he could not become immortally evil and lose his ability to repent from the evil which he had embraced.

"For the great mystery hidden within mankind which none could yet see was twofold," said Diakrina. "The first mystery was that we were completely time bound. We touched eternity only by an ever-moving *Now* within time.

"We were imprisoned in this *Now*. Therefore, mankind could succumb to evil in one particular *Now*, and could, with the King's help, reverse that choice in a different *Now*. Mankind was alterable in not one direction, but two. He could repent. He could be lifted. He could reverse his moral direction in more than one way. He could descend, and, if he accepted the Living One's help, he could re-ascend.

"Of course Anomos did not fully understand this, but he feared man nonetheless. He became obsessed with the idea of taking mankind out of the King's hand as a weapon and making him a weapon in his own hand. He was determined to infect mankind with his self-centering nature— his lie.

"Yet, unknown to Anomos, no matter which path men would take, both could be used to vindicate the heart of the Creator to His creation. In a sense it was a win-win for the Creator.

"Yet risks did indeed exist for all mankind. Men could be used as a weapon against evil in love, light and joy or they could be used for evil in fear, darkness and suffering. Either way, however, the Creator would destroy evil's hold on every part of His creation. Anomos' challenge would be crushed by mere truth acting through love."

Then Diakrina looked up and said, "This is where my quest became necessary. Anomos soon realized that man could not be made immortal in his fallen form: death would begin undoing mankind, dissolving his soulical union of spirit and body. To become immortal weapons in Anomos' hands, mankind would need access to the tree in the Garden, *after* he was infected with evil. And Anomos was certain the King would not allow it.

"In this he was right, for if men ate immortal fruit after being infected with evil, they would become immortally evil. That would put humankind forever in Anomos' realm and would give Anomos another powerful hold over the material realm through the nature of this composite being who could move both in the spiritual and material realms.

"So, before he attempted his temptation of man, Anomos sent one of his principalities into the Garden to steal a single fruit from the Tree of Life. This Immortal Fruit he gave to Thanatos and told him to guard it in his domain until it was called for."

As it turned out, Anomos did manage to deceive and infect man with evil, and here is where the second of the mysteries concerning human nature became important. Diakrina saw the King's Hand take up the quill again. On the blank page to the right, opposite the dark page, He wrote these words in very bright crimson letters: σωθησεται αγαπη δια τον λογος. This she was made to understand meant, *"Shall be saved Love by reason of the Word."* Or as we would phrase it, *"Love shall be saved by means of the Word."*

This referred to the second aspect of the great mystery concerning the nature of mankind: a mystery such that neither angel, demon nor man could have imagined it. Mankind—even in his fallen deformity, in all his weakness and ignorance, enslaved and subject to the power of Anomos and his lies—was to be the object of something so wonderful and unimaginable that no creature had ever considered it even possible. (But with the King all things are possible.)

Mankind, though weak and fallen, was to be united with the Creator in a way no creature had ever been. The human race would be saved by a condescension of which only the King could conceive! And this condescension would exalt weak mankind to a place no other created race could ever claim. Mankind could say, as no others had been able to say before it, that numbered among their race was the uncreated Creator, Himself!

Diakrina said in a tone of utter reverence, "It was here the King bound two great issues together into a mystery kept hidden for centuries of time. The central piece of this mystery was the fact that if mankind did fall under evil's power, not only could the Living One still answer evil's challenge and destroy its power, He would also save mankind from evil in the process. *It would be in rescuing mankind that the universe would see the Accuser's slander undone and the creation redeemed back from corruption.*"

Here Diakrina's face began to shine with joyful astonishment. It was clear she deeply felt the power of the truths that next came to her lips.

"The King was willing to do what no creature could imagine before He performed it. He was willing to become a man—a perfect man—while remaining Himself. By putting Himself within the context of evil, He would use the nature of evil as a background against which to reveal His true nature to His creatures.

"In fact, the very heart of the Creator would be willingly ripped open and put on display before the whole universe. His love for us, His creatures, and His willingness to become one of us—to unite with our utterly corrupted nature in its shattered weakness—He would use as the weapon of weakness by which He would forever vindicate His heart to all His creatures.

"And the rage that evil would maniacally unleash on His willing vulnerability—His chosen and acquired weakness—would forever discredit evil. At one and the same moment evil would be unmasked and the Creator's Name vindicated.

"It would be a single master stroke. The weakness of love would prove stronger than the greatest powers of evil. Love, Himself, in acquired weakness would tread underfoot evil's poisonous head forever.

"So, do you see it? Our weakness—at its weakest—would be used to put on display the perfect Love of the Creator for all His creatures. Yet, it was not by means of His power. It would be through submission to injustice, shame, torture and murder that the Creator would refute evil's slander. The power of the Serpent would be finished. His poisonous head would be crushed and his cause exposed for the fraud it is."

Then she paused and looked into the sky and with a gleaming tear of joy rimming her eye added, "And it would all happen with two simple cross-intersected pieces of wood! In those beams love and justice would meet and kiss each other, and evil would be undone."

Here Diakrina, in telling it to me, began to walk back and forth like an attorney making the final argument.

"The King has overcome all the Serpent's schemes. He has reversed the distrust and suspicion with which Anomos had infected us at the beginning. Anomos' slander against the King is undone! All men who choose to trust this display of God's heart can be forever united with the Creator through the God/Man: the incarnate, enfleshed, King.

"This King, who could not die, took on human weakness so that He could die: die for us. This Man He became, who could die, remained the Eternal Living One whom death could not hold!

"And because the Creator has the right to the deepest areas of all His creatures' hearts—because their very existence is His constant provision—He has the right to do *all* for them. *And He has done all for all*!

"He took his deathless Life, bound it to our death-imprisoned life and carried us through the grave and out the other side. Anomos' claims were undone, the penalty of death was satisfied, and his control over us by death—by which he kept us severed from relationship with the Living One—has come to an end.

"The Living One has come out of death to give us His deathless Life—Life that has conquered death: resurrection Life. He does this by giving us His Spirit that has overcome death.

"He has become resurrection. He *IS* resurrection, and He has returned to give us this death-conquering power now. Therefore we can walk toward the mouth of Thanatos' realms knowing that we can walk through it by means of the death-*immune* Life He has placed within us. He makes us, even now, part of the society of Resurrection! For we are spiritually resurrected through Him when we put our trust in Him and what He has done for us. This spiritual resurrection is only the beginning!

"However," she reminded, "The Living One will not coerce. Even after disproving Anomos' slander and nullifying his claims over us and all creation, He has determined to offer His conquest, not impose it. He empowers us to believe Him and accept it. The proof of it stands on the horizon of history by means of the intersected beams.

"Yet, He will not make it irresistible. To do so would destroy the possibility of it being received on the merits of love, and He will have none of us on any terms but love. For it is our love life, itself, He is bringing back to life. This is what He values, and this is what He is saving. To *save* by decree would be a non-salvation, a non-deliverance from evil. He saves by enabling grace not by coercing decrees. His sovereignty is so great, and so complex, it conquers by love and love alone."

Then Diakrina looked up and seemed to be seeing beyond space and time.

"If in gazing upon His proof of love we open our hearts to Him, His victory becomes ours. The symbol of His love for us stands on the horizon of all time shouting to any who will listen, 'You can trust the heart of the King!'

"We are set free from evil's power by the King's conquest. Through His absolute trust of His Father, as a man facing evil's ultimate weapon—death—He has tread Adam's distrust backwards and has undone the distorting spell evil casts over us all. He has made it possible to be cleansed of the infectious suspicion of evil that plagues our race."

At this point Diakrina rose in a kind of poetic wonder. She was clearly seeing things invisible to most.

"By looking to the One slain for us out of love for us, our suspicions are cured and our perception healed. The lie is undone. The penalty we had incurred by being part of Anomos' rebellion, which was punishable by death—which is separation from the Creator forever—has been paid in full.

"Amazing! It is paid by the very act of weakness by which the Creator's Life and Love for us is spilled out for all to see. Even His weakness has proven stronger than Anomos' strength!"

Diakrina's amazing story was entrancing. And what is even more astonishing is she affirmed that all this, and more, was communicated in just a few encyclopedic expressions! Cosmological history contained in *supercomprehensive* words!

One of the things Diakrina also mentioned later was how she was immediately immersed and overwhelmed with a sense of timelessness while in the Living One's immediate presence. There was no hurry, no impatience. She was surrounded by the deepest sense of care and concern: pure, unselfish giving rooted in an infinite surplus of all there is and ever could be.

She was not hurried or dismissed. She was surrounded and delighted in—celebrated and welcomed. She was cherished with a deep passion that burst beyond all her previous notions of being valued and desired. She inhabited a lifetime of joy and fulfillment in the context of a single flash of radiance.

Yet, at the same moment, as hard as it is to conceive, while drenched in this unconditional love, she was still in the presence of an awful holiness: a purity and passion for goodness that is infinitely intense. This holiness must hate evil for this holiness is produced by love. Because He loves all in His creation so deeply, He hates all that threatens and corrupts them. He despises all that diminishes their beauty and potential.

This is fierce love. It is a love that Diakrina intuitively knew would never compromise. His is a love that will not lower the standard He has set for His children. This love instead stoops to guide, correct and discipline in order to lift. This love, guided by infinite wisdom that cannot err, insists on the best and is satisfied with nothing less, even if the creature is yet too dull to understand and desire the best. So, patiently, He works, seeking to create a willing creature of admirable beauty.

Diakrina was suspended between this unrestrained delight taken in her and the uncompromising ambition He felt for her. Yet, it was not contradictory. Somehow, neither would be fully true without the other. Then as immediately as He had come, the glory vanished; she was left kneeling in the grass in the lesser light of a blazing sun.

Diakrina added later one more very important exchange between her and the Living One who said, "STRATEIA WILL GIVE YOU YOUR ORDERS CONCERNING THE IMMORTAL FRUIT. YOU MUST FOLLOW THEM EXACTLY. I GIVE MYSELF TO YOU TO PROSECUTE THIS QUEST. IT WILL BE NO SMALL UNDERTAKING. YET, IT WILL BE ACCOMPLISHED IF YOU TRUST YOUR WEAKNESSES TO MY STRENGTH."

When the circle of blinding radiance faded, Diakrina sat nearly motionless for over an hour as she tried to process all she had felt, learned and experienced in those indescribable moments. When she came to herself, Strateia was seated on the table-like stone not far from her.

She stood up and slowly walked over to where Strateia sat. He smiled warmly at her but said nothing. He knew nothing needed to be said and that words would only impoverish the beauty that still riveted her mind and heart.

Diakrina sank down cross-legged onto the green turf and became lost in thought again. She was not sure how long she sat there, but presently she looked up at Strateia's face. It struck her she knew little about this handsome, noble warrior. The content of his life and the realms he constantly moved and functioned in were beyond her conception.

Why did she trust him so? Yet, she did trust him as she had never trusted any other created person before. His very presence was peace and security.

She found herself asking questions about him she could not answer. There were things that she wanted to know; hundreds of questions that tumbled over each other. Each question was trying to get to the front of her mind.

The problem was while she gazed at the bronze warrior every question seemed to be canceled and, so to speak, have its question mark straightened into an exclamation point as it surfaced in her mind. There was something about his very presence that was more profound than the answers her questions could seek. He was already an answer given to a question she could not form.

It wasn't that she had lost the desire to know things about him. It was rather the essence of whom and what he was transcended such questions and made them all seem small, and maybe even foolish.

She felt like a small child sitting there in the grass looking up at some profound physicist and mathematical genius. The child wanted to know what was going on in the thoughts of the great thinker. But what does a child ask of such things as he is thinking? The realms of his experience, thoughts and knowledge—his equations and formulas—were so far beyond her; she didn't know enough even to form a question that made sense.

He could stoop to relate to her simple two-plus-two world, but she could not rise and relate to his normal mode of life and his differential calculus of quantum values. The great could descend. The child could only wonder and hope to grow in knowledge.

For the rest of the day Diakrina relaxed, deep in reflection, near the quiet stream. The songs of the birds in the treetops mixed pleasantly with the sound of the water and her unfolding thoughts. These thoughts were interrupted when Strateia walked up to her.

"Little one," he said, "the sun will be setting soon."

With that he walked over to an area near the stream where some tall grass, about four feet high, was growing. He took out his sword, and bending over, pushed the grass back with his large forearm and began cutting it close to the ground. He repeated this several times until a rather large square of grass had been mowed down like hay. He then sheathed his sword and began gathering the grass up in a bundle.

When he had formed a bundle so large only his arms could reach around it, he picked it up and walked back to an area where the edge of the green turf nestled up close to some oak trees. He laid the grass down, took a moment to clear any acorns or sticks from a small area, and then began weaving a loose, but well formed, mat of grass several inches deep.

Diakrina, who was still trying to come back to the reality around her, watched all this with interest but never actually inserted herself into any of the activity. But then a thought came to her that brought her to full awareness of the moment and what was going on.

"Strateia," she said as she rose and walked over to where he was weaving together the last corner of the mattress of grass, "the last time you bid me take a nights rest under a tree, I awoke to a most terrifying earthquake, and nothing has ever been the same since." She didn't need to ask the question that was now hanging in the air. Strateia knew exactly why she had raised this point.

"You need have no fear, little one," answered Strateia. "Both the night and the morning will pass without incident. When you awake I will still be here, and we will engage the day before us together."

That was all she needed to hear. The threatening thoughts were vanquished and she found herself filled with a sense of great relief, joy and a kind of child-like delight.

Diakrina gathered her sword, shield, crystal container and the page from the glowing book and carried them over to the base of the great oak tree near one end of the grass mat. She set them down between some of the roots that served like a narrow container to hold them for the night. However, the crystal container, with the Immortal Fruit within it, Diakrina kept in her hand.

She walked to the end of the grass mattress just as Strateia stood from his weaving task and, turning with her back to the skillfully woven *sofa*, threw her arms out to the side and fell backwards. When she hit the soft grass a gust of air puffed out all around her and the sweetest fragrance of the freshly cut grass filled the air. Diakrina giggled almost like a child.

Strateia smiled at her. "Rest well, little one. Tomorrow we begin the journey." Diakrina sat up, turned toward Strateia and crossed her legs on the mat. "Where?"

"We will speak of that tomorrow," answered Strateia. "In the morning I have something very wonderful to show you about this spring. After that we will begin our journey to a place called by many names."

"I feel there must be something very special indeed about the water of this spring. I have never had water affect me in this way before."

"You will learn tomorrow that this is indeed true."

With that Strateia walked back to the table-like stone in the middle of the clearing and took his station for the night. Diakrina glanced at this mountain of nobility that now set watch over her. She then fell back into the fragrant grass as the first stars were starting to twinkle through the branches of the great oak trees.

She turned onto her side and laid the crystal container next to her face so she could see the soft glow of the Immortal Fruit through it. It was only her recent time spent in the Living One's presence that gave her power to withstand its allure. Even so, it was hard not to get lost in desiring it. The light coming from it seemed to fill one with stories just out of reach. It was like hearing the echo of haunting music but never being able to hear the music itself. It was like the captivating meter of a great story being told in a language unknown to you that was both strange and marvelous.

It was maddening! Diakrina found herself starting to look deeper and deeper into the surface of the Fruit. How she longed to get just one small hint of its fragrance!

It was this last thought that jolted Diakrina out of her trance in realization of how the Fruit was again starting to affect her. She quickly pulled some of the grass from the mattress over the crystal container so she could not see the Fruit, and then turned again onto her back to look up into the sky.

It had been a long time since she had slept. She sank down into the sounds of the bubbling stream, and the song of a nightingale began off in the distance. The stars only twinkled a few more times before she was fast asleep.

## CHAPTER TWENTY-ONE

# The HOLE in the WORLD

When Diakrina slowly became conscious, it was to the sound of a crackling fire mixing with the laughter of the stream. As she opened her eyes she smelled something cooking. It was tantalizing.

She sat up to see that Strateia had indeed built a fire at the edge of the green turf near the bank of the stream. Two sticks were stuck in the ground, trimmed so they each had a short V shape at its top. Across the V's rested a limb with three large perch-like fish cooking over the flames.

The sun was just starting to turn the eastern sky a golden hue, blended with ever-changing shades of blue. In the west the sky was still somewhat dark as the last few stars slowly faded in the growing light.

As Diakrina stood up, Strateia, who was tending the fire with his back to her, greeted her without turning around. "Good morning, little one. I trust the first of the day has filled you with strength for the rest of it."

She paused in thought at this unusual greeting, and didn't immediately reply. Strateia then turned around, and seeing her standing there with what had to be a quizzical look, stood up.

"Sorry, Strateia," Diakrina said coming to herself. "Good morning to you. But you said something just now about the *first of the day.*" Her inflection on those final words had the effect of turning the statement into a question.

"Yes, little one. The first of the day began when the sun went down. That is when you fell asleep and let the Living One, the Giver and Sustainer of all Life, heal you and renew you. Now as the sun rises, you will serve Him during the rest of this day on the strength that He has provided." And then he added in a tone of voice that made it clear he was quoting, *"The evening and morning were the first day."*

Diakrina recognized the quote as coming from the first book of the Bible, Genesis, and she was struck with a sense of wonder that she had never given much thought as to how a day should be defined. Like many in the modern western world, she had always divided the days technically at 12:00 a.m., and more practically when she awoke in the morning.

"There is a symmetry to all things, little one," continued Strateia. "The very creation of a day follows the order of all things. He is the Source. He is the Overflow. He is the Bread and the Water. We are the receptors: the needy who are empty, full only of weakness and hunger and thirst. The day, like every other part of the poem that is creation, must be formed to follow the meter of the whole and reflect its character."

Diakrina smiled and then stretched her limbs. "Thank you, Strateia, for that wonderful morning lesson. And, yes, He has quite filled me with strength, and I am eager for the day to unfold."

"Good! But first, you must break the fast."

*"Break the fast?"* questioned Diakrina. And then, as the meaning became instantly clear to her, she nearly shouted, "Oh! Breakfast! Break-the-fast! Of course, Strateia, but if you don't stop startling me with all this education into the true meaning of things, I shall never have the presence of mind to get to it."

Strateia smiled and turned toward the fire. "You will experience a warrior's breakfast, this morning: fish, cucumbers and some fruit. But I trust you will find it most pleasing."

"Pleasing" would hardly be a strong enough word. Delicious and utterly satisfying was more how Diakrina put it. After the hardy feast, she waded into the spring again and washed in the refreshing water. She then came out and found a place where the morning sun provided some warmth as she dried near the fire.

Diakrina was always surprised how quickly her dress of woven grass dried in the sun. It never seemed to turn brown or brittle but stayed as soft and green as the day Strateia had given it to her.

In a few minutes she had dried enough to strap on her sword and tuck the page from the glowing book inside her dress. She then went to the mat and pulled the crystal container out from under the grass she had placed over it, and lifted the strap over her left shoulder and head. Then, picking up her shield, she turned toward Strateia and announced, "I am ready."

"Indeed you are, little one," responded Strateia with a look of approval. "But before we begin our journey come with me in this direction." And with that he started walking upstream toward where the spring poured from the hillside, out of an opening like the mouth of a cave, nearly concealed by vegetation.

Strateia proceeded to cut away some of the vegetation with his sword and Diakrina joined in with hers. Within thirty seconds they had cleared an area more than adequate for entrance. The ceiling of the tunnel from which the spring flowed stretched about 12 feet high. On their side of the water, which was the left side as they faced the hill, a small path ran back into the tunnel alongside the spring.

Strateia led the way and they both kept their swords drawn to illuminate their path alongside the spring, as it grew darker the farther they traveled from the entrance. The spring, thought Diakrina, could easily be called an underground river.

The deeper they ventured into the tunnel, the larger and higher the roof of the cavern became. Soon Diakrina detected the sound of falling water up ahead; not a roar like Nekus had been, but a more earth-size sound. The sound increased as they advanced further into the tunnel, until they nearly had to shout to communicate with each other.

As they rounded a bend the waterfall came into sight, and Diakrina was surprised to see light up ahead. The light seemed to be coming from the vertical shaft of water falling to the cavern floor. She could not see the top of the fall, and assumed that the cavern ceiling must be higher at the fall, and that she was only seeing the lower part of the cascading waters.

Her assumption proved to be correct, though strikingly inadequate. When they stepped out of the tunnel into a full display of the waterfall, Diakrina stood in awe at the sight before them. A shaft of water and light flowed from a portal in the ceiling of the cavern about 70 feet up and descended straight down to the floor. This shaft of illuminated water looked almost like an enormous tube, nearly perfectly round and about 40 feet in diameter. It fell dead center into a pool of water, also nearly perfectly round, about 80 feet in diameter.

"Wow!" was all Diakrina could say at first. Then taking several steps around the left side of the pool and feeling the mist tickle her face, she turned toward Strateia and asked, "Where does it come from?"

Strateia looked up to the ceiling and said, "From a higher realm."

"What do you mean, Strateia? Do you mean from some high mountain or something? Is this opening the end of a long downward tunnel?"

"No, little one, I mean literally *from another realm*—a realm not of this world. As far as any material perception is concerned, above this opening of cascading light and water there is nothing but solid rock. This water does not come from this world."

"Then from what world, Strateia?"

"From the land of beginnings. You are looking, Diakrina, at *The Hole in the World*. And through this hole the Living One is pouring Life and Light into the Severed Lands to sustain it until His purposes are accomplished. Only because you have been brought to this side of reality, so that you see also the spiritual realities, are you able to perceive it.

"This spring is a form of grace—life sustaining ability—given to all in these severed realms. It flows out of this hillside, down the stream in which you bathed, and then down the valley on a long journey past Sapient Castle and ultimately into Nekus. Along the way, branches off this stream flow into many different parts of the Severed Lands. The waters of this spring are soon mixed and mingled with the natural waters of this realm to give life to everyone and everything here. It rises in vapors to the clouds and makes them sing a silent song of another world. It dances on a roof as spring rain and turns the rhythm of it into a haunting hint of the Great Dance.

"Without this continual source of Light and Life being graciously provided by this spring, the Severed Lands would become dead and uninhabitable very quickly. This spring, though invariably diluted by the severed waters of these realms, replenishes the light and life that are constantly being used up and not renewed. It becomes diluted light and life; but light and life all the same."

"No wonder I felt so renewed by the waters of this spring as I bathed in them."

"Yes, little one, more than you know. For the very infection of death was upon you and in you when you came from the realms of Thanatos. It would have continued to dissolve your life and health if you had not washed in this living water. It cleansed, healed and restored you in ways you can hardly comprehend. And besides," he added with a wink, "you no longer stink."

Diakrina chuckled at this witticism by Strateia and also blushed a little.

"One of the effects of this water," added Strateia, "is to engender and keep alive a desire and passion for something from beyond. The smallest drop of this water can awaken a soul, deadened by sensuality or materialism and the boundaries of this severed world, to the world beyond. Here in the Severed Lands your race needs this healthy discontentment to keep you from descending into the lower possibilities of your corrupted nature. The smallest taste of this living water can make the eyes of your heart sensitive to Heavenly light and awaken your inner thirst for the world above.

"This water gives dreams and visions that point over the world's rim. Men almost always corrupt them into something that has to do with this world, but that is not their true purpose.

"For those who come to know and love the Living One, this constant hint of something more from their true Homeland causes them joy even in this world. For in every tree, in every flower, in the strength of a lion or the grace of an eagle, they can glimpse a small reflection of glory and catch the subtle hints of that land's fragrance. For them, every proper melody has hidden within it a small echo of the music from their true country.

"For some who do not yet know Him, they mistake these glimpses in the nature around them as coming from nature itself. That is the corruption I spoke of. They chase after nature in multitudes of ways as they dream of finding a less diluted form of this water somewhere in the messengers that conveyed these glimpses to them.

"But they never find it in nature or in the object through which it came because it is not there. It came *through* them but they are not it. A landscape in the right light will manifest the presence of this living water from within. And the thirsty soul will, for a moment, see, just out of reach, the tantalizing thing they were born desiring. When it fades they grasp at the medium through which it came and try to squeeze more of this water and light from it.

"But it never works. It is not meant to lead to the tree or the landscape or the flower or the music through which it came. It is intended to point beyond itself over the rim of this world."

"Strateia," interrupted Diakrina, "in the place and time from which I came, I have heard people say that those who long for a better world are useless for making the present world better. They say that believing in *'pie in the sky'* keeps one from really working hard to change what needs to be changed in the here and now."

"Diakrina, it is not so. In fact, if you will read your own histories well, you will discover that it is the people who hope most of the world to come that cherish and work hardest for the present world. Those who reduce all of life to this present world—these present Severed Lands—and see no value in any world to come, soon see little value in the present one. They descend into a reductionistic perception that cares for almost nothing and cannot find a reason to believe anything really matters.

"It is those who believe people are immortal that do most for people. Those who consider them mere animals soon treat them as mere animals. Those who believe there is no ultimately lasting and meaningful world soon treat this world as a mere insignificant *hiccup* between two voids.

"They have lost the Story. And without the Story—the grand narrative that comes before and after—what they experience here can only be perplexing.

"Diakrina, they will characterize believing in something beyond as being a *hole in the world*. And in a sense they are right. But they misunderstand still.

"They imagine this hole to be like a whirlpool that sucks the attention and effort that should be expended in the here and now into a Never Never Land of wishful thinking. But in reality it is, as you see, a source of all things meaningful and valuable. It is that which gives men a glimpse of something from beyond. It constantly resupplies value and purpose back into these Severed Lands. It is a spring that pours beauty and meaning into the world. It takes nothing from the world and invalidates nothing about it except the lies that have twisted how men see, understand and use it.

"Diakrina, this spring is called the *Spring of Longings*, which enters through *The Hole in the World*. It is a common, efficacious and unmerited favor given to the rebellious race of men so they can be restored. It is a grace that leads to grace. The effect of this spring is to sustain in men an ability to desire and perceive the remedy the Living One brings to these Severed Lands. But it does not force any to embrace Him or His gift. It gives them power to discern their need by rekindling longings for a place unsevered from Light and Life. But while each is enabled to embrace the cure, none are forced to do so. All His conquests are by love. It is thus a preventing—prevenient or antecedent—grace in its effect.

"Diakrina, even the outer darkness—that will ultimately confine evil, and those forever infected with evil by their own choice, from all access to the Living One's restored creation—is a last gift, the only gift He can give to those who are self-imprisoned and self-severed from Life."

Diakrina walked to the edge of the pool around the *Spring of Longings* and knelt down. She scooped a handful of the water up to her mouth and drank it. She repeated this several times until she could feel herself tingling with inner life.

"Strateia, I desire to be filled with these longings. For I know they draw me toward my true country."

Strateia smiled at Diakrina and placed his hand on her shoulder. "It is a thirst He creates so that He can satisfy it. It is a thirst that, in the end, connects with unending joy."

Then turning Diakrina more fully around so she was facing the noble warrior who towered over her, Strateia said with a sudden sense of gravity, "It is time we talk of our journey. As you have been told Diakrina, the Immortal Fruit is presently a curse to your race. Not until you are fully healed can you consume it with joy. Now it would lead to unending despair.

"In fact, from this moment we will give it a different name to be used as long as it is in the Severed Lands and poses a terrible threat to your race. It is to be called, from this moment forward, until it is again safe within the Garden, *Atheos*. *Atheos* means to be severed from the knowledge, worship and enjoyment of the Living One. And this Fruit's curse, here in the Severed Lands, would lead to an eternal severing from the Living One. And this terrible curse is so important for you to understand that it would not be enough for me simply to describe the consequence it could have for those in the Severed Lands if they were to eat it as Anomos intends. You must be shown in a way that will deeply impact you with understanding: a knowledge which will be almost experiential.

"And there is another reason, Diakrina. The journey ahead of us shall take several weeks. During that time the crystal of the container will become saturated with the Atheos' essence. Its light and fragrance will gradually soak through the crystal and create a maddening thirst in you to consume it. You have to know, beyond all doubt, that you must resist it at all cost. Only in this way will you be desperate about seeking and accepting the strength offered you by the Living One. Only through Him can you resist and overcome this great corruption."

"Strateia, you talk as if the Fruit—Atheos—is, itself, evil," interrupted Diakrina.

"For you it *is* the greatest possible evil, at present. Diakrina, as I have tried to teach you, all evil is spoiled goodness. And the greater the goodness spoiled, the greater the evil it becomes. Goodness is like a capacity. If it is inverted and perverted it has great potential to do harm.

"The power of the Atheos is so great that your kind will live by means of the gift of it, as Immortal Fruit, forever and ever. This will be when all things are renewed and the Severed Lands cease to be. But this particular Fruit, as long as it stays in the Severed Lands, is Atheos to you. It possesses one of the greatest dangers that can be imagined for your race.

"In Anomos' hand, it could become a weapon of unspeakable tragedy. It would give him the power to doom all future races of mankind to the chains of his infernal ignorance and darkness. He could extinguish all hope. It has the power to make those who would taste it, or who would come of those who have tasted it, immortally *severed*—dead. There would be no hope; there never could be hope: no redemption. They would exist forever dead to Life, ultimate meaning and joy.

"The Living One, in accordance with His purpose to defeat evil and its slander with His weakness instead of His power, has chosen you to carry the Atheos back to the Garden beyond the Chasm. Only there will Atheos again be the Immortal Fruit renewed to its true purpose. You are to give it back to the great Guardian of the Gates, whom you met when you first came through the Door of the Rose."

"You mean the great flaming angel which stood over 300 feet tall?"

"Yes. It is his trust that has been violated by Anomos. You will help him recover and make whole his keep."

"Surely there must be a way back to the Tree Bridge that does not go back through Nekus Canyon?" questioned Diakrina with a shiver.

"We cannot speak of this now, but we will later, though I believe that Nekus may yet be part of the path home. What you must focus on now is that you will need the help of a people that are still faithful to the Living One in these Severed Lands if the quest is to succeed.

"There is a great Lord, whose title is Lord Mazzaroth, who keeps the knowledge of the Living One alive in these lands by prophecy and understanding given him by the Spirit of the Living One. He has written these prophecies upon the stars with the help of his father. In your time this message has been so corrupted that it can no longer be trusted. For it is a fact that Anomos, down through time, will attempt to corrupt every revelation and message that is sent.

"As you would know from the history of Israel in your day, when the Law is given, Anomos will corrupt it through abuse and misuse. What is intended to drive men to the Creator in recognition of their great loss and need, will be turned on its head as an attempt to establish, through human effort, their own self-redemption and self-righteousness.

"This was a complete corruption of the Law's purpose, which was to testify to the beauty and holiness of the Living One, which your race was created to reflect. The Law, by means of its testimony to the true beauty and holiness of the Living One, was intended to reveal in each person the terrible loss of that beauty and holiness, so as to drive them to the Living One seeking His provision and healing. Instead, in their pride, which blinded them to the true extent of their loss, they inverted the Law's intended purpose and imagined themselves capable of self-restoration by means of observing it.

"And when the good news of the Living One's rescue of men is revealed, the people who carry that message will continually fight against a corrupting force. Even among them Anomos will seek to turn the good news of who the Living One is and what He has accomplished into a twisted caricature of the original. Only by the Creator's promise and power to protect His Good News will the truth survive down to your time and beyond."

"So, Strateia, going back to the Tree Bridge is the destination of our journey?" asked Diakrina. "And then we will cross back into the Garden?"

"Yes, but it is not as you think. No mortal of the Severed Lands can cross that Bridge back to the Garden. A great Guardian, whose name is Nemesis, guards it. She guards the unspoiled realms against all evil, no matter what its form. She guards it with the power of the Living One's justice behind her. Any who try to cross must be able to satisfy the claim of His perfect justice, for evil will not be allowed to reenter the unspoiled realms; it has been forever cast out.

"What is more, Anomos, knowing the Living One has a plan to help you, is already alerted by Thanatos to your taking of the Atheos. He has sent out platoons of his fiercest and deadliest demons to intercept you on every possible path to the Bridge."

"Do you mean to say, Strateia," interrupted Diakrina with grave concern in her voice, "that Anomos has sent devils to kill me and keep me from the Tree Bridge? And even if I could fight through them and get to the Tree Bridge, I would not be allowed to cross—that I am trapped here in the Severed Lands?"

"Yes . . . and no. If you try to cross on your own, you will fail. But if you trust the Living One and follow His directions, He will provide a way over. He alone can satisfy the claims of absolute justice. They must be satisfied in order to protect the coming creation from every form of evil.

"Nemesis is empowered to enforce this absolute claim of justice with authority that none can undo with mere might. Anomos cannot challenge her; nor could I withstand her on your behalf. Only the Living One can provide a satisfaction that will cause her to stay her sword against you."

Diakrina was much troubled by these revelations, and her whirling mind tried to take it all in.

"When do we begin?" asked Diakrina, suddenly feeling very much like staying encamped by the Spring of Longings for several more days.

"Today. For the time is short," answered Strateia. "Anomos is already on the move. And the Atheos is already starting to penetrate its confinement. This will increasingly endanger you, Diakrina. And the Atheos' fragrance will also endanger the men you will necessarily have to be around once we reach Lord Mazzaroth's land."

Diakrina did not like the answer. She knelt down once again and lifted some of the crystal clear water to her lips and drank in deeply. She did this several times, pausing between each dip to stare into the light-filled water.

As she felt the tingling deep within her she stood up, and taking a deep breath, let it out slowly. "I guess I am as ready as I'll ever be, Strateia."

"Almost," corrected Strateia. "You will be even more prepared once the knowledge concerning the Atheos, of which I spoke earlier, is given to you."

And with that Strateia turned and pointed with his sword down toward the surface of the pool. "Move close to the edge and look deep into the surface of the Spring of Longings. A vision has been prepared for you."

"A vision?" question Diakrina.

"Yes, a vision. By means of it you will live through a very important truth about the Atheos and the Severed Lands. You will return from this vision with an understanding almost as complete as if you had been one who has lived as an *Atheon*—an eternally severed human. But in your case, it will only *seem* real.

"Your senses are about to be saturated with the effect of living as an Atheon. You will know something of the Atheos' power to thrill and fill. But you will also be shown something of its curse of utter emptiness."

Diakrina was not sure she wanted to experience this "vision" of which Strateia spoke. Yet, she knew she must need it or it would not have been prepared for her.

Slowly, she moved to the edge of the pool. Kneeling down on one knee she peered into the surface of the water.

At first all she saw was her own reflection and the reflection of Strateia as he walked up close behind her. Then he reached past her with his sword and touched the tip of the water with the blade. Mist began to rise from the surface of the pool.

All went dark.

CHAPTER TWENTY-TWO

# IMMORTAL SEVERING

The darkness slowly lifted, turned to mist and then dissipated. Diakrina stood in a large hall, like in a castle; the kind of hall in which a ruler might receive guests for functions of state. It was very long—about 150 feet she guessed—and about half that wide. Twenty massive columns lined the hall on each side, and a wide corridor ran on the outside of each set of columns.

The hall was quite dark where Diakrina stood, somewhere near the back. Toward the front of the room a few candles leaned out toward the center from the face of the two farthest columns on each side, and one bright light lit up the center at the very front.

This center light immediately caught Diakrina's eye. She recognized the golden glow. It was identical to the light she had seen as she entered the cave where Thanatos kept the Atheos.

Diakrina felt around behind her for the crystal container. It was not there. She then realized that neither was she in possession of her sword or her shield. She reminded herself this was only a vision. If she had needed them surely they would have been included in the vision.

This *vision*, thought Diakrina, was incredibly tangible. She *knew* she was having a vision, and yet her senses wanted to convince her that everything around her was completely real.

She took several steps toward the front of the hall, veering slightly to the right as she did so, to within arm's length of a column. Reaching out, she felt a hard, cool, and *very real* smooth surface. As she walked past it, she curled her fingernails inward and scraped them around the column toward her, feeling the small cracks in the cold granite that spread like hair-thin rivulets over its polished surface.

She had taken only a few more steps toward the golden light when the familiar fragrance of the Fruit encircled her like a wave washing up a beach. Instinctually, she stopped and literally pushed backwards against some strong forward inclination. Yet try as she may, she was pulled by an untiring force step by step toward the Atheos, which she now knew for certain was the source of the golden glow.

As she neared the front, she clearly saw the Atheos sitting on a throne seat, about six steps up onto a raised platform. She could no longer resist its pull and now walked without hesitation straight up the steps and stopped within inches of the throne chair. The Atheos' beauty was breathtaking. Light flowed from its surface like liquid and a rainbow of colors swirled within its core.

Something made Diakrina glance slightly upward for a moment. There, just above the fruit, a face—like the one she had encountered in the cave, only smaller—was carved into the backrest of the throne. Instantly, its eyes flashed open. A smile, not unwelcoming but still troubling, altered its carved expression.

"Welcome, chosen one. You are called to live among the Immortals. Reach out your hand and take what will forever become yours; no one can take it from you. What you are, you will always be. Power and pleasure will be heaped on your unchanging person and none will deny you. Take and eat!"

It was at this point Diakrina noticed a marked difference between her and the person she was in the vision. Everything inside of her pulled back from the face and the impact of its words. But the *Diakrina* of the vision continued without hesitation to flow with what seemed a prewritten story that could not be altered. It was as if she was imprisoned inside this *Diakrina* and could not escape. She felt what this *Diakrina* felt and knew what *she* knew. But somehow she knew herself distinct from *her,* and she also knew that the *Diakrina* of the vision was unaware of her—the true Diakrina.

From this point forward Diakrina experienced a kind of split-identity. She was both the *Diakrina* of the vision and the Diakrina seeing the vision. She experienced everything within the vision as if it were actually happening to her; she was watching through the *Diakrina* of the vision's eyes, hearing with her ears, feeling through her skin, smelling with her nose and tasting with her tongue. Yet she was, at the same time, like a hovering ghost outside of the *Diakrina* of the vision watching *herself.*

Diakrina, herself, was no longer in control. All she could do was watch and experience the vision taking place before her. Repulsed by what she knew must happen next, she desperately longed for some way to disassociate herself from the *Diakrina* of the vision. Suddenly, she remembered the word *Atheon* from Strateia's description of one who eats the Atheos. Not knowing what else to do, and frantic for some space between herself and this vision, so as to not let it madden her altogether, she renamed the *Diakrina* of the vision, *Atheon.* Ever after, whenever she retold the story, she would describe it as happening to *Atheon,* though she experienced every vivid detail of it herself.

The sensations of smelling and tasting suddenly overwhelmed everything else as *Atheon* leaned forward over the Golden Fruit and the fragrance filled both her nose and mouth. Then she lifted the Golden Fruit from the seat of the throne chair. Just the touch of the Fruit sent powerful waves of pleasure, mixed with a trill of surging strength, all through every facet of her body.

The light from the Fruit invaded *Atheon's* body and the swirling rainbow of colors ran up her arm and hit like an atomic bomb of delight and thunderous power inside her head. But for the power and strength flowing into her, she would have fallen over, for the force was like being hit in the chin by an upward swing of a 20-pound sledgehammer. But so full of strength and invincible delight was she, that she felt nothing but utter joy and power.

*Atheon's* eyes widened and she turned her hand over as she lifted the Fruit to her face. For a moment she was frozen, looking wide-eyed into the glorious sphere. Suddenly, she lifted it to her lips and, pausing with her mouth ever so slightly open, caressed its surface while her eyes dilated wider and wider with the touch. Then, slowly and firmly she sank her teeth into the fruit.

Diakrina recoiled as she watched, felt and experienced the transformation happening in her counterpart. It was nothing short of a metamorphosis. *Atheon* dropped the Fruit onto the floor and turned around with her back to the throne chair. Diakrina, who was five feet, seven inches tall, watched as *Atheon* began to grow slowly until she was around eight feet tall. At the same time Diakrina experienced being *Atheon* and felt herself growing and watched as the floor receded several feet from her head as she now stood taller than she had ever wished to be.

She felt power, ability, unbridled ambition and immortal pride surge from within her and erupt into a flow of light and heat from her whole body. Out of her mouth rose arrogant words that echoed from the ceiling of the hall.

"I am a goddess! I will take all I want! None shall hold my allegiance! I will take hold of the limits of the universe and make them mine. All shall come to fear and revere me!"

*Atheon* sat down slowly onto the throne chair, and the rainbow of light pouring from her body caused the chair to turn to a dark crystal, pulsing with greenish light. Diakrina gasped as the unmistakable color of nauseous, green light, which she had seen in the sword of Thanatos and the eyes of Tuphoo, came radiating from the throne chair.

Then she knew, instantly, that *Atheon* summoned some power she—Diakrina—as yet did not know. As *Atheon* she did know it, and in a flash she shot upward through the ceiling of the great hall through a laser of green light, in an ecstasy of power and delight which she had never known and could never find words to describe. What followed will have to be explained in large generalities, as the details of the vision and its progression are too many and long to be included here.

The immortal *Atheon* had thirst for knowledge, pleasure and beauty like Diakrina had never imagined. Plus, she had a capacity to take these in which would have been inconceivable to all mortal mankind.

With immortal powers to move around, she explored the face of the whole earth for generations, interacting with the most intricate beauties and mysteries of the creation. But soon her thirst for knowledge and beauty outgrew what the earth could provide. It seemed that every satisfaction gave birth to a greater hunger and thirst: an ever-growing need, which could not be quenched.

*Atheon* then looked toward the heavens and shot upward at what seemed the speed of light. She traveled outward beyond the earth and turned toward the Sun. In a matter of minutes she was beholding its brilliance from its very surface as flames of fire leaped up around her higher than a hundred earths from its boiling gas surface. The heat was not too much, nor the lack of atmosphere any cause of need or discomfort.

With powers of perception and mental knowledge that made all earthly modes of knowing seem silly and childish, *Atheon* felt the whole essence of what the Sun was and what it would become flow into her at every glance. She knew all. And she drank it in with great passion.

Absorbing knowledge of this great object was like drinking in crystal clear water. *Atheon's* immortal mind thirsted for knowledge, her senses craved stimulations as never before. Her body demanded sensations and experiences.

When the stream of experiences from the Sun had exhausted itself—at the first hint of a repeat—*Atheon* rushed outward toward the first planet, Mercury. It was too mundane, too small and too basic in design—a large hot, pitted rock—to warrant stopping on its surface. She circled it twice and took in all it had to offer in a split second.

Then she rushed on toward the orbit of Venus, but since Venus was not on this side of the Sun, she blasted past its orbit, past the earth and came within minutes to the surface of the Red Planet. It had mountains higher than any on earth and canyons greater than earth's oceans. There were places of great beauty for one who had no fear of its cruel atmosphere, for immortality carries its own atmosphere of comfort. The planet's full essence was soon known, yet her hunger and thirst were greater still.

In the same manner she flew to the great gaseous giant, Jupiter, and plunged into its red eye, where the atmospheric gases were circling in that great storm at over 380 miles an hour. But in like manner as before, soon it was all experienced and her hunger and thirst were larger still. This continued until she had explored every planet, every asteroid, and every comet in our solar system.

Then for what must have covered eons of time, *Atheon* flew from star to star in our galaxy, exploring systems and worlds beyond description. And all the while a growing dissatisfaction filled her within as it all began to look alike and the features of the last planet or star could be predicted to be the features of the next.

Diakrina said this continued until *Atheon* had frantically searched the whole of the universe, from galaxy to galaxy, for something new— something more. All of creation felt like it was closing in on her. She needed more and there was no more.

As Diakrina watched *Atheon*, and also felt and saw through her body, it became increasingly apparent that being such an immortal, forever severed from the presence of the Living One and the glory of His Great Dance, one could never find anything to fill the need which had been created in the human soul. Eternity is in human hearts and only the Infinite One can fill it to utter satisfaction.

Diakrina felt a growing horror fill *Atheon*. The whole cosmos seemed to be shrinking in on her until it felt like a dingy, little coffin. With accelerating madness she screamed, "More! There must be more!"

She returned to earth and there, with Anomos—filled like him with a raging thirst for something more—began to feed on the souls of men by means of Anomos' schemes. Diakrina watched in utter despair as *Atheon* committed crimes beyond belief. Driven by an insane need that could not be supplied, she destroyed and devoured. She turned in anger and bitterness on the One she most needed and desired, but now hated because she was forever banished from His presence. Crime after crime piled up as innocence was devoured and blood ran deep in the streets of many a city.

And then, suddenly, it all faded and Diakrina watched as the universe became old. She realized if the Living One allowed it to do so, it would in billions and billions of years all turn dark and cold, with not a star or sun left to light a single corner of space. Those who bind themselves to such a dying universe are, like passengers on the Titanic, doomed.

But the Living One did not allow it to linger. For at a certain point, a circular wave of energy flowing from the universe's center, like someone dropping a large rock into a pond, began warping all of space-time. The whole fabric of space, matter and energy imploded, enveloped in a fierce conflagration. Then suddenly, with a great noise, the cosmos vanished.

*Atheon*, though immortal, could no longer live as a soul, for there was no longer any space-time or matter in which her powers could operate. She was instantly a disembodied spirit confined in an inexplicable darkness, completely void of all sight, sound, feeling, taste and smell. No senses—no substance to be sensed—remained. It was, as she remembered reading in the Bible as a child, a true "outer darkness."

And she was alone; totally and forever alone. In this darkness, this sensory vacuum, no relationship could exist. *Atheon* tried to groan in her utter pain, but there could be no sound. She tried to weep, but she had no body to produce tears. The raging hunger and thirst of her inner being began to consume her sanity as there was nothing, whatsoever, to answer these demanding and all-consuming cravings which had long ago taken possession of her.

From without, Diakrina experienced all this with *Atheon*, who had become like a conscious and tormented black hole floating in a nearly infinite blackness where utter *nothingness* was the only reality her spirit could encounter. She was reduced to the absolute despair of total hopelessness, complete and irrevocable aloneness, with no other reality available to her but the dictatorship of mad cravings that tormented her and consumed her in a kind of unending self-cannibalism.

Flames of despair turned every pleasure she could ever remember into a mocking realization of her perpetual banishment from such delights. No remembered pleasure was now a pleasure. No joy was now joy. All memory of former gratification only heightened the horror of the complete impossibility of ever knowing them again. She was endlessly consumed by the flames of her deprivation, generating greater torments than any earthly fires could have inflicted on the flesh of a mortal. And worst of all, they could never stop. All was Hell.

Then, all changed. Diakrina saw a scene where a glorious One sat on a Throne and every creature of all time came before Him to be judged. *Atheon* was given a body again, and was summoned before Him. As she was brought before this glorious King she knew, instantly, this was the One she had been truly longing for all her existence. He was the One who could have quenched her thirst and satisfied her deep hunger completely and continuously.

But the horror of utter hopelessness came over her as she realized she was now condemned to never look on His face again or ever have access to Him or His creation. She had made herself His enemy. She had severed the only thread by which she had been bound to beauty and infinite joy.

Diakrina watched as *Atheon* was condemned along with Anomos and his fallen angels. And from within *Atheon*, she felt the absolute finality of hopelessness—like a steel cable binding her and crushing her by its endless *mass*. This hopelessness was now her only truth: her only future. Hopelessness forever buried its talons inside her soul and it could not be banished.

The heaviest blow of all came in the fact that the Living One gave to each condemned being a capacity to understand the totality of their condition. They understood the justice of their sentence and the justice of every other creature's sentence. Each, in unqualified clarity—though it confirmed their greatest possible horror—bowed their knee, dammed human and devil alike, and confessed that the Living One was just in His judgments and is the true and righteous Lord of all that is or ever will be.

Diakrina watched as a great lake of fire opened up, and one by one each condemned soul and spirit was cast into it. All who were self-obsessed in their contamination with evil were forever banished to the outer darkness of unmitigated aloneness with the self they had chosen.

Somehow she knew that a new universe of incredible beauty and glory was being called into existence. It would never know evil or pain of any kind. But she—*Atheon*—and all like her, were forever outside and denied access. They would each be confined alone, forever, to their own totally dark, yet conscious, existence. There they would have only memory, regret and hopelessness in an unending black prison—the outer darkness, which was itself the flames of ceaseless shame and remorse.

Diakrina watched as *Atheon's* time to be cast into the burning lake came. It would disembody her again into the outer darkness as a damned spirit exiled from all the joys and beauties of the New Creation or any creation whatever. She would exist in sheer isolation without end. A horror that no earthly experience can create or comprehend came over *Atheon* as she watched the darkness of absolute unchangeable hopelessness open its mouth to receive her.

Diakrina said that *Atheon* began to scream. And at the same moment she realized that she—the real Diakrina—was also screaming in horror, begging for the vision to stop.

And stop it did.

All went dark. Slowly she felt calmed. And in the darkness a beautiful voice spoke to her: "Trust Me, Diakrina, and follow Me. I gave Myself to rescue you from such a fate. Remember what you have felt and learned. It will be your anchor to truth when Anomos tries to spin his illusions around you. His promises are all lies. He cannot even retain for himself what he pretends he can give to you. He spins an illusion around himself and tries to strengthen it into reality by selling it to others. But in the end, his insanity will fail."

Then the darkness faded. Once again she was kneeling beside the Spring of Longings and looking into its mirror-like surface seeing the reflection of Strateia standing behind her. She was so overcome with relief she buried her face in her hands and wept.

Strateia knelt beside her and placed his arm around her shoulder.

"Welcome back, little one. You have endured a severe mercy."

He then held her as she sobbed. "Why? Why? Why did I have to experience this?"

"It is given to you out of love," Strateia said softly. "Because of the great danger to your soul in this quest, and the great danger to mankind, and because the Living One is determined to help you succeed, He has given you a thorn in your flesh. It is one that will only be removed when you are beyond this danger."

Strateia reached down into the cool waters of the pool, lifted a large cupped handful of water and poured it over Diakrina's bowed head. Instantly the sense of horror left her. Strateia's words flowed over her like fragrant oil. She felt strength coming into her from his touch.

Diakrina stood, pulled her brown hair back in a long ponytail and dropped it onto her back. She looked up into Strateia's face and her eyes said, "Thank you." But she spoke not a word.

They retraced their steps back along the spring and out into the bright morning sunlight. As they were making their way back to the grassy area alongside the stream, Strateia paused in mid stride and turned to face Diakrina.

"The first phase of the quest is ended. The Atheos is in our hands and safely in the crystal container.

"Now, however, the first phase gives birth to the second. And once again all will balance on a knife's edge. Everything gained, Diakrina, can be lost. Yet, everything gained can also be secured."

Then pausing and looking deeply into Diakrina's eyes so as to fully engage her in the gravity of what he was saying, Strateia continued. "The next phase has to do with Sapient Castle, and Sapient Castle has to do with *you* in ways you cannot yet understand.

"On our way to seek the help of the Sons of El—whom you will need if the quest is to succeed—you must first make a conquest within Sapient Castle. This castle is a key to unlocking the abilities you will need for this next phase of the quest. We must get there and achieve our purpose before Anomos can discover us. Time is short."

Then Strateia walked over to the edge of the spring and motioned for Diakrina to take a seat on the soft grass beside him. Diakrina could sense everything was about to change.

———————————— 🍎 ————————————

————End of Book One————

*Book Two*
*The Conquest of Sapient Castle*
*(The Quest Continues)*

# APPENDIX to Chapter Six

While they were talking about the place of reflection in the Great Dance, Strateia also taught Diakrina another important aspect of reflection, which he called myth.

"In a sense, Diakrina, we can each write a myth—a reflection—that mirrors some aspect of the Speaking Music. This is how we create: as sub-creators reflecting His inexhaustible beauty, we retell again and again His ever-new Unending Story. The Living One lovingly edits and redeems our myths and actualizes them, weaving them into the themes of the Great Dance.

"But Anomos wishes to author his *own* story outside and contrary to the Great Story; to create independent of the Great Dance. Such a foolish, diseased and defiant myth corrupts the Story and shall be excluded. It must ultimately be expelled and shredded or the whole Story would collapse into a nonstory: a plotless, chaotic scramble of meaningless words.

"Myth, like us, Diakrina, is a kind of mirror. It is a lesser story designed to reflect and illuminate obscure aspects of the real Story. In that sense we are all a myth: a myth that the Living One is transforming into actual existence as we reflect the Story He is singing. And like us, myth has meaning *only* if it reflects reality."

"Strateia," said Diakrina, "I have always thought of myths in much less noble terms. I assumed they were deceptive, or at best, silly stories."

"They can be; they often have been. But many are also a kind of shadow dance that hints at truths far beyond themselves. The great mistake is to miss this deeper meaning. Where there are shadows, there must be reality no matter how distorted the shadow may be.

"Often, a myth reflects some aspect of reality that is unknown to us. It may, at first, seem strangely preternatural. But if it is a reflection of what is true and what is coming to be, it shines a light on the creation that enriches our knowledge of the Great Dance.

"But any *mirror*, no matter what kind, devoid of light—isolated from light—is meaningless. Isolated from the Great Dance, all meaning and content of a myth—or a life—are lost. A mirror cannot find reality by looking into a mirror, nor can a created *self* find meaning by looking within. When a *self* severed from its Life Source looks within, it discovers only a dead myth of *self* and falls into an abyss where every image is a lie that forever recedes from reality like a hall of mirrors."

Diakrina knew she had often fallen into such an abyss of mirrors as she had tried to find her identity. Her culture had trained her to, "Look within." Now she realized it was the advice of Anomos by which he hoped to fill every soul with despair.

"What is more, Diakrina," continued Strateia, "if a creature severed from the Great Dance—wishing to be like the Creator—stands face to face with a myth in order to be, himself, reflected, he creates only an infinite regression into delusional madness, for he is, himself, a reflection. Each regression generates a reflection of a reflection that further distorts reality. With each replication, this ever-imploding myth moves ever further from the Great Story where all things actually live.

"By this self-perpetuating un-creation, the inverted *self* retreats into delusion as both the reflected and the reflection lose all connection with the Great Dance and its reality. This fantasy of meaning breaks the heart.

"Anomos has become such an inversion. He has replaced the Great Dance with a myth about himself. As a severed reflection that longs to be reflected, he stands in front of his lie-birthed myth hoping for identity. But he can never find it.

"Such is the plight of every creature severed from the Great Dance. He degenerates into a lie: a creature which cannot ultimately sustain its own identity. No self-sustaining creature exists. We must be sustained. A creature severed from the Great Dance propagates the meaningless myth that we can govern and provide for ourselves apart from the Living One. This myth merely reflects his own empty reflection and forms the pathology of a creature collapsing into *nonidentity*.

"Down, down, down the gravity of madness pulls him. Deeper and deeper it draws him into a black hole of *selfism*. His ever-increasing density of self-idolatry—which is pride—collapses him into insignificance.

"Yet, from within this shrinking prison of *self*, an illusion grows. In his own perception, this deluded *self* becomes greater and greater as he increasingly fills up the sum of his diminishing inner world, and his inflated sense of imagined self-importance leaves little room for anything else."

All this was turning Diakrina's whole understanding of reality upside down—or, as she later said, "Right side up!" and awakening her to facets of reality she had never before considered. But it was also very hard to follow and took all her will power to keep in step with Strateia.

She would later say, "Understanding evil is difficult because the thing to be understood is so convoluted and such a twisted version of reality. Evil seems to continually complicate everything without adding meaning or purpose. And as it becomes more and more intricate it also becomes more and more ugly."

Nonetheless, her thirst had awakened. Determined to know these things, she simply fixed her eyes on Strateia's chiseled features and listened as he made these difficult ideas come to life like a powerful drama inside her head.

"Diakrina," continued Strateia, "the *self* of each creature has a hunger and thirst which the Living One delights to continually fill. All our pleasures, all our joys come from Him. And He gives to us abundantly so we can also know His kind of joys and pleasures (which are the highest): the joys and pleasures of sharing.

"But when a hunger or thirst is isolated from its only possible Source of satisfaction, it implodes into ever-intensifying poverty. Such a *self* becomes like a black hole that can only take, not receive; steal, but never give; lust, yet never love.

"And what is worse," Strateia added, "all that it sucks out of everyone and everything around it can never give it satisfaction. The gravity of *self*, as it pulls anything over the *event horizon* between reality and delusion, crushes all meaning. When we isolate anything from its true Source, meaning is sucked out of it and digested in the gut of a lie, where it is replaced by the ever-receding mirage of the lie of self-generated self-actualization.

"And so this raging, voracious hunger and thirst—which Anomos has become and with which he infects your race—continually steals from the Speaking Music to create a façade of substance, beauty and purpose. The façade is used to entice the next victims he needs to feed upon. Like any parasite, he must prey on, and live off of, what he is trying to destroy."

"Strateia," said Diakrina, finally interrupting, "it is interesting that even in his attempts at independence from the Speaking Music, Anomos is forced to try to replicate from what already exist. He has no power to cause something totally new. So, in that sense, he is still a captive to the Speaking Music. In fact, it seems to me, that his opposition to the Speaking Music is what makes him captive to it. He becomes its slave unwillingly chained to it instead of a son in delighted submission."

"You speak well, little one. For he both needs and hates the Speaking Music. What he steals—because he must—he digests and corrupts so it will *not* serve its original purpose. If he takes in light, he extinguishes it into darkness. If he utilizes knowledge, he misapplies it so it becomes foolishness. In him all joys become pain and all health collapses into disease.

"Without the Creator, he is empty, like the empty mirror we spoke of. He is a meaningless, reflected redundancy, reduced to a parasitic essence. He sucks out life intended for nobler purposes and enslaves it to give the illusion of substance to his shameful schemes. Parasitical distortion is his only originality. Distortion of the good is his sole achievement.

"Diakrina, there is another way to say this is. The only thing he has *created* is corruption, and corruption has no existence in itself. It must have something real to twist, something living from which to suck life, some existence to diminish. This *real*—this Life—only the Living One can, and does, continually create and sustain.

"But Diakrina," and here Strateia caught her eye with a penetrating gaze, "never think this principle of opposition and corruption means that evil is always ugly. It replicates beauty. It enslaves beauty. It uses beauty as a cover for its cancerous center. The mask of evil is often attractive. It is a duplication of something beautiful from the Speaking Music. It is used like bait to hide the terrible, poisonous hook evil always places inside.

"So, Diakrina, remember this. Never, never forget it. Evil is most itself— most dangerous—when it most closely replicates good but does not submit to the good. When it takes on the appearance of good in order to subdue others to its will. When it replicates the themes of beauty in order to prostitute beauty. When it caricatures truth to smuggle in a lie. Evil's subtleties are the hollows in the fangs of the parasite by which it slowly sucks life out of its victims. Or to say it another way, it is the small deviations, the little slips of the foot, that lead ultimately to the plunge over the precipice."

Diakrina's eyes widened. The whole world suddenly seemed much more dangerous than before.

"Do you now notice, Diakrina, how he led you, little by little, more and more out of step with the Great Dance?" asked Strateia.

"Yes. But it didn't seem out of step at the time," said Diakrina. "Only now, looking back with your help, do I realize that it was."

"Because you began to listen to his counterfeit music, he made you feel as if you were still in step. Had you changed suddenly and listened again to the Speaking Music you would have noticed immediately that you were involved in a corruption.

"But at least now this lie is undone."

# ABOUT the AUTHOR

*Dr. Gary L. Durham*

Gary L. Durham is the Senior Pastor/Teacher of New Hope Fellowship, in Palm City, Florida and is distinguished for his captivating speaking and teaching. In the past he has served his denomination as a conference speaker, teacher, missionary and pastor and has taught in many different denominations. He holds three earned degrees, including the Doctorate of Theology and has pursued a post-doctoral Ph.D. in Philosophy with a focus on Apologetics. He served for many years as theologian and master teacher for Freedom Ministries International, a pastoral training institute. He has been a speaker at C. S. Lewis Foundation events and a presenter at their academic forum at Oxford and Cambridge University. In what he calls his "hobby life" he is an inventor, along with his brother Steve, and together they hold several patents worldwide in the field of electromagnetics and energy generation technology. He has a daughter and son-in-law, Pastor David and Janet Russell, a son and daughter-in-law, Pastor Ryan and Colleen Durham and three grandchildren, Gavin and Ethan Russell and Kaia Grace Durham. He and his wife Sheryl of 42 years live in Stuart, Florida.

# COMING SOON!

### The Other Side of Reality, Book Two
*The Conquest of Sapient Castle: The Quest Continues*

### The Other Side of Reality, Book Three
*The Door of Dorogon: The Quest Revealed*

**www.osortrilogy.com**

Watch for these and other truth-empowered resources from
**Veritas Resurgence**
**Media and Publishing**